Copyright Acknowledgments

The authors and publisher are grateful for permission to reproduce portions of the following copyrighted material:

"Evolutionary Psychology: A New Paradigm for Psychological Science," by David Buss, 1995, *Psychological Inquiry, 6*, pp. 1–30. Copyright © 1995 by Lawrence Erlbaum Associates. Reprinted with permission of Lawrence Erlbaum Associates.

Figure 3.1, "Ajax and Hector as Boys Throwing Rocks," from *The Legend of Odysseus* by Peter Connolly (Oxford: Oxford University Press, 1986). Copyright © by Peter Connolly. Reprinted by permission of Peter Connolly, author and illustrator.

Figure 3.2, "Central and Distributed Processor Models," from *Handbook of Child Psychology* (4th ed.), edited by Paul Mussen (New York: John Wiley & Sons, 1983). Copyright © 1983 by Laboratory of Comparative Human Cognition. Reprinted by permission of John Wiley & Sons, Inc.

Figure 9.1, "Franz von Stuck, *Sin*, 1893, Oil on Canvas," from *The Symbolists,* translated by M. Gibson (New York: Harry N. Abrams, 1988, p. 85). Copyright © 1988 by Franz von Stuck Estate. Reprinted by permission of Museum Villa Stuck, Munich, Germany.

Evolution
of the Psyche

Evolution
of the Psyche

EDITED BY
David H. Rosen AND
Michael C. Luebbert

HUMAN EVOLUTION, BEHAVIOR, AND INTELLIGENCE
Seymour W. Itzkoff, Series Editor

Westport, Connecticut
London

Library of Congress Cataloging-in-Publication Data

Evolution of the psyche / edited by David H. Rosen and Michael C. Luebbert.
    p. cm.—(Human evolution, behavior, and intelligence, ISSN 1063–2158)
  Includes bibliographical references and index.
  ISBN 0–275–96312–8 (alk. paper)
  1. Genetic psychology. 2. Behavior evolution. I. Rosen, David H., 1945– . II. Luebbert, M. C. (Michael C.) III. Series.
BF701.E96 1999
155.7—dc21   98–24561

British Library Cataloguing in Publication Data is available.

Library of Congress Catalog Card Number: 98–24561
ISBN: 0–275–96312–8
ISSN: 1063–2158

First published in 1999

Praeger Publishers, 88 Post Road West, Westport, CT 06881
An imprint of Greenwood Publishing Group, Inc.

Printed in the United States of America

The paper used in this book complies with the Permanent Paper Standard issued by the National Information Standards Organization (Z39.48–1984).

10 9 8 7 6 5 4 3 2 1

Contents

Acknowledgments

This book resulted from an Evolution of the Psyche Conference held on September 13 and 14, 1996, at Texas A&M University, which was co-sponsored by Paul Wellman, Head of the Department of Psychology at Texas A&M; Arnold Vedlitz, Director of the Center for Public Leadership Studies at Texas A&M; and Russell Gardner, Head of the Texas Region of the Across-Species Comparisons and Psychopathology Society. We sincerely thank these three individuals for their generous support and assistance. David Rosen, McMillan Professor of Analytical Psychology, Professor of Psychiatry & Behavioral Science, and Professor of Humanities in Medicine, organized the conference. A special acknowledgment goes to Lisa Anderson, who functioned as the coordinator for the conference.

We also express our gratitude to Russell Gardner, Harry K. Davis Professor of Psychiatry & Behavioral Sciences at the University of Texas Medical Branch in Galveston, who critically reviewed two of the thirteen chapters in this book. In addition, we are appreciative of Jeffry Simpson's editorial assistance.

We are extremely grateful to Professor Seymour Itzkoff, Editor of the Human Evolution, Behavior, and Intelligence Series, for selecting our manuscript for inclusion in his series, and to Dr. James Sabin, Director of Academic Research and Development at Greenwood Publishing Group (Praeger) for facilitating the publication of this volume.

We are beholden to, and extremely appreciative of, the creative efforts of all the contributors to this book.

Finally, a heartfelt thank you to Angela Lozano for typing various parts of this manuscript.

Introduction

DAVID H. ROSEN and MICHAEL C. LUEBBERT

> According to phylogenetic law, the psychic structure must, like the anatom-
> ical, show traces of the earlier stages of evolution it has passed through.
> (Jung, 1966, p. 97)

What emergent path has the psyche taken in the course of human evolution?
Attempting to address such a vast, speculative, and controversial topic is for
any group of researchers a daunting task. Indeed, many social scientists would
balk at the very use of the word "psyche," viewing it as an anachronistic
throwback to a prescientific age. While we ourselves are firmly committed to
the ultimate value of scientific analysis, we have chosen to retain "psyche" as
an objective locus of human psychological evolution. This choice is motivated
by the shared belief that the human person, even after valid reductive analysis,
remains greater than the sum of his or her parts. The decision to retain this term
reflects our strong belief in the uniqueness of human psychic life, despite our
sharing of an evolutionary past and present with infrahuman species.

Psyche, as we use it, refers not only to the psychological but also to the social
and biological realms. Indeed, psyche (soul and mind), like soma (body), has
evolved in a social context and is grounded in biology. Despite its rootedness
in biology, the difficulties in tracing psychic evolution are manifold. Whereas
biological evolution has left clear structural markers, identifiable through an
examination of skeletal remains, psychic evolution can be inferred only from
psychological and cultural evidence already partially contaminated by humankind's establishment of a world of human meaning. The difficulty of tracing
psychic evolution is compounded by the accumulation of thousands of years of
human history and cultural development that both obscure as well as elucidate

the evolutionary pathways. The authors contributing to this current volume walk the fine line that separates the contiguous and interpenetrating worlds of human evolution and development. The success of their creative forays into the realm of psychic evolution will be left to the judgment of the individual reader.

In Chapter 1, Buss maintains that psychological science is currently in conceptual disarray, characterized by unconnected mini-theories and isolated empirical findings. He addresses the need for a paradigm shift in psychology. Buss posits that evolutionary psychology provides the integrative conceptual tools for emerging from this fragmented state. He outlines the fundamental premises of evolutionary psychology, illustrates the application of evolutionary psychology to domains such as reasoning, social exchange, language, aggression, sex, and status, discusses jealousy in detail, and then considers the implications of evolutionary theory for psychology. Buss, the author of a pioneering text (Buss, 1998) in this field, concludes by focusing on the future of evolutionary psychology as our field matures into the twenty-first century.

Chapter 2, by Campbell, Simpson, and Orina, explores how different, evolutionary-based theories address patterns of mating in humans. They review and evaluate Trivers's (1972) Parental Investment and Sexual Selection Theory, focusing on important and often overlooked nuances in his theory. Then the authors review and critique Buss and Schmitt's (1993) Sexual Strategies Theory, which attempts to explain variation in mating strategies between and within women and men. Subsequently, they review theory and research from a "female-centered" perspective. For instance, they examine recent models of mating proposed by Hrdy (1997), Gowaty (1992a, 1992b), and Waage (1997). Then the authors present Gangestad and Simpson's (1997) Strategic Pluralism Theory, which melds ideas from good-provider and good-genes models of sexual selection. Lastly, the Strategic Pluralism Theory, which attempts to explain why so much within-sex variation exists in human mating, is evaluated, and suggestions for future research and theory development are proposed.

In Chapter 3, Graziano and Tobin discuss the challenge of integrating a person's individual history with evolutionary approaches to psychology, giving special attention to social narratives. The authors set out to answer these questions: How can we reconcile historical accounts that assign a high priority to the powerful role of individual experience with evolutionary accounts of psychological structure that give meaning to persons and events, presumably transcending time and place? How do history and individual experience constrain evolved psychological structure, and vice versa? Why do some characters and narratives from antiquity still speak to us? The authors argue that for persons of all ages, meaning must be forged on the anvil of existing psychological structures and life experiences. They maintain that the meaning would not be filtered passively through existing structure but created in concert with existing structure. Further, they claim that from a developmental perspective, an individual's life experiences can even shape and alter psychological structure. The authors conclude with a discussion of narratives and stories as tools for uncovering evolved psychological structures.

Chapter 4, by Skowronski and Sedikides, argues that the human capacity to construct a self is an evolutionary adaptation. Specifically, they suggest that the symbolic self is a trait that was selected and distributed in the human population because of its considerable adaptive value. Indeed, they propose that the symbolic self evolved from a more primitive form of self-concept that has close analogues in species near to humans on the evolutionary tree. Citing evidence that the higher primates possess a kind of objective self-awareness, they argue that objective self-awareness was present in the early ancestors of humans but was altered and amplified in response to evolutionary pressures: (1) the exigencies of food procurement (especially hunting) and (2) new social pressures related to the rise of large, stable social groups. Central to this perspective is the idea that the symbolic self is formed, in part, by an internalization of the group's perception of the individual.

In Chapter 5, Smith and Ward posit that human creativity is a uniquely adaptive trait that continues to serve us in our rapidly changing environments. The authors describe evidence of cognitive and motivational components of creativity that can be seen throughout evolution. A recently evolved cognitive mechanism of central importance in creative thought is environmental suppression, which is the ability to suppress one's processing of the immediate environment to free up cognitive resources necessary for conceptualization. Neoteny, a prolonged period of immaturity, is described as another critical contributor to creativity. Smith and Ward conclude their chapter by speculating that in a metaphoric sense, creativity recapitulates both ontogeny and phylogeny, re-creating similar patterns within the thought process as are found developmentally and evolutionarily.

Chapter 6, by Pierce, examines the concept of insight from a cognitive psychologist's perspective and provides a possible evolutionary account for the phenomenon. He begins with the seminal studies of intelligent chimpanzee behavior by Wolfgang Köhler (1925) and then provides possible examples of insightful behavior in other species. Selective advantages of insight are discussed, particularly in regard to insight learning as an adaptive alternative to purely random or "blind" trial-and-error learning. Distinctions are drawn between insight and other forms of intelligent behavior. Then, using the work of Stephen Fiore and Jonathan Schooler (1998), Pierce discusses a possible neuropsychological basis for insight. In particular, he discusses the parallels pointed out by Fiore and Schooler (1998) between insight problem-solving characteristics and cognitive functioning in the right hemisphere of the brain. Pierce concludes that those processes involved in insight problem solving may have evolved in conjunction with specialized functions of the brain's right hemisphere.

Chapter 7, by Vaid, explores the nature and functional significance of humor in relationship to its presumed survival value. In a review of the extant literature, she presents and critiques four distinct hypotheses regarding the adaptive significance of humor, suggesting possible avenues for empirical testing. As a disabling mechanism, humor appears to display a survival value by interfering with habitual, schema-based reasoning that, if unmodified, might lead to disastrous results. Viewed as a source of social stimulation, humor can be seen as providing exposure to fitness-enhancing scenarios in a nonserious context, facilitating the attainment of invaluable survival skills. Humor is also thought to promote survival by enabling the individual to manipulate his or her status in a group, thereby ensuring access to resources necessary for reproductive success. Lastly, the development of language in general and humor specifically have been viewed as a vocal extension of physical grooming. By facilitating the release of endogenous opiates, both physical grooming and laughter promote social bonding necessary for survival in a dangerous environment. Vaid concludes by suggesting possible directions for empirical research, addressing whether humor possesses a different adaptive significance for males and females involved in the mate selection process.

In Chapter 8, Huston, Rosen, and Smith maintain that, although Descartes artificially separated psyche and soma, actually they are two aspects of the same, integrated whole. In fact, the evolution of the psyche (mind) parallels the evolution of the soma (body). Hence, it is postulated that the mind has an unconscious collective memory of its evolutionary past. In other words, the collective unconscious can be thought of as the evolutionary memory of humankind. Empirical cognitive studies indicate that while individuals do not consciously (explicitly) know what archetypal or ancient symbols mean, they do share an implicit, unconscious knowledge of their universal meanings. A possible mechanism is discussed, and it is proposed that this type of evolutionary memory is innate.

Chapter 9, by Cooke, presents a biopoetics that purports to link the purposes of art with the genetic imperatives of evolution. Specifically, Cooke proposes that one can use the tenets of natural selection to account for differential interest, namely, the uneven attention we give to diverse facets of our environment. With limited time, mental capacity, energy, and focus, we necessarily preselect foci for attention, but this preselection follows contours closely related to the survival needs of humans in the original environment of evolutionary adaptedness. Taking into account the regularity of phobic reactions to snakes both in humans and non-human primates close to us on the evolutionary chain, Cooke explores artistic expression connected with three largely snakeless realms as evidence for survival-oriented, differential interest: ancient Ireland, the age of nineteenth-century European decadence, and the twentieth-century genre of science fiction.

In Chapter 10, Luebbert explores the development of forgiveness from an evolutionary point of view, establishing evidence for ''forgiveness'' behaviors among non-human primates. He argues, as well, that the twin theories of kinship selection and reciprocal altruism, when viewed as a product of natural selection occurring within humankind's original context of evolutionary adaptedness, help explain forgiveness behavior. A human capacity to forgive developed originally to cope with environmental pressures associated with food acquisition, mating, predation, and marauding bands. Cooperation among kin and non-kin alike ensured that one's genes passed on to succeeding generations. Luebbert also suggests that as humankind moved beyond the original environment of evolutionary adaptedness, the internalization of literacy led to a more highly differentiated and interiorized personal identity and a lessening of the agonistic character of primary oral consciousness. An increased capacity for separating the knower from the known encouraged by literacy led, in part, to a guilt-based morality and, consequently, to new possibilities for forgiveness. So-called dialectical forgiveness could now be imagined and practiced. Likewise, an increasing capacity for abstraction laid the groundwork for the articulation of universal religious appeals for forgiveness. However, the author maintains that only from a contemporary perspective can we fully appreciate the survival value of forgiveness.

Chapter 11, by Huston, provides an introduction to Jung's archetypal psychology. She also operationally defines archetypal dreams and explains how they are different from other kinds of dreams. In addition, Huston maintains that archetypal dreams are evolutionary in that they serve an adaptive purpose that has helped human beings to survive. Finally, the author discusses some of her own dreams as an aid to understanding and appreciating the value of archetypal dreams and their adaptive nature.

In Chapter 12, Price and Stevens take an evolutionary approach to psychiatric disorders, arguing that the genetic tendency underlying schizophrenia and affective disorders performs different, even opposite survival-enhancing functions. They portray both disorders as by-products of vital group processes, concerned with the multiplication and integrity of human groups during the course of evolution. According to their view, the capacity for mood change served as a primitive mechanism, enabling the individual to accept lesser sanctions protecting group homeostasis (i.e., the loss of status or prestige), thereby avoiding the ultimate sanction of group expulsion. In like manner, an evolutionary approach to schizophrenia suggests that as human social groups reached a certain size, a need for group splitting or colonization arose. Bearing the schizophrenic genotype, a successful leader would attract followers and persuade them to accept his or her unique beliefs, thus promoting an orderly process of group splitting that favored the evolution of the human species.

Chapter 13, by Stevens and Price, brings a new orientation to the treatment of disorders of the psyche. Initially, the authors outline the following position, which is the premise of their important new text (Stevens & Price, 1996): psychiatric disorders are an ancient adaptive response that for some contemporary reason has become maladaptive. Then they discuss how treatment ought to parallel this evolutionary view of mental conditions. Stevens and Price contend that the key factor in all treatment is to take the patient's history beyond purely personal predicament and relate it to the story of humankind. They illustrate their perspective with a case history involving a depressed patient.

The chapters in this volume provide a diverse sampling of scientific and theoretical approaches to understanding some of the most important markers connected with the evolution of the psyche. Markers from our evolutionary past can be discerned in our similarities to our infrahuman ancestors, in the structure of the human brain, and in contemporary capacities that, upon reflection, continue to serve purposes best understood in our original environment of evolutionary adaptedness. Indeed, evolutionary psychology can help chasten our acceptance of Western enlightenment ideas by reminding us that the legacy of our evolutionary past continues to shape our human responses and by serving as a new integrative paradigm for psychology in the twenty-first century.

REFERENCES

Buss, D. M. (1998). *Evolutionary psychology: The new science of the mind.* Boston: Allyn & Bacon.

Buss, D. M., & Schmitt, D. P. (1993). Sexual Strategies Theory: A contextual evolutionary analysis of human mating. *Psychological Review, 100,* 204–232.

Fiore, S. M., & Schooler, J. W. (1998). Right hemisphere contributions to creative problem solving: Converging evidence for divergent thinking. In M. Beeman & C. Chiarello (Eds.), *Right hemisphere language comprehension: Perspectives from cognitive neuroscience* (pp. 349–371). Mahwah, NJ: Lawrence Erlbaum.

Gangestad, S. W., & Simpson, J. A. (1997). *On the evolutionary psychology of human mating: Trade-offs and strategic pluralism.* Unpublished manuscript, University of New Mexico, Albuquerque.

Gowaty, P. A. (1992a). Evolutionary biology and feminism. *Human Nature, 3,* 217–249.

Gowaty, P. A. (1992b). What if within-sex variation is greater than between-sex variation? *Behavioral and Brain Sciences, 15,* 389–390.

Hrdy, S. B. (1997). Raising Darwin's consciousness: Female sexuality and the prehominid origins of patriarchy. *Human Nature, 8,* 1–49.

Köhler, W. (1925). *The mentality of apes.* New York: Liveright.

Jung, C. G. (1966). Vol. 15 in H. Read, M. Fordham, & G. Adler (Eds.), *The collected works of C. G. Jung.* Princeton, NJ: Princeton University Press.

Stevens, A., & Price, J. (1996). *Evolutionary psychiatry: A new beginning.* London and New York: Routledge.

Trivers, R. (1972). Parental investment and sexual selection. In B. Campbell (Ed.), *Sexual selection and the descent of man, 1871–1971* (pp. 136–179). Chicago: Aldine.

Waage, J. K. (1997). Parental investment—Minding the kids or keeping control? In P. A. Gowaty (Ed.), *Feminism and evolutionary biology* (pp. 527–553). New York: International Thomson.

Evolution
of the Psyche

1

Evolutionary Psychology: A New Paradigm for Psychological Science

DAVID M. BUSS

> After more than a century, the social sciences are still adrift, with an enormous mass of half-digested observations, a not inconsiderable body of empirical generalizations, and a contradictory stew of ungrounded, middle-level theories expressed in a babel of incommensurate technical lexicons. (Tooby & Cosmides, 1992, p. 23)

Anyone familiar with the broad field of psychology knows that it is in theoretical disarray. The different branches—such as cognitive, social, personality, clinical, and developmental—proceed in relative isolation from one another, at most occasionally borrowing, like a cup of sugar, a concept here and a method there from a neighbor. Within each branch, psychologists also fail to reach consensus. Mini-theories proliferate unconnected, each conceived to account for a particular set of phenomena, such as obedience to authority, children's concepts of mind, or the effects of priming on categorization tasks. Although psychologists assume that the human mind is a whole and integrated unity, no metatheory subsumes, integrates, unites, or connects the disparate pieces that psychologists gauge with their differing calipers.

An important new theoretical paradigm called *evolutionary psychology* is emerging that offers to provide this metatheory. This chapter describes the basic features of evolutionary psychology and draws out several key implications for psychological science. It covers recent empirical work conducted using the principles of evolutionary psychology in the areas of jealousy, reasoning abilities, social exchange, decision rules, language, mate preferences, status, aggression, and sex. It considers some of the consequences for branches of psychology such as social, personality, cognitive, clinical, developmental, and cultural. It concludes by looking to the future of evolutionary psychology—its promises, its pitfalls, its illuminations, its limitations.

FUNDAMENTAL PRINCIPLES OF THE NEW PARADIGM

All Psychological Theories Imply Evolved Mechanisms

It does not seem to be generally known among psychologists that all manifest behavior depends on underlying psychological mechanisms—information-processing devices, decision rules, and so on—in conjunction with contextual input into those mechanisms. No behavior can be produced without them. If dogs and cats respond to the same stimuli with different responses, it is because the psychological mechanisms of dogs and cats differ. If a child and an adolescent respond differently to the same stimulus, it is because they differ in their psychological mechanisms. If a man and a woman differ in their behavior in response to identical input, it is because they possess somewhat different psychological mechanisms. A person obeys authority, conforms to the group, values particular mates, and responds with rage when provoked in particular ways— and a blank slate does not—because the person possesses a particular set of psychological mechanisms absent in the blank slate.

All psychological theories, even the most ardently environmental ones, imply the existence of psychological mechanisms (Quine, 1981; Symons, 1987). Skinner's theory of operant learning, for example, implies the existence of domain-general mechanisms that cause organisms to alter their behavioral output in accordance with the history of reinforcement they have experienced. The mechanisms Skinner implies are among the most domain-general ever proposed— they are presumed to operate in the same manner across different domains such as feeding and mating and, remarkably, also are presumed to be the same across different species. Festinger's (1957) theory of cognitive dissonance, to take another example, implies the existence of internal psychological mechanisms that cause discrepant thoughts or behaviors to feel uncomfortable and that cause people to alter one of those thoughts or behaviors to make the two more consistent. Latané's (1981) theory of social loafing implies the existence of human psychological mechanisms that cause people to diminish effort at a project as a function of the presence of others.

All psychological theories—be they cognitive, social, developmental, personality, or clinical—imply the existence of internal psychological mechanisms. Unfortunately, the precise nature of these mechanisms is often left implicit. Despite the lack of explicitness, it is clear that no behavior can be produced in the absence of psychological mechanisms. Because all psychological theories imply underlying mechanisms, they also imply a human nature. What are the origins of basic psychological mechanisms that constitute human nature?

Evolution by Natural Selection Is the Only Known Causal Process Capable of Producing Complex Physiological and Psychological Mechanisms

Only a few causal processes have been proposed over the past two centuries to account for the origins of these complex organic mechanisms known as adaptations (Dawkins, 1986; Mayr, 1982). Several of these, such as orthogenesis and Lamarckism, have been shown to be false and are no longer considered viable possibilities. Three remaining possibilities have some adherents. The first is *evolution by natural selection* (Darwin, 1859, 1871; Hamilton, 1964). The second is *creationism*. The third is *seeding theory*—the idea that extraterrestrial organisms visited Earth many years ago and planted the seeds of life. Creationism is largely incapable of being verified or disproved by observation or experiment and is not a scientific theory. Seeding theory, although it cannot be excluded as a possibility, is not an explanation in itself but, rather, pushes the problem back a step to the causal process that created the origins of the seeds and the extraterrestrial beings that planted them. Evolution by natural selection, in contrast, is a powerful and well-articulated theory that has successfully organized and explained thousands of diverse facts in a principled way (Mayr, 1982).

Because all behavior depends on complex psychological mechanisms, and all psychological mechanisms, at some basic level of description, are the result of evolution by selection, then all psychological theories are implicitly evolutionary psychological theories.[1] No psychological theories imply basic psychological mechanisms that were created by some other causal process. As Symons (1987) phrased it, "we're all Darwinians" in the sense that all (or nearly all) psychologists believe that evolution is responsible for who we are today. If another causal process exists that is capable of producing complex mechanisms, it has not been made generally known to the scientific community.

Levels of Analysis in Evolutionary Psychology

When I give colloquia about my evolution-based research on human mating strategies, I am sometimes asked questions such as "What evidence would falsify 'the theory'?" or "Doesn't the existence of people helping total strangers falsify 'the theory'?" In order to answer these questions, one must first distinguish between at least four levels of analysis (see Figure 1.1). The first level is *general evolutionary theory—evolution by natural selection*, as understood in its modern form as *inclusive-fitness theory*. Now, at this level, even though general evolutionary theory is called a *theory*, it is widely regarded by biologists as so well established that it is simply assumed to be correct in its general outlines, and then work proceeds from that assumption but does not test the assumption, at least not directly. There have been thousands of tests of the

Figure 1.1
Simplified Depiction of a Hierarchy of Levels of Analysis in Evolutionary Psychology

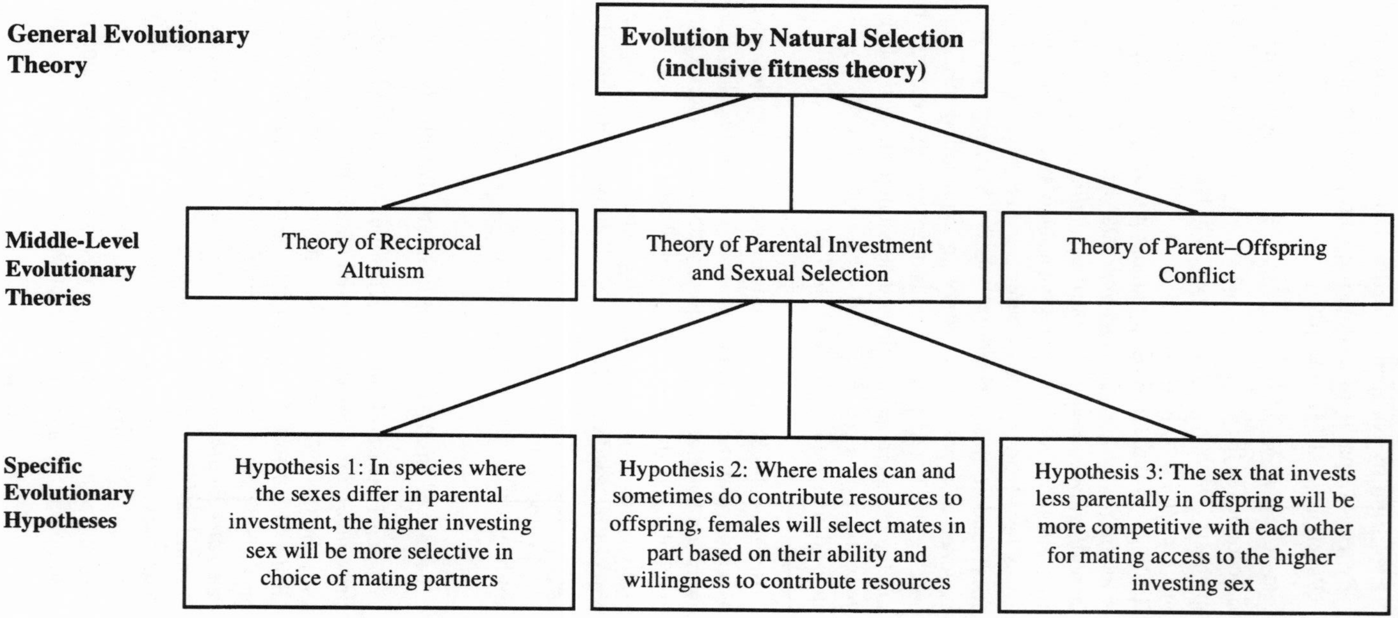

General Evolutionary Theory

Middle-Level Evolutionary Theories

Specific Evolutionary Hypotheses

	Evolution by Natural Selection (inclusive fitness theory)	
Theory of Reciprocal Altruism	Theory of Parental Investment and Sexual Selection	Theory of Parent–Offspring Conflict
Hypothesis 1: In species where the sexes differ in parental investment, the higher investing sex will be more selective in choice of mating partners	Hypothesis 2: Where males can and sometimes do contribute resources to offspring, females will select mates in part based on their ability and willingness to contribute resources	Hypothesis 3: The sex that invests less parentally in offspring will be more competitive with each other for mating access to the higher investing sex

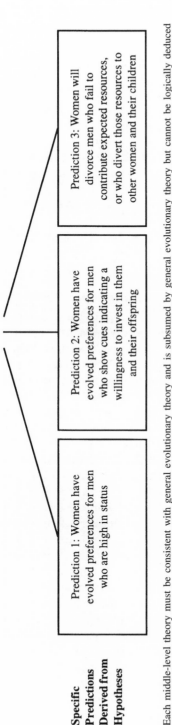

Specific Predictions Derived from Hypotheses

Prediction 1: Women have evolved preferences for men who are high in status

Prediction 2: Women have evolved preferences for men who show cues indicating a willingness to invest in them and their offspring

Prediction 3: Women will divorce men who fail to contribute expected resources, or who divert those resources to other women and their children

Each middle-level theory must be consistent with general evolutionary theory and is subsumed by general evolutionary theory but cannot be logically deduced from general evolutionary theory. A variety of specific evolutionary hypotheses can be derived from each middle-level theory, just as a variety of specific empirical predictions can be generated from each evolutionary hypothesis. Standards of "normal paradigm science" hold for testing each level in the hierarchy.

5

general theory. New species can be created in the laboratory using its principles. Evolution by natural selection is the guiding metatheory for the entire field of biology. There are phenomena that could falsify the general theory—if complex life forms were found to be created in time periods too short for natural selection to have operated (e.g., in seven days) or if adaptations of organisms were found that evolved for the benefit of intrasexual competitors or for the benefit of other species (Darwin, 1859; Mayr, 1982; Williams, 1966). But no such phenomena have ever been observed or documented.

So, when an evolutionary psychologist tests an evolutionary proposition, she or he is not testing "general evolutionary theory," just as, when an astronomer tests a particular hypothesis (e.g., about the amount of critical mass in the universe), she or he is not testing "general relativity theory" with each experiment. That theory is assumed to be true, just as evolution by natural selection is assumed to be true for the present purposes. Because no compelling alternatives have been proposed over the past 130 years, and because there is overwhelming evidence supporting general evolutionary theory, these assumptions are reasonable.

Moving one level down, we find *middle-level evolutionary theories*, such as the theory of reciprocal altruism (Trivers, 1971), the theory of parental investment and sexual selection (Trivers, 1972), and the theory of parasite-host co-evolution (Hamilton & Zuk, 1982). These middle-level theories are still fairly broad in that they are theories about entire domains of functioning—for example, the conditions under which parents and their offspring will conflict with one another. These theories are fair game for testing and possible falsification. I'll examine just one to illustrate this point—Trivers's theory of parental investment and sexual selection (see Figure 1.1).

This theory, which is itself an elaboration of Darwin's (1871) theory of sexual selection, provided one of the key theoretical ingredients for predicting the operation of mate choice and the operation of intrasexual competition. Leaving aside the logical and reproductive underpinnings of Trivers's theory (which would require a major treatise to spell out), he essentially argued that the sex that invests more in offspring (often, but not always, the female) will evolve to be more choosy about mating, whereas the sex that invests less in offspring will evolve to be more competitive with members of their own sex for sexual access to the valuable, high-investing opposite sex. Women, whose minimum parental investment includes a nine-month gestation period, for example, are predicted to have evolved mechanisms that lead to greater choosiness than men, whose minimum parental investment is the contribution of his sperm. The asymmetries between the sexes, in fitness currencies, of the costs of making a poor mate choice and the benefits of making a wise mate choice would have created selection pressure for sex-differentiated psychological mate preferences. Trivers and others have developed additional hypotheses about the precise content of mate choice—various forms of resources, for example, when certain contextual conditions were met, such as resource defensibility, variance in resource holdings among potential mates, or whether a long-term or short-term mate is being pursued (Buss & Schmitt, 1993). Some of the *specific hypotheses* derived from Trivers's theory are shown in Figure 1.1. *Specific predictions* can be derived from each of these hypotheses—predictions about evolved psychological mechanisms or behavioral strategies in a particular species.

In testing these predictions, all the conditions of "normal paradigm science" hold. If the predictions do not pan out empirically, then the hypothesis on which they were based is called into question. If key hypotheses are called into question by several predictive failures, then the truth or value (depending on one's philosophy of science) of the middle-level theory that generated the hypotheses is doubted. Theories that are consistently supported—as, for example, Trivers's theory of parental investment and sexual selection has been in hundreds of empirical studies—are hailed as major middle-level theories, especially if they prove highly generative of interesting and fruitful avenues of research. Theories that are not generative or that produce a series of predictive failures are abandoned or replaced by better theories.

This is a highly oversimplified account, of course, and several additional levels of analysis are often involved. Evolutionary psychologists, for example, develop hypotheses about the psychological mechanisms that have evolved in humans to solve particular adaptive problems that humans have faced under ancestral conditions. This often involves a detailed task analysis of the sorts of information-processing mechanisms needed to solve particular adaptive problems, conjoined with an analysis of the relevant ancestral cues that would have been available to organisms in those environments. In my work, for example, I have developed hypotheses about psychological mate preferences of men and women, based in part on Trivers's theory of parental investment but also based on a task analysis of the adaptive problems that men and women would be required to solve if they were pursuing a short-term or a long-term sexual strategy (Buss & Schmitt, 1993). Some have been supported by dozens of studies; a few have not. But, for the present purposes, the key point is that when one asks "What evidence could falsify the theory?" one must locate the question in the hierarchy of levels. My particular hypothesis about a psychological mechanism could be wrong, even if the theory one level up, which led me to the hypothesis, is entirely correct. As in the rest of science, all levels are evaluated by the cumulative weight of the evidence—rarely is a single study definitive one way or the other.

Thus, the empirical methods used by an evolutionary psychologist to evaluate hypotheses and predictions are exactly the same as those used by other psychologists. They include experimental methods (e.g., Sadalla, Kenrick, & Vershure, 1987), questionnaire methods (e.g., Buss, 1989a, 1989b; Kenrick, Sadalla, Groth, & Trost, 1990), analysis of public documents such as homicide statistics or divorce statistics (e.g., Betzig, 1989; Daly & Wilson, 1988), observational methods (e.g., Buss, 1988a, 1988b; Hill & Kaplan, 1988), psychophysiological techniques (Buss, Larsen, Westen, & Semmelroth, 1992; McGuire & Troisi,

1987), and many others. Empirical methods, as in other areas of psychology, are tailored to the specific hypothesis being tested. As always, results that transcend several methods are seen as stronger than results limited to a single method. Results found across different populations and cultures are seen as stronger than results limited to a single population or culture.

Before leaving the level-of-analysis issue, it should be noted that some evolutionary investigations take as their starting point a phenomenon or an observation and then try to test hypotheses about its function or about why it evolved. The fact of sexual reproduction itself, for example, remains a major enigma to evolutionary biologists, and there are several competing theories about why sex evolved (e.g., Hamilton, 1980; Tooby, 1982). No previous evolutionary theory "predicted" in advance that sex would exist, but the fact of its existence is fair game for subsequent evolutionary analysis, just as observations in other fields (e.g., the observation of galaxies moving away from one another in astronomy) are fair game for subsequent theoretical scrutiny.

To take another example, the existence of the orgasm among women has provoked substantial theoretical interest among evolutionists (e.g., Baker & Bellis, 1989; Gould, 1987; Rancour-Laferriere, 1985; Symons, 1979). Several competing evolutionary hypotheses have been advanced, including hypotheses of (1) paternity confidence, (2) cue to selecting the right male, (3) "sealing the pair-bond," and (4) sperm upsuck. At least two prominent evolutionists, in contrast, have argued that the female orgasm is not in itself an adaptation but rather an incidental by-product of male orgasm, much as male nipples apparently have no function and are incidental by-products of the fact that females have nipples (Gould, 1987; Symons, 1979). The key point is that it is rare that one can refer to the evolutionary hypothesis. Just as there are competing theories in other areas of science, so there are often competing evolutionary hypotheses about the same set of observations. Testing among competing hypotheses involves generating additional predictions about phenomena as yet unobserved and proceeds in the same fashion as "normal paradigm science." The value of evolutionary theories and hypotheses, like the value of all theories and hypotheses, must be gauged by their conceptual and empirical harvest.

The Nature of Psychological Mechanisms

Symons (1987) asked, If we are all Darwinians, what is the fuss about? If all behavior depends on mechanisms, and evolutionary processes are the only ones capable of producing basic mechanisms, then the key question cannot be Is evolution relevant to human behavior? The answer to that question must necessarily be yes, and hence it is an uninteresting question. Instead, the key questions become, What is the nature of the psychological mechanisms that evolution by selection has fashioned? Why do these mechanisms exist in the form that they do—what adaptive problems did they arise to solve, or what are their functions?

At the core of the debate between evolutionary and nonevolutionary psychologists are their answers to these questions. The key issues of this debate have been obscured by false dichotomies that must be jettisoned before we can think clearly about the issues—false dichotomies such as "nature versus nurture," "genetic versus environmental," "cultural versus biological," and "innate versus learned." These dichotomies imply the existence of two separate classes of causes, the relative importance of which can be evaluated quantitatively. Evolutionary psychology rejects these false dichotomies.[2] All humans have a nature—a human nature that differs from cat nature, rat nature, and bat nature. That nature requires particular forms of environmental input for its development. Once developed, all mechanisms require particular forms of input to be activated and to function properly. The mechanisms of learning that make humans responsive to immediate and developmental contingencies owe their existence to evolution by natural selection. The evolved mechanisms and the input that they were designed to be activated by both owe their existence to causal evolutionary processes (Tooby & Cosmides, 1990a). They are not two separate causal processes but rather part and parcel of the same evolved package. In order to see why these previous dichotomies are false, it is first necessary to provide a provisional definition of *psychological mechanisms* and to discuss several key conceptual issues about their nature.

An *evolved psychological mechanism* is a set of processes inside an organism that:

1. Exists in the form it does because it (or other mechanisms that reliably produce it) solved a specific problem of individual survival or reproduction recurrently over human evolutionary history.

2. Takes only certain classes of information or input, where input (1) can be either external or internal, (2) can be actively extracted from the environment or passively received from the environment, and (3) specifies to the organism the particular adaptive problem it is facing.

3. Transforms that information into output through a procedure (e.g., decision rule) in which output (1) regulates physiological activity, provides information to other psychological mechanisms, or produces manifest action and (2) solves a particular adaptive problem.

Species have evolved psychologies to the degree that they possess mechanisms of this sort (modified from Buss, 1991, p. 464; but see Fodor, 1968; Marr, 1982; Newell & Simon, 1961; Pylyshyn, 1980).

Because all behavior owes its existence to underlying psychological mechanisms, the central task, according to evolutionary psychologists, is to discover, describe, and explain the nature of those mechanisms. Many mainstream psychologists implicitly set this as their agenda already. The difference between evolutionary and nonevolutionary psychologists is not so much the agenda they set—although there are some key differences, noted later—but rather in the conceptual tools they bring to bear on pursuing that agenda.

A central premise of evolutionary psychology is that the main, nonarbitrary way to identify, describe, and understand psychological mechanisms is to articulate their functions—the specific adaptive problems they were designed by selection to solve. Consider the human body. In principle, the mechanisms of the body could be described and parsed in an infinite number of ways. Why do anatomists identify as separate mechanisms the liver, the heart, the larynx, the hand, the nose, the eyes, and the ears? What makes these divisions nonarbitrary compared with alternative ways of parsing the body, such as those based solely on physical proximity? The answer is function. The liver is recognized as a mechanism that performs functions different from those performed by the heart and the larynx. The eyes and the nose, although spatially proximate, perform different functions and operate according to different input and different principles. A partition that failed to be based on function would be seen by anatomists and physiologists as failing to cleave nature at its natural joints. Evolutionary psychologists argue that similar principles should be applied to analyzing the mechanisms of the human mind. Although an infinite number of descriptions may be used to describe and parse the mind, a powerful and nonarbitrary description identifies mechanisms by function.

Although, at this incipient stage of development in evolutionary psychology, no psychological mechanism has been fully or completely described—in terms of all its procedures or decision rules, the precise range of events that trigger its activation, and the events that affect its development—several illustrations of potential candidates for evolved psychological mechanisms are shown in Table 1.1, along with their hypothesized functions. An evolved disposition to fear snakes, for example, exists in the form that it does because it solved a specific problem of survival in human ancestral environments. The fear is triggered only by a narrow range of inputs, such as long, slithering organisms perceived to be within striking distance. Once a snake is perceived to be dangerous and within striking range, this information is transformed via decision rules that activate physiological activity, such as autonomic arousal. The eventual output is manifest action—such as freezing or fleeing—that in ancestral environments would have solved an adaptive survival problem by reducing the risk of a potentially deadly snakebite. That human phobias tend to be concentrated heavily in the domains of snakes, spiders, heights, darkness, and strangers provides a window for viewing the survival hazards that our ancestors faced (Marks, 1987).

Preferences are evolved psychological mechanisms of a sort different from fears. Preferences motivate the organism to seek things rich in the "resource-providing potential" needed for survival or reproduction (Orians & Heerwagen, 1992). Landscape preferences provide an illustration. Research has shown that savanna-like environments are consistently preferred to other environments. In particular, landscapes are liked that provide food, water, safety, protection from hazards (e.g., bad weather or landslides), and relative freedom from predators,

Table 1.1
Evolved Psychological Mechanisms: Ten Illustrations

Psychological Mechanism	Function	Author
1. Fear of snakes	Avoid poison	Marks (1987)
2. Superior female spatial-location memory	Increase success at foraging/gathering	Silverman & Eals (1992)
3. Male sexual jealousy	Increase paternity certainty	Buss, Larsen, Westen, & Semmelroth (1992); Daly, Wilson, & Weghorst (1982); Symons (1979)
4. Preference for foods rich in fats and sugar	Increase caloric intake	Rozin (1976)
5. Female mate preference for economic resources	Provisioning for children	Buss (1989a, 1989b)
6. Male mate preferences for youth, attractiveness, and waist-to-hip ratio	Select mates of high fertility	Buss (1989a, 1989b); Singh (1993)
7. Landscape preferences for savanna-like environments	Motivate individuals to select habitats that provide resources and offer protection	Kaplan (1992); Orians & Heerwagen (1992)
8. Natural language	Communication/manipulation	Pinker & Bloom (1990)
9. Cheater-detection procedure	Prevent being exploited in social contracts	Cosmides (1989)
10. Male desire for sexual variety	Motivate access to more sexual partners	Symons (1979)

parasites, toxic foods, and unfriendly humans (Orians & Heerwagen, 1992). Furthermore, people prefer places where they can see without being seen—places providing multiple views for surveillance and multiple ways of moving through space for escape. As a human ambulates through a variety of potential habitats, some particular landscape constellations fail to activate, fulfill, or embody these evolved preferences. Those that do embody the preferences presumably trigger a set of cognitive procedures or decision rules, depending in part on other contextual input, such as one's state of hunger or thirst, the size of one's group, and knowledge about the presence of hostile humans in the vicinity. Eventually, these procedures produce output in the form of a behavioral decision to remain in the habitat or to continue one's search for a better habitat. These behavioral decisions presumably led the possessors of landscape preferences to survive and reproduce better than those lacking landscape preferences or those who possessed alternative preferences that were less effective at securing resources and reducing risk.

Although psychological mechanisms such as landscape preferences clearly differ in important ways from mechanisms such as snake fears, they share critical ingredients that qualify them as evolved psychological mechanisms—they solved specific adaptive problems in human ancestral environments; they are triggered only by a narrow range of information; they are characterized by a particular set of procedures or decision rules; and they produce behavioral output that presumably solved the adaptive problem in ancestral times.

Given the infinite courses of action a human could pursue in principle, evolved psychological mechanisms are necessary for channeling action into the narrow pockets of adaptive choices: "Animals subsist on information. The single most limiting resource to reproduction is not food or safety or access to mates, but what makes them each possible: the information required for making adaptive behavioral choices" (Tooby & Cosmides, 1990b, p. 408). Psychological mechanisms are necessary for seeking and extracting particular forms of information; decision rules are necessary for producing action based on that information.

Evolved psychological mechanisms are likely to be large in number and complex in nature, and many will be domain-specific. There are several rationales for these premises, but I mention only two—one conceptual and one empirical. Conceptually, the adaptive problems that humans had to solve in their environment of evolutionary adaptedness were many, complex, and different from one another. A fear of snakes may solve the adaptive problem of avoiding a dangerous environmental hazard but does nothing to solve the adaptive problem of which foods to consume (e.g., berries and nuts, not twigs or gravel). Similarly, solutions to the problem of "how to attract a mate" do little to solve the problem of "how to socialize children." Different adaptive problems typically select for different adaptive solutions. As Symons (1992) put it, there is no such thing as a "general solution" because there is no such thing as a "general problem."

Mechanisms vary, of course, along many dimensions—some more domain-general, others more domain-specific; some more cognitively penetrable, others less cognitively penetrable; some easily overridden by other mechanisms, others more difficult to override. What constitutes a successful solution to an adaptive problem, however, differs across adaptive domains (e.g., avoiding a snake versus selecting a mate), individual circumstances (e.g., presence of powerful kin and alliances versus absence of social resources), different species (humans versus spiders), different ages (prepubescent versus adolescent), and different sexes (male versus female).

There can in principle, therefore, be no fully domain-general solution mechanism—one that can be used across all adaptive domains, by all ages, by all sexes, and under all individual circumstances. A carpenter's flexibility comes not from having a single, domain-general, "all-purpose tool" for cutting, poking, sawing, screwing, twisting, wrenching, planing, balancing, and hammering but rather from having many, more specialized, tools. The number and specificity of the tools in the entire tool kit give the carpenter great flexibility, not a single, highly "plastic" tool. Similarly, we display great flexibility in dealing with our social environments not because we have just a few domain-general psychological mechanisms, but rather because we possess a large number of complex and specific ones, which can be deployed singly and in complex combinations depending on circumstances.

On conceptual grounds, therefore, evolutionary psychologists assume that—because (1) adaptive problems are many and distinct, (2) successful solutions to one problem are different from the solutions needed for other problems, and (3) what will be successful depends heavily on species, age, sex, context, and individual circumstances—the solution mechanisms will be numerous and complex. Evolutionary psychology offers a powerful heuristic for identifying some of these human adaptive problems (Buss, 1991).

The second rationale for the complexity-numerosity premise is empirical. In the past 30 years, psychologists have demonstrated again and again violations of proposed principles of domain generality. In learning theory, for example, violations of equipotentiality have been demonstrated by Garcia and others. Indeed, Garcia's findings at first were so startling to editors and reviewers of the major journals—mainly because the findings violated domain-general learning principles—that they refused to believe or to publish them until they were replicated many times (Garcia, 1981). We now know that some things are extraordinarily difficult to learn, requiring thousands of trials; others can be learned in a single trial. We now know that humans are predisposed to learn some things more readily and rapidly than other things (Seligman & Hagar, 1972). More people learn fears of snakes, heights, spiders, and darkness, for example, than fears of cars or electrical outlets, which are currently more hazardous.

The existence of many domain-specific mechanisms, of course, does not rule out the possibility that some mechanisms will be relatively more domain-general than others—mechanisms such as the capacity for induction, the ability to perceive means-ends relations, and perhaps the perception of certain forms of covariation (Holland, Holyoak, Nisbett, & Thagard, 1986; Nisbett, 1990; but see Pinker, 1994, for a discussion of the need for domain-specific similarity metrics to guide generalizations). An evolutionary psychological perspective, however, suggests that the human mind cannot be solely composed of domain-general mechanisms—most adaptive problems require more complex and specialized psychological machinery to successfully solve. Moreover, the relatively more domain-general mechanisms will not be deployed randomly. Instead, these mechanisms are co-opted for very specific goals, such as forming reciprocal alliances or friendships, selecting mates, achieving or maintaining position within social hierarchies, helping family members, and building coalitions.

Many empirical findings that point to domain specificity have been discovered, and I list just 20 samples now for illustrative purposes:

1. A highly patterned distribution of fears and phobias that corresponds to hazards faced by humans in ancestral environments—the "fear of strangers" that emerges reliably between 8 and 24 months of age and fear of snakes, spiders, heights, open spaces, and darkness (Marks, 1987).

2. Particular mechanisms of color vision (Shepard, 1992).

3. Universal psychological adaptations to terrestrial living (Shepard, 1987).

4. Perceptual adaptations for entraining, tracking, and predicting animate motion (Freyd & Miller, 1993).

5. Children imitate high-status models much more than they do low-status models (Bandura, 1977).

6. Preschoolers reliably develop a specific theory of mind that entails the use of inferences about the beliefs and desires of others to predict their behavior (Wellman, 1990).

7. Autism results in a highly domain-specific psychological impairment—namely, the inability to formulate a concept of mind involving inferences about the beliefs and desires of others (Leslie, 1991).

8. Child abuse is 40 times greater among preschoolers in stepfamilies than in "intact" families in which there are two genetic parents—not implying dedicated mechanisms for child abuse but rather mechanisms for the preferential allocation of resources and imposition of costs (Wilson & Daly, 1987).

9. The causes of marital dissolution across cultures are highly predictable on evolutionary psychological grounds, centering heavily on infidelity and infertility (Betzig, 1989).

10. Male sexual jealousy occurs in all known cultures and is the leading cause of spousal homicide across cultures—not suggesting dedicated mechanisms for spousal homicide but rather male mechanisms designed to increase paternity certainty (Daly & Wilson, 1988).

11. Men and women worldwide show preferences for mates who are kind, intelligent, and dependable (Buss et al., 1990).

12. Men and women show consistent differences in what qualities they desire in potential mates (e.g., cues to resource investment potential, cues to reproductive value); these differences are closely linked with the social adaptive problems that men and women have confronted in mating contexts and are highly consistent across cultures (Buss, 1989a).

13. Women and men show predictable shifts in mate preferences when moving from brief sexual encounters to committed mating relationships (Buss & Schmitt, 1993).

14. Men and women differ dramatically in the frequency and content of sexual fantasy in ways predicted by evolutionary psychologists (Ellis & Symons, 1990).

15. Men inseminate more sperm after a separation from their wives in which an opportunity for infidelity might occur—a possible solution to the adaptive problem of lowered paternity certainty (Baker & Bellis, 1989).

16. Women of high reproductive value are more intensely guarded, sequestered, veiled, cloistered, and restrained than women of lower reproductive value (Dickemann, 1981).

17. Men engage in more risk-taking activity than women do, particularly between the ages of 16 and 24, when men are entering the arena of mate competition (Wilson & Daly, 1985).

18. Morning sickness shows a degree of design specificity such that one can reasonably infer that it represents an adaptation to prevent the ingestion of teratogens (Profet, 1992).

19. Women show superior spatial-location memory compared with men—a possible adaptation to gathering (Silverman & Eals, 1992).

20. Men show greater spatial-rotation ability compared with women—a possible adaptation to hunting (Silverman & Eals, 1992).

Although no one of these findings tells a definitive story, in the aggregate they point strongly to the existence of a large number of specialized psychological mechanisms. A mushrooming body of empirical evidence, in other words, supports the conceptual expectations of evolutionary psychologists—numerous mechanisms have evolved because of the large number and extreme diversity of adaptive problems that humans needed to solve in our evolutionary environments.

Many Important Adaptive Problems for Humans Are Social

The social group constituted at least one of the crucial "selection environments" for humans. Brewer and Caporael (1990), for example, argued that the cooperative group may have been the primary survival strategy of humans, and this would have selected for adaptations suited for cooperative group living— adaptations such as cooperativeness, loyalty, and fear of social exclusion (see also Alexander, 1987; Baumeister & Tice, 1990; Buss, 1990). Individuals whose mechanisms led them to be uncooperative, deviant from group norms, or disloyal presumably would have had more trouble surviving than those with the opposite set of mechanisms, and hence their mechanisms would have been selected against. This does not rule out mechanisms that lead people to be selectively disloyal or uncooperative, depending on particular circumstances. Indeed, analyses of the evolution of cooperation anticipate the existence of precisely such discriminative mechanisms (Axelrod, 1984; Cosmides, 1989).

But survival is only the beginning. Because natural selection operates by a process of differential reproductive success (not differential survival success), there are many reproductive problems that we had to solve, and many of these are inherently social in nature. Examples include successful intrasexual competition, mate selection, mate attraction, sexual intercourse, mate retention, reciprocal dyadic alliance formation, coalition building and maintenance, prestige and reputation maintenance, hierarchy negotiation, parental care and socialization, and extraparental kin investment (Buss, 1986, 1991).

Within each of these large classes of social adaptive problems lie dozens of subproblems. Forming a successful dyadic alliance, for example, may require identifying key resources possessed by potential friends, assessing which individuals possess these resources, modeling the values of those individuals, gauging potential sources of strategic interference, initiating sequential and incremental chains of reciprocity, and detecting signs of "cheating" or nonreciprocity (see Cosmides & Tooby, 1989). All these subproblems require solutions for the formation of a successful friendship.

Humans are probably unique in the duration and complexity of the social relationships they form. Humans sometimes form lifelong mating relationships, develop friendships that last for decades, and maintain contact with their brothers, sisters, and other relatives over great expanses of time and distance. Because social adaptive problems were so crucial for human survival and reproduction, many of the most important features of our evolved psychological mechanisms will necessarily be social in nature. Social adaptive problems have been so important over human evolutionary history that many of the dedicated psychological mechanisms currently studied by cognitive, personality, clinical, and developmental psychologists, in addition to those studied by social psychologists, are inherently social.

The Centrality of Context in Evolutionary Psychology

A common misconception of evolutionary approaches is that they postulate "instincts"—rigid, genetically inflexible behavior patterns that are invariantly expressed and unmodifiable by the environment. Although this view may have characterized some evolutionary approaches in the past and in some cases is erroneously thought to characterize contemporary evolutionary approaches, nothing could be further from the current views in evolutionary psychology.

Indeed, few other perspectives within psychology place greater importance on a detailed and complex treatment of environmental, situational, and contextual factors. Contextual evolutionary analysis takes place at several levels in the causal sequence. One is the *historical selective context*—the selection pressures that humans and their ancestors have faced over thousands of generations. Because we share part of our evolutionary history with other species—humans and chimps share common ancestors—we share some mechanisms with those species, such as our mechanisms of vision, which are similar. But, because human evolutionary history differs from that of all other species, and the selection pressures we have experienced are unique in many ways, some of our evolved psychological mechanisms are unique to us and are not shared by any other forms of life. Evolutionary psychology requires an analysis of these shared and unique features of our historical context.

A second context for evolutionary psychological analysis is the *ontogenetic context*. Evolutionary analyses of ontogenetic context have taken two forms, although these by no means exhaust the possibilities. One is analysis of the experiences during development that can shunt individuals toward different strategies (Buss, 1991; Tooby & Cosmides, 1990a). There is some evidence that father absence during childhood shunts individuals toward a more promiscuous mating strategy, whereas the presence of an investing father during childhood shunts individuals toward a more monogamous mating strategy (Belsky, Steinberg, & Draper, 1991; Draper & Belsky, 1990). The environmental input during development—presence versus absence of investing fathers and the reliability or unpredictability of resources—presumably provides information about the probability of securing a high-investing, committed mate and hence whether or not the pursuit of a series of short-term mates might be more advantageous. Second, developmental experiences set differing thresholds on species-typical psychological mechanisms. The threshold for responding to a threat with extreme violence, for example, may be lowered in some cultures, such as the Yanomamo Indians of Brazil (Chagnon, 1983), and raised in others, such as the !Kung San of Botswana (Shostack, 1981). Ontogenetic context includes, of course, variations by sex (due to sex-differentiated socialization) as well as variations due to culture (Low, 1989).

The third form of contextual analysis entails an analysis of the *immediate situational inputs* that activate the operation of particular psychological mechanisms. Just as callus-producing mechanisms are activated only if an individual experiences repeated friction to the skin, so psychological mechanisms such as sexual jealousy (Buss et al., 1992), cheater detection (Cosmides, 1989), and discriminative parental solicitude (Daly & Wilson, 1988) are activated only by particular contextual input such as cues to infidelity, nonreciprocation, and the simultaneous presence of biological children and stepchildren. A central goal of evolutionary psychology is to explicate all these forms of contextual input—historical, ontogenetic, and experiential.

The Core of Human Nature: Why Our Basic Psychological Mechanisms Are Likely to Be Species-Typical

There are compelling reasons for the view that our basic psychological mechanisms are likely to be species-typical, shared by most or all humans (Tooby & Cosmides, 1990a). Essentially, all complex mechanisms require dozens, hundreds, or thousands of genes for their development. Sexual recombination, by shuffling genes with each new generation, makes it exceedingly unlikely that complex mechanisms could be maintained if genes coding for complex adaptations varied substantially between individuals. Selection and sexual recombination tend to impose relative uniformity in complex adaptive designs. This is readily apparent at the level of physiology and anatomy—all people have two eyes, a heart, a larynx, and a liver. Individuals can vary quantitatively in the strength of their hearts or in the efficiency of their livers but do not vary in their possession of the basic physiological mechanisms themselves (except by unusual genetic or environmental accident). This suggests that individual dif-

ferences, including heritable individual differences, are unlikely to represent differences in the presence or absence of complex adaptive mechanisms—that is,
mechanisms containing many elements that are functionally integrated and likely
to be polygenic (Dawkins, 1986). Individual differences cannot be understood
apart from human nature mechanisms any more than differences in the turning
radius and stopping ability of cars can be understood apart from the basic car-
nature mechanisms such as steering wheels and brakes.

Discovering Evolved Psychological Mechanisms

Psychological mechanisms are usefully regarded as evolved solutions to adaptive problems. Analogy to the human body is useful. We have sweat glands and
shivering mechanisms that solve problems of thermal regulation; callus-
producing mechanisms that solve the problem of repeated friction to the skin;
taste preferences that solve the problem of what substances to ingest. Standards
for inferring that these mechanisms are solutions to adaptive problems include
economy, efficiency, complexity, precision, specialization, and reliability (Tooby
& Cosmides, 1992; Williams, 1966). Mechanisms that solve adaptive problems
are like keys that fit particular locks. The efficiency, detail, and complex structure of the key must mesh precisely with the inner "problem" posed by the
lock.

Evolutionary analysis of psychological mechanisms proceeds in two directions—form-to-function and function-to-form (Tooby & Cosmides, 1992).
Imagine finding a key but not knowing which of the thousands of possible locks
it might fit. Its size, its shape, its details might suggest tentative hypotheses and
rule out others. It might be too large to fit some locks, yet too small to fit others.
The shape of its tines must have a corresponding mirror-image shape in the
internal workings of the lock. Eventually, through an iterated process of hypothesis generation and empirical testing, we might eventually discover the exact
lock that the key was designed to fit. The precision, reliability, and specialization
with which a particular key fits a particular lock provide the researcher with
reasonable standards for inferring that a particular key was designed to fit a
particular lock.

Alternatively, one might identify a lock (adaptive problem) and then search
for a key that might fit it. Here, the same standards would apply—precision,
efficiency, complexity of design. The "bottom line" is whether the key one
discovers (adaptive mechanism proposed) actually fits the lock (solves the adaptive problem with reasonable precision, efficiency, and reliability) and whether
alternative hypotheses about its origin (e.g., incidental by-product of some other
adaptation) and function (other adaptive problems the mechanism might solve
or other mechanisms capable of solving the adaptive problem) can be reasonably
ruled out.

Evolutionary psychologists proceed in both directions, form-to-function and
function-to-form. Sometimes a phenomenon or form is discovered—fever, fear

of snakes, male sexual jealousy, mate preferences for "kindness"—and re-searchers generate and test hypotheses about its function. Often, there are com-peting functional theories about the same phenomenon, and these may be pitted against one another in critical empirical tests. This method is sometimes erro-neously derided as telling "just-so stories," but it is an essential process of science. The discovery of three-degree black-body radiation sent astronomers scrambling for cosmological theories or "stories" to explain it. The discovery of continental drift sent geologists scrambling for a theory, such as plate tec-tonics, that could explain it. The power of a theory rests with its ability to explain known facts and to generate new predictions, which are then subjected to empirical test. Specific evolutionary psychological theories should be evalu-ated by these rigorous scientific standards. Some will pan out. Others will be jettisoned on conceptual or empirical grounds.

Evolutionary analysis provides psychologists with a powerful heuristic, guid-ing them to important domains of adaptive problems and guiding the develop-ment of hypotheses about adaptive mechanisms heretofore unobserved. Because fertilization and gestation occur internally within women, for example, an adap-tive problem for ancestral men would have been ensuring confidence in their paternity as a condition for heavy investment. Men who were indifferent to this adaptive problem are not our ancestors. Such men would have devoted valuable effort to children who possessed copies of other men's genes rather than their own. Identifying this adaptive problem has led evolutionary psychologists to search for adaptive solutions in psychological mechanisms such as mate pref-erences for chastity, fidelity, and faithfulness (Buss, 1989a; Buss & Schmitt, 1993) and mechanisms involved in male sexual proprietariness such as sexual jealousy (Buss et al., 1992; Daly, Wilson, & Weghorst, 1982; Symons, 1979). Function-to-form and form-to-function are both viable methods for discovering our evolved psychological mechanisms.

Culture

When I give colloquia on my cross-cultural research on human mating strat-egies, at least one member of the audience will raise the following issue, phrased variously as "I have an alternative explanation for your findings—culture" or "Doesn't the existence of cross-cultural variability undermine your explanatory account?" When asked to elaborate on precisely what causal mechanisms are being invoked by culture as an alternative explanation, the questioner typically cannot supply additional details. Is "culture" really an alternative explanation? How can evolutionary psychologists deal with cultural variability?

Let us start with a common observation: "Humans everywhere show striking patterns of local within group similarity in their behavior and thought, accom-panied by profound intergroup differences" (Tooby & Cosmides, 1992, p. 6). These local within-group similarities and between-group differences can be of any sort—physical, psychological, behavioral, attitudinal, and so on. How can we understand and explain these cultural differences? It is useful to start with a physical example—calluses. The number and thickness of calluses that individuals have certainly show patterns of local within-group similarity and between-group differences. The warring Yanomamö have thicker and more numerous calluses than the missionaries who proselytize them.

The cultural differences can often be traced to environmental differences—Yanomamö experience more repeated friction on certain parts of their skin than do the missionaries. These differences, in turn, may be traced to other differences, such as the ways that the two groups secure food, the nature of the protective garments they use, and perhaps even the performance of certain rituals and leisure activities.

A causal explanation of these "cultural differences" requires the following ingredients: (1) evolved callus-producing mechanisms that were "designed" to receive as input only certain forms of external information (repeated friction), (2) local, within-group similarities and between-group differences in exposure to these forms of external information, and (3) an account of why some groups of individuals receive this exposure more than others. In this example, it is clear that any reasonably complete causal explanation requires a description of the evolved callus-producing mechanisms. Without these mechanisms, the "cultural differences" literally could not occur. Two profound implications follow: (1) cultural variability, far from constituting evidence against evolved psychological mechanisms, depends on a foundation of evolved mechanisms for its very existence; and (2) cultural variability is not explained merely by invoking "culture" (which merely mystifies the actual causal processes involved) but rather represents phenomena that require explanation.

Cultural differences in the number and thickness of calluses represent physical differences, but the logic applies with equal force to psychological, attitudinal, ideational, and behavioral differences. Certain Yanomamö groups display high levels of aggression, whereas the !Kung are notably peaceable (Chagnon, 1983; Shostack, 1981). The Ache of Paraguay are highly promiscuous, whereas the Hiwi show high levels of monogamy—a difference perhaps attributable to the high ratio of men to women among the Hiwi and the low ratio of men to women among the Ache, providing input into mechanisms that are sensitive to the relative availability of mates (Buss, 1994; Hill & Hurtado, 1989; Pedersen, 1991). These cultural differences are real and important, but explanatory accounts of them cannot ignore evolved psychological mechanisms underlying aggression and sexuality—mechanisms that are differentially activated in some contexts more than in others. Explanations require a specification of precisely what those context differences are and, ideally, a historical account of how they came to pass. Recognizing the role of evolved mechanisms provides a necessary foundation for cultural analyses of this sort.

Evolutionary psychology advocates integration and consistency of different levels of analysis, not psychological or biological reductionism: "By themselves, psychological theories do not, and cannot, constitute theories of culture.

They only provide the foundations for theories of culture'' (Tooby & Cosmides, 1992, p. 88). But those foundations are critical and the sine qua non of cultural phenomena:

It is especially important . . . to recognize that the environmental factors that cause contentful mental and behavioral organization to be expressed are not necessarily the processes that constructed the organization. . . . The claim that some phenomena are ''socially constructed'' only means that the social environment provided some of the inputs used by the psychological mechanisms of the individuals involved. (Tooby & Cosmides, 1992, pp. 89–90)

Not all cultural phenomena can be explained as ''evoked culture'' in the manner in which callus differences are explained. A different subset of cultural phenomena may be restricted to:

(1) those representations or regulatory elements that exist originally in at least one mind that (2) come to exist in other minds because (3) observation and interaction between the source and the observer cause inferential mechanisms in the observer to recreate the representations or regulatory elements in his or her own psychological architecture. In this case, their representations and elements inferred are contingent: They could be otherwise, and in other human minds, they commonly are otherwise. (Tooby & Cosmides, 1992, p. 91)

Tooby and Cosmides referred to these cultural phenomena as ''adopted culture.''

But phenomena described by adopted culture, like all other human behavioral phenomena, require an account of what psychological mechanisms underlie them and why such mechanisms have evolved. Tooby and Cosmides have suggested that such mechanisms are advantageous, conferring upon individuals an adaptive responsiveness to local conditions that is difficult to gain through only individual experience. Indeed, more often than not, an individual's predecessors in a particular social environment have developed a useful information base that others are able to reconstruct through social observation. However, it appears that such inferential reconstruction

would be unsolvable if the child did not come equipped with a rich battery of domain-specific inferential mechanisms, a faculty of social cognition, a large set of frames about humans and the world drawn from the common stock of meta-culture, and other specialized adaptations designed to solve the problems involved in this task . . . [thus] culture is also shaped by the details of our evolved psychological organization . . . there is no radical discontinuity inherent in the evolution of ''culture'' that removes humans into an autonomous realm. (Tooby & Cosmides, 1992, p. 91)

''Culture,'' ''learning,'' and ''socialization'' do not constitute explanations, let alone alternative explanations to those anchored in evolutionary psychology. Instead, they represent human phenomena that require explanation. The required explanation must have a description of the underlying evolved psychological mechanisms at its core.

The Evolutionary Psychology of Jealousy: An Illustration

No evolved psychological mechanism has been explored comprehensively in all its facets—the historical selection pressures that forged it, its development, the inputs that activate it, its species-typical nature, and its sex-differentiated, age-differentiated, culturally differentiated, and individually differentiated features. In this sense, evolutionary psychology offers a promissory note, and it is reasonable to hold it to a rigorous theoretical standard—what new insights are gained by adopting this perspective? Its value, like the value of all theoretical perspectives, must be gauged by its conceptual and empirical harvest.

Here I explicate one case I believe illustrates the potential payoff of evolutionary psychology—the case of jealousy. Jealousy is neither a peripheral nor a trivial emotion, for it is experienced in all known cultures and is the leading cause of spousal battering and homicide worldwide (Daly & Wilson, 1988). Why do humans experience jealousy? Do the sexes differ in its expression? What contexts activate jealousy? Of what value is evolutionary psychology in shedding light on this pervasive and pernicious mechanism?

Jealousy is a cognitive-emotional-motivational complex activated by threat to a valued relationship. It is considered ''sexual jealousy'' if the relevant threatened relationship is a sexual one, but some types of jealousy do not involve sex. Jealousy presumably is activated by cues to the loss of key resources provided by the relationship—cues such as eye contact between one's mate and a rival, decreased sexual interest, and a mate's increase in flirting with same-sex competitors. Jealousy channels attention, calls up relevant memories, and channels thought in particular directions. Ultimately, it motivates actions designed to reduce or eliminate the threat and retain the valuable relationship and the resources it provides.

Because both men and women over human evolutionary history have been damaged by relationship loss, both sexes have faced adaptive problems to which jealousy may have evolved as a solution. There are no evolutionary grounds for predicting that one sex will be more jealous than the other, and, indeed, almost all studies have shown that the sexes are equally jealous (White & Mullen, 1989). Jealousy appears to be a species-typical mechanism in both men and women in all known cultures (Daly & Wilson, 1988).

But evolutionary psychologists have long predicted that the sexes will differ in the events that activate jealousy (Daly et al., 1982; Symons, 1979). Specifically, because fertilization and gestation occur internally within women and not men, men over evolutionary history have faced an adaptive problem simply not faced by women—less than 100% certainty of parenthood. The reproductive threat for the man comes from the possibility of sexual infidelity by his mate. In species such as ours, in which the male sometimes invests heavily in a female and children, the female's certainty of genetic parenthood is not compromised if the male has sex with other females. The woman may risk the loss of her mate's time, attention, commitment, involvement, protection, and resources—resources that can be diverted from her and her children toward another woman. For these reasons, evolutionary psychologists have predicted that the inputs that activate jealousy for men will focus heavily on the sex act per se, whereas for women they will focus on cues to the loss of the men's commitment and investment.

A recent series of studies provided powerful confirmation. Consider this question: What would upset or distress you more: (1) imagining your mate having sexual intercourse with someone else or (2) imagining your mate forming a deep emotional attachment to someone else? The overwhelming majority of women endorsed emotional attachment; most men endorsed sexual intercourse. These sex differences were also observed in physiological arousal to imagining the two different scenarios. In measures of heart rate, electrodermal activity, and frowning, men showed greater physiological arousal and distress to imagined sexual infidelity than to emotional infidelity (Buss et al., 1992). Women tended to be more distressed by emotional than by sexual infidelity.

Individuals also vary within sex in jealous responses. For example, in the study just described, although some 60% of the men reported that they would be more distressed by their partner's sexual infidelity, the other 40% reported that they would be more distressed by their partner's emotional infidelity. These individual differences provide an important avenue for testing evolutionary psychological hypotheses. One such hypothesis is that the relevant ontogenetic experiences must occur before the mechanism is activated. In the case of men, the relevant experience might be whether or not the man had experienced a committed sexual relationship. We found that the majority of men who had not experienced such a relationship reported that they would be more upset by emotional, rather than sexual, infidelity (Buss et al., 1992). In contrast, most men who had experienced a committed sexual relationship reported that they would be more upset by sexual infidelity. So, individual differences within sex may be due, in part, to differing developmental experiences—in this case, whether or not the relevant activating context had been experienced—although obviously the opposite causal arrow (i.e., men upset by infidelity preferentially seek committed relationships) and other alternative explanations (e.g., men lower in mate value have more difficulty securing committed sexual relationships and so may not be able to insist on sexual fidelity) cannot be ruled out.

What about cross-cultural evidence? Sex differences in jealousy are not limited to American samples. Gottschalk (1936) found that 80% of the Central European men in his sample expressed fears of sexual threat, such as fantasies about the man's mate having sexual intercourse with another man or fears about his own sexual adequacy. Only 22% of the women in this sample expressed sexual concerns, focusing instead on relationship themes such as emotional closeness between the woman's mate and other women. A study of Dutch,

English, and American divorce cases found that men more frequently cited infidelity by their spouses as a cause of divorce, even though such men were less likely to encounter infidelity than their female counterparts (Buunk, 1987; see also Kinsey, Pomeroy, & Martin, 1953). Betzig (1989) found similar results in a massive study of 89 cultures from around the world.

Cross-culturally, a wife's infidelity is viewed as a provocation so extreme that a "reasonable man" may respond with lethal violence (Daly & Wilson, 1988, p. 196). In Texas up until 1974, for example, it was legal for a husband to kill his wife and her lover if he did so while the adulterers were caught flagrante delicto (in the actual act). It was considered a reasonable response to a powerful provocation. Laws exonerating men from killing adulterous wives are found worldwide and throughout human history, despite myths propagated by some anthropologists that there are cultures in which men are not sexually jealous. Consider this description of Greek culture:

The wife's infidelity . . . brings disgrace to the husband who is then a Keratas—the worst insult for a Greek man—a shameful epithet with connotations of weakness and inadequacy. . . . While for the wife it is socially acceptable to tolerate her unfaithful husband, it is not socially acceptable for a man to tolerate his unfaithful wife and if he does so, he is ridiculed as behaving in an unmanly manner. (Safilios-Rothschild, 1969, pp. 78–79)

Daly and Wilson (1988) scrutinized in detail the ethnographies for cultures that scholars such as Margaret Mead, Frank Beach, Marvin Whyte, and others have asserted have no bars to sexual conduct other than the universal incest taboo. Daly and Wilson found evidence for sexual jealousy in every one of these supposedly "nonjealousy" cultures. Among the Marquesa Islanders, for example, in which anthropologists have asserted that there are no bars to adultery other than the incest prohibition, we find this striking contradiction: "When a woman undertook to live with a man, she placed herself under his authority. If she cohabited with another man without his permission, she was beaten, or, if her husband's jealousy was sufficiently aroused, killed" (Handy, 1923, p. 100; cited in Daly & Wilson, 1988, p. 204).

Another example of the supposed absence of sexual jealousy involved the practices of wife sharing by Eskimo men. Contrary to popular myths, however, male sexual jealousy is the leading cause of spouse homicide among the Eskimos—homicides that occur at an alarmingly high rate. Eskimo men share their wives only under highly circumscribed conditions—when there is the reciprocal expectation that the favor is to be returned in kind. Nowhere are wives shared freely. Paradises populated with sexually liberated people who share mates and do not get jealous apparently exist only in the minds of optimistic anthropologists and their unsuspecting readers. Sexual jealousy has been found to be a leading motive behind homicide in Sudan (Lobban, 1972), Uganda (Tanner, 1970), and India (Bohannan, 1960). Daly et al. (1982) concluded that "the majority of cases in each society was precipitated either by male accusations of adultery or by the woman's leaving or rejecting the husband'' (p. 16).

These studies are clearly just the start of the exploration of this important psychological mechanism. Additional evolutionary psychological questions being explored currently include: Does male sexual jealousy vary in intensity across cultures according to the magnitude of male parental investment? Does female jealousy decrease as a function of decreases in a mate's resources? Does male sexual jealousy decrease as the reproductive value of his mate decreases? Is the partner who is relatively lower in mate value more jealous than the partner who is higher in mate value? All these questions were guided by evolutionary psychological thinking, and answers to them over the next few years should provide an even greater understanding of the workings of this complex mechanism—its species-typical features, its sex-differentiated features, and its individually different features.

Several important theoretical points can be drawn from this case example. First, evolved mechanisms do not determine behavior invariantly or rigidly but rather require relevant contextual information for their activation. Second, not all individuals respond to the same input in the same manner; just as men and women weight differing signs of infidelity somewhat differently, so different individuals within sex also weight cues differently (e.g., based on different developmental experiences, different assets such as mate value). Third, different cultures are likely to provide somewhat different input into evolved mechanisms—highlighting phenomena that require explanation rather than invoking ''culture'' as an alternative explanation. Fourth, mechanisms such as those subsumed by the concept of ''jealousy'' cut across traditional disciplinary boundaries within psychology. It is clearly a social phenomenon, because it involves mates and intrasexual rivals; it is clearly a cognitive phenomenon, because its mechanisms process informational input; it clearly has important developmental features, because varying ontogenetic experiences appear to affect the operation of the mechanisms; and, because individuals differ in consistent ways over time in the manner in which their jealousy mechanisms are activated, it is clearly a personality phenomenon as well. This implies that the traditional disciplinary boundaries within psychology do not cleave nature at its functional joints.

THE FUTURE OF EVOLUTIONARY PSYCHOLOGY

Scientific success in uncovering the mysteries of life has been based on three critical foundations—mechanism, natural selection, and historicity (Williams, 1992). Since the cognitive revolution, psychologists have moved away from behaviorism's unworkable antimentalism, making it respectable to study information-processing mechanisms inside the head. Nonetheless, we have been handicapped in failing to consider the profound importance of natural selection and historicity in the creation of those mechanisms. The neglect of natural selection has led psychologists to ignore the adaptive functions of mechanisms and hence has hindered the quest to unravel the mystery of why these mechanisms exist at all and, more specifically, why they exist in the particular forms that they do.

Currently, evolutionary psychology is viewed from the mainstream as a relatively new theoretical perspective within psychology—a perspective that generates some novel insights perhaps and that includes a lot of promise perhaps but is just one perspective among many. A prominent, open-minded psychologist I know said, "At some point in the future, every psychology department will need to have at least one evolutionary psychologist on its rosters."

At the other extreme, a well-known evolutionary psychologist once remarked that, at some point in the future, the term *evolutionary* would be dropped entirely from *evolutionary psychology* because the entire field of psychology will be evolutionary, and the qualifier would be superfluous. Although I do not share the latter view, I do believe that evolutionary psychology provides a coherent metatheory for the different branches of psychological science, and it is unlikely to be supplanted by another unless some radically new causal process, heretofore entirely unknown and unobserved, is discovered to account for the origins and particulars of the complex adaptations that characterize humans and other species.

Most of us are aware that the field of psychology is currently in a fragmented state. Disciplinary boundaries are strange, unnatural, misleading, and distorting. A plethora of mini-theories within each discipline clamors like a babble of incommensurate tongues. Experimentalists use stimuli that are convenient but often arbitrary—many only marginally more meaningful than the nonsense syllables used in hundreds of memory drum experiments in earlier decades. Furthermore, many psychologists assume a high degree of domain generality of psychological mechanisms—an unfortunate assumption carried over from behaviorism. When I recently asked a distinguished categorization researcher whether he thought that the cognitive mechanisms that humans use to categorize kinship relationships (e.g., father, mother, daughter, brother) were the same as those used to categorize plants or foods (e.g., edible versus nonedible, fruit versus meat), he answered in the affirmative. To an evolutionary psychologist, however, it would be astonishing to find that degree of domain generality with no specialized procedures for dealing with radically different adaptive domains such as kinship categories and consumption categories. Despite the mainstream assumptions, cutting-edge cognitive psychologists are making great strides in the evolutionary analysis of perception (Shepard, 1992), language (Pinker, 1994), reasoning (Cosmides, 1989), cognitive heuristics (Gigerenzer & Hug, 1992), and cognitive neuroscience (Gazzaniga, 1992).

Social psychologists have mapped out reaction times to trait words shown to college sophomores on cathode-ray tubes, but the mainstream seems to have lost sight of the social interactions and social relationships that properly form the core content for the field. Recently, however, there are signs of increasing commitment to the study of social relationships (e.g., Berscheid & Snyder, 1989;

Hazan & Shaver, 1991; Hendrick & Hendrick, 1991; Rusbult, 1987; Snyder, Gangestad, & Simpson, 1987). A veritable cottage industry has sprung up around the evolutionary psychology of human mating (Baily, Gaulin, Agyei, & Gladue, 1994; Buss, 1994; Gangestad & Simpson, 1990; Kenrick, Groth, Trost, & Sadalla, 1993). The evolutionary psychologies of friendships (Lusk, Mac-Donald, & Newman, 1993), kinships (DeKay, 1991), and coalitions (Cosmides & Tooby, 1993) are starting to receive increasing attention.

Personality psychologists historically have endlessly created scale after scale to measure yet more dimensions of investigator-defined and often arbitrary individual differences. Taxonomic efforts at individual differences remain atheoretical and isolated from the basic species-typical psychological functioning that occupies much of the rest of the field. Individual differences too, however, are starting to yield to an evolutionary psychological analysis (e.g., Belsky et al., 1991; Buss, 1993; Gangestad & Simpson, 1990; Hogan, 1983; Kenrick et al., 1993; McDonald, 1992; Nesse & Lloyd, 1992; Waller, 1994).

Explanations advanced as causal (e.g., "culture," "learning," and "socialization") are at best descriptions of phenomena awaiting explanation and at worst empty names given to ignorance of actual causal processes that give the illusion of having explained something—and hence have the pernicious effect of halting the causal investigation (D. Symons, personal communication, 1991). Cultural and socialization phenomena, too, are starting to yield to evolutionary psychological analysis (Belsky et al., 1991; Brown, 1991; Low, 1989; Tooby & Cosmides, 1992).

Despite these important advances, the program advocated by evolutionary psychology would dissolve the traditional disciplinary boundaries. Human beings cannot be neatly partitioned into discrete contents such as personality, social, developmental, clinical, or cognitive. Stable individual differences have been relegated traditionally to the personality branch, but they often involve social orientations, have particular developmental antecedents, and are undergirded by particular cognitive mechanisms. Social exchange and reciprocity have traditionally been regarded as quintessentially belonging to social psychology, but the mechanisms that underlie them are information-processing devices that have developmental trajectories. The rapid changes occurring at puberty have traditionally been the province of developmental psychologists, yet individuals differ in onset of puberty, many of the most important changes are social, and all are undergirded by evolved psychological mechanisms that get suddenly activated. From the perspective of evolutionary psychology, many traditional disciplinary boundaries are not merely arbitrary but are misleading and detrimental to progress. They imply boundaries that cleave mechanisms in arbitrary and unnatural ways. Studying human psychology via adaptive problems and their solutions provides a natural means of "cleaving nature at its joints" and hence crossing current disciplinary boundaries.

A critical task in this new psychological science will be the identification of the key adaptive problems that humans confronted repeatedly over our evolutionary history. We have barely scratched the surface by identifying some of the problems most obviously and plausibly linked with survival and reproduction. Most adaptive problems remain unexplored; most psychological solutions, undiscovered. It is not unreasonable to expect that the first scientists to explore these uncharted territories will come away with a great bounty.

Evolutionary psychology provides the conceptual tools for emerging from the fragmented state of current psychological science. It provides the key to unlocking the mystery of where we came from, how we arrived at our current state, and the mechanisms of mind that define who we are.

NOTES

This chapter owes a profound conceptual debt to Leda Cosmides, Martin Daly, Don Symons, John Tooby, and Margo Wilson. I also thank the Center for Advanced Study in the Behavioral Sciences for supporting our Foundations of Evolutionary Psychology project. Tim Ketelaar, Richard Nisbett, Larry Pervin, Steve Pinker, and Todd Shackelford offered insightful suggestions on the substance of the article.

Selected portions of this chapter were adapted and updated from papers published by the author in *Motivation and Emotion* (1990) and *Annual Review of Psychology* (1991) or presented by the author at the NATO Conference on Biological and Social Approaches to Personality (1993).

1. Of course, evolutionary processes other than selection—including mutation, drift, and pleiotropic effects—affect physiological and psychological mechanisms, but they are extremely unlikely to fashion complex, precise, efficient, well-sculpted mechanisms. Of all evolutionary processes, only selection has the causal power to produce such complex mechanisms.

2. The exception to this statement, of course, occurs when one is interested in partitioning variance among individuals at a sample or population level, in which case behavioral genetic methods can be used to generate quantitative estimates of the relative size of the genetic and environmental variance components (see Plomin, DeFries, & Loehlin, 1977, for a useful discussion of this issue). This is a different level of analysis, however, from the individual level that is the focus of the present discussion.

REFERENCES

Alexander, R. D. (1987). *The biology of moral systems*. New York: Aldine de Gruyter.

Axelrod, R. (1984). *The evolution of cooperation*. New York: Basic.

Baily, J. M., Gaulin, S., Agyei, Y., & Gladue, B. A. (1994). Effects of gender and sexual orientation on evolutionarily relevant aspects of human mating psychology. *Journal of Personality and Social Psychology, 66,* 1081–1093.

Baker, R. R., & Bellis, M. A. (1989). Number of sperm in human ejaculates varies in accordance with sperm competition theory. *Animal Behaviour, 37,* 867–869.

Bandura, A. (1977). *Social learning theory*. Englewood Cliffs, NJ: Prentice-Hall.

Baumeister, R. F., & Tice, D. M. (1990). Anxiety and social exclusion. *Journal of Social and Clinical Psychology, 9,* 165–195.

Belsky, J., Steinberg, L., & Draper, P. (1991). Childhood experience, interpersonal development, and reproductive strategy: An evolutionary theory of socialization. *Child Development, 62*, 647–670.

Berscheid, E., & Snyder, M. (1989). The Relationship Closeness Inventory: Assessing the closeness of interpersonal relationships. *Journal of Personality and Social Psychology, 57*, 792–807.

Betzig, L. (1989). Causes of conjugal dissolution: A cross-cultural study. *Current Anthropology, 30*, 654–676.

Bohannan, P. (1960). *African homicide and suicide*. Princeton, NJ: Princeton University Press.

Brewer, M. B., & Caporael, L. R. (1990). Selfish genes versus selfish people: Sociobiology as origin myth. *Motivation and Emotion, 14*, 237–243.

Brown, D. E. (1991). *Human universals*. Philadelphia: Temple University Press.

Buss, D. M. (1986). Can social science be anchored in evolutionary biology? *Revue Europeene des Sciences Sociales, 24*, 41–50.

Buss, D. M. (1988a). The evolution of human intrasexual competition: Tactics of mate attraction. *Journal of Personality and Social Psychology, 54*, 616–628.

Buss, D. M. (1988b). From vigilance to violence: Tactics of mate retention. *Ethology and Sociobiology, 9*, 291–317.

Buss, D. M. (1989a). Sex differences in human mate preferences: Evolutionary hypotheses tested in 37 cultures. *Behavioral and Brain Sciences, 12*, 1–49.

Buss, D. M. (1989b, June). *A theory of strategic trait usage: Personality and the adaptive landscape*. Paper presented at the Invited Workshop on Personality Language, University of Groningen, Groningen, The Netherlands.

Buss, D. M. (1990). The evolution of anxiety and social exclusion. *Journal of Social and Clinical Psychology, 9*, 196–201.

Buss, D. M. (1991). Evolutionary personality psychology. *Annual Review of Psychology, 45*, 459–491.

Buss, D. M. (1993). Strategic individual differences: The role of personality in creating and solving adaptive problems. In J. Hettema & I. J. Deary (Eds.), *Foundations of personality* (pp. 175–189). Dordrecht, The Netherlands: Kluwer Academic.

Buss, D. M. (1994). *The evolution of desire: Strategies of human mating*. New York: Basic.

Buss, D. M., Abbott, M., Angleitner, A., Asherian, A., Biaggio, A., et al. [45 additional authors]. (1990). International preferences in selecting mates: A study of 37 societies. *Journal of Cross-Cultural Psychology, 21*, 5–47.

Buss, D. M., Larsen, R. J., Westen, D., & Semmelroth, J. (1992). Sex differences in jealousy: Evolution, physiology, and psychology. *Psychological Science, 3*, 251–255.

Buss, D. M., & Schmitt, D. P. (1993). Sexual strategies theory: A contextual evolutionary analysis of human mating. *Psychological Review, 100*, 204–232.

Buunk, B. (1987). Conditions that promote break-ups as a consequence of extradyadic involvements. *Journal of Social and Clinical Psychology, 5*, 237–250.

Chagnon, N. (1983). *Yanomamo: The fierce people* (3rd ed.). New York: Holt, Rinehart, & Winston.

Cosmides, L. (1989). The logic of social exchange: Has natural selection shaped how humans reason? *Cognition, 31*, 187–276.

Cosmides, L., & Tooby, J. (1989). Evolutionary psychology and the generation of culture,

Part II: Case study: A computational theory of social exchange. *Ethology and Sociobiology, 10*, 51–98.

Cosmides, L., & Tooby, J. (1993, August). *Cognitive adaptations for threat, cooperation, and war.* Paper presented at the meeting of the Human Behavior and Evolution Society, Binghamton, NY.

Daly, M., & Wilson, M. (1988). *Homicide.* New York: Aldine de Gruyter.

Daly, M., Wilson, M., & Weghorst, S. J. (1982). Male sexual jealousy. *Ethology and Sociobiology, 3*, 11–27.

Darwin, C. (1859). *On the origin of the species by means of natural selection, or, Preservation of favoured races in the struggle for life.* London: Murray.

Darwin, C. (1871). *The descent of man and selection in relation to sex.* London: Murray.

Dawkins, R. (1986). *The blind watchmaker.* New York: Norton.

DeKay, W. T. (1991, July). *Sibling cooperation and conflict.* Paper presented at the meeting of the Human Behavior and Evolution Society, Hamilton, Canada.

Dickemann, M. (1981). Paternal confidence and dowry competition: A biocultural analysis of purdah. In R. D. Alexander & D. W. Tinkle (Eds.), *Natural selection and social behavior* (pp. 417–438). New York: Chiron.

Draper, P., & Belsky, J. (1990). Personality development in evolutionary perspective. *Journal of Personality, 58*, 141–163.

Ellis, B. J., & Symons, D. (1990). Sex differences in sexual fantasy: An evolutionary psychological approach. *Journal of Sex Research, 27*, 527–556.

Festinger, L. (1957). *A theory of cognitive dissonance.* New York: Row Peterson.

Fodor, J. A. (1968). *Psychological explanation.* New York: Random House.

Freyd, J. J., & Miller, G. F. (1993, August). *Human perceptual adaptations for entraining, tracking, and predicting animate motion.* Paper presented at the meeting of the Human Behavior and Evolution Society, Binghamton, NY.

Gangestad, S. W., & Simpson, J. A. (1990). Toward an evolutionary history of female sociosexual variation. *Journal of Personality, 58*, 69–96.

Garcia, J. (1981). Tilting at the paper mills of academe. *American Psychologist, 36*, 149–158.

Gazzaniga, M. S. (1992). *Nature's mind.* New York: Basic.

Gigerenzer, G., & Hug, K. (1992). Domain-specific reasoning: Social contracts, cheating and perspective change. *Cognition, 43*, 127–171.

Gottschalk, H. (1936). *Skinsygens problemer* [Problems of jealousy]. Copenhagen: Fremad.

Gould, S. J. (1987). Freudian slip? *Natural History, 2*, 14–21.

Hamilton, W. D. (1964). The evolution of social behavior. *Journal of Theoretical Biology, 7*, 1–52.

Hamilton, W. D. (1980). Sex versus non-sex versus parasite. *Oikos, 35*, 282–290.

Hamilton, W. D., & Zuk, M. (1982). Heritable true fitness and bright birds: A role for parasites? *Science, 218*, 384–387.

Handy, E. S. C. (1923). *The native culture in the Marquesas* (Bulletin No. 9). Bernice A. Bishop Museum.

Hazan, C., & Shaver, P. R. (1991). Love and work: An attachment-theoretical perspective. *Journal of Personality and Social Psychology, 59*, 270–280.

Hendrick, C., & Hendrick, S. (1991). Dimensions of love: A sociobiological interpretation. *Journal of Social and Clinical Psychology, 10*, 206–230.

Hill, K., & Hurtado, A. M. (1989). Hunter-gatherers of the new world. *American Scientist, 77*, 437–443.

Hill, K., & Kaplan, H. (1988). Tradeoffs in male and female reproductive strategies among the Ache. In L. Betzig, M. Borgerhoff Mulder, & P. Turke (Eds.), *Human reproductive behavior* (pp. 277–306). Cambridge, England: Cambridge University Press.

Hogan, R. (1983). A socioanalytic theory of personality. In M. M. Page (Ed.), *Nebraska Symposium on Motivation.* Lincoln: University of Nebraska Press.

Holland, J. H., Holyoak, K. J., Nisbett, R. E., & Thagard, P. R. (1986). *Induction: Processes of inference, learning, and discovery.* Cambridge: MIT Press.

Kaplan, S. (1992). Environmental preference in a knowledge-seeking, knowledge-using organism. In J. Barkow, L. Cosmides, & J. Tooby (Eds.), *The adapted mind* (pp. 555–580). New York: Oxford University Press.

Kenrick, D. T., Groth, G. E., Trost, M. R., & Sadalla, E. K. (1993). Integrating evolutionary and social exchange perspectives on relationships: Effects of gender, self-appraisal, and involvement on level of mate selection. *Journal of Personality and Social Psychology, 64*, 951–969.

Kenrick, D. T., Sadalla, E. K., Groth, G., & Trost, M. R. (1990). Evolution, traits, and the stages of human courtship: Qualifying the parental investment model. *Journal of Personality, 58*, 97–116.

Kinsey, A. C., Pomeroy, W. B., & Martin, C. E. (1953). *Sexual behavior in the human female.* Philadelphia: Saunders.

Latané, B. (1981). The psychology of social impact. *American Psychologist, 36*, 343–356.

Leslie, A. M. (1991). The theory of mind impairment in autism: Evidence for modular mechanisms of development? In A. Whiten (Ed.), *The emergence of mind reading.* Oxford, England: Blackwell.

Lobban, C. F. (1972). *Law and anthropology in the Sudan (An analysis of homicide cases in Sudan)* (African Studies Seminar No. 13). Khartoum: Khartoum University, Sudan Research Unit.

Low, B. S. (1989). Cross-cultural patterns in the training of children: An evolutionary perspective. *Journal of Comparative Psychology, 103*, 311–319.

Lusk, J., MacDonald, K., & Newman, J. R. (1993, August). *Resource appraisals among self, friend, and leader: Toward an evolutionary perspective on personality and individual differences.* Paper presented at the meeting of the Human Behavior and Evolution Society, Binghamton, NY.

Marks, I. M. (1987). *Fears, phobias, and rituals.* New York: Oxford University Press.

Marr, D. (1982). *Vision.* San Francisco: Freeman.

Mayr, E. (1982). *The growth of biological thought.* Cambridge: Harvard University Press.

McDonald, K. (1992). Warmth as a developmental construct: An evolutionary analysis. *Child Development, 63*, 753–773.

McGuire, M., & Troisi, A. (1987). Physiological regulation-deregulation and psychiatric disorders. *Ethology and Sociobiology, 8*, 9–27.

Nesse, R. M., & Lloyd, A. T. (1992). The evolution of psychodynamic mechanisms. In J. Barkow, L. Cosmides, & J. Tooby (Eds.), *The adapted mind* (pp. 601–624). New York: Oxford University Press.

Newell, A., & Simon, H. (1961). Computer simulation of human thinking. *Science, 134*, 2011–2017.

Nisbett, R. E. (1990). Evolutionary psychology, biology, and cultural evolution. *Motivation and Emotion, 14,* 255–263.

Orians, G. H., & Heerwagen, J. H. (1992). Evolved responses to landscapes. In J. Barkow, L. Cosmides, & J. Tooby (Eds.), *The adapted mind* (pp. 555–580). New York: Oxford University Press.

Pedersen, F. A. (1991). Secular trends in human sex ratios: Their influence on individual and family behavior. *Human Nature, 3,* 271–291.

Pinker, S. (1994). *The language instinct.* New York: Morrow.

Pinker, S., & Bloom, P. (1990). Natural language and natural selection. *Behavioral and Brain Sciences, 13,* 707–784.

Plomin, R., DeFries, J. C., & Loehlin, J. C. (1977). Genotype-environment interaction and correlation in the analysis of human behavior. *Psychological Bulletin, 84,* 309–322.

Profet, M. (1992). Pregnancy sickness as an adaptation: A deterrent to maternal ingestion of teratogens. In J. Barkow, L. Cosmides, & J. Tooby (Eds.), *The adapted mind* (pp. 327–366). New York: Oxford University Press.

Pylyshyn, Z. W. (1980). Computation and cognition: Issues in the foundations of cognitive science. *Behavioral and Brain Sciences, 3,* 111–132.

Quine, W. V. (1981). *Theories and things.* Cambridge: Belknap Press of Harvard University Press.

Rancour-Laferriere, D. (1985). *Signs of the flesh: An essay on the evolution of hominid sexuality.* New York: Mouton de Gruyter.

Rozin, P. (1976). Psychological and cultural determinants of food choice. In T. Silverstone (Ed.), *Appetite and food intake* (pp. 286–312). Berlin: Dahlem Konferenzen.

Rusbult, C. E. (1987). Responses to dissatisfaction in close relationships: The exit-voice-loyalty-neglect model. In D. Perlman & S. Duck (Eds.), *Intimate relationships: Development, dynamics, and deterioration* (pp. 209–237). Newbury Park, CA: Sage.

Sadalla, E. K., Kenrick, D. T., & Vershure, B. (1987). Dominance and heterosexual attraction. *Journal of Personality and Social Psychology, 52,* 730–738.

Safilios-Rothschild, C. (1969). Attitudes of Greek spouses toward marital infidelity. In G. Neubeck (Ed.), *Extramarital relations* (pp. 78–79). Englewood Cliffs, NJ: Prentice-Hall.

Seligman, M. E. P., & Hagar, J. L. (Eds.). (1972). *Biological boundaries of learning.* New York: Appleton-Century-Crofts.

Shepard, R. N. (1987). Toward a universal law of generalization for psychological science. *Science, 237,* 1317–1323.

Shepard, R. N. (1992). The perceptual organization of colors: An adaptation to regularities of the terrestrial world? In J. Barkow, L. Cosmides, & J. Tooby (Eds.), *The adapted mind* (pp. 495–532). New York: Oxford University Press.

Shostack, M. (1981). *Nisa: The life and words of a !Kung woman.* Cambridge: Harvard University Press.

Silverman, I., & Eals, M. (1992). Sex differences in spatial abilities: Evolutionary theory and data. In J. Barkow, L. Cosmides, & J. Tooby (Eds.), *The adapted mind* (pp. 533–549). New York: Oxford University Press.

Singh, D. (1993). Adaptive significance of waist-to-hip ratio and female attractiveness. *Journal of Personality and Social Psychology, 65,* 293–307.

Snyder, M., Gangestad, S., & Simpson, J. A. (1987). Personality and sexual relations. *Journal of Personality and Social Psychology, 51,* 181–190.

Symons, D. (1979). *The evolution of human sexuality.* New York: Oxford University Press.

Symons, D. (1987). If we're all Darwinians, what's the fuss about? In C. Crawford, M. Smith, & D. Krebs (Eds.), *Sociobiology and psychology: Ideas, issues, and applications* (pp. 121–146). Hillsdale, NJ: Lawrence Erlbaum Associates.

Symons, D. (1992). On the use and misuse of Darwinism in the study of human behavior. In J. Barkow, L. Cosmides, & J. Tooby (Eds.), *The adapted mind* (pp. 137–159). New York: Oxford University Press.

Tanner, R. E. S. (1970). *Homicide in Uganda, 1964: Crime in East Africa.* Uppsala, Sweden: Scandinavian Institute of African Studies.

Tooby, J. (1982). Pathogens, polymorphism, and the evolution of sex. *Journal of Theoretical Biology, 97,* 557–576.

Tooby, J., & Cosmides, L. (1990a). On the universality of human nature and the uniqueness of the individual: The role of genetics and adaptation. *Journal of Personality, 58,* 17–68.

Tooby, J., & Cosmides, L. (1990b). The past explains the present: Emotional adaptations and the structure of ancestral environments. *Ethology and Sociobiology, 11,* 375–424.

Tooby, J., & Cosmides, L. (1992). Psychological foundations of culture. In J. Barkow, L. Cosmides, & J. Tooby (Eds.), *The adapted mind* (pp. 19–136). New York: Oxford University Press.

Trivers, R. (1971). The evolution of reciprocal altruism. *Quarterly Review of Biology, 46,* 35–57.

Trivers, R. (1972). Parental investment and sexual selection. In B. Campbell (Ed.), *Sexual selection and the descent of man: 1871–1971* (pp. 136–179). Chicago: Aldine.

Waller, N. G. (1994). Individual differences in age preferences in mates. *Behavioral and Brain Sciences, 17,* 578–581.

Wellman, H. M. (1990). *The child's theory of mind.* Cambridge: MIT Press.

White, G. L., & Mullen, P. E. (1989). *Jealousy: Theory, research, and clinical strategies.* New York: Guilford.

Williams, G. C. (1966). *Adaptation and natural selection: A critique of some current evolutionary thought.* Princeton, NJ: Princeton University Press.

Williams, G. C. (1992). *Natural selection: Domains, levels, and challenges.* New York: Oxford University Press.

Wilson, M., & Daly, M. (1985). Competitiveness, risk-taking, and violence: The young male syndrome. *Ethology and Sociobiology, 6,* 59–73.

Wilson, M., & Daly, M. (1987). Risk of maltreatment of children living with step-parents. In R. J. Gelles & J. B. Lancaster (Eds.), *Child abuse and neglect* (pp. 215–232). Hawthorne, NY: Aldine de Gruyter.

2

Sex and Mating: Sexual Strategies, Trade-offs, and Strategic Pluralism

LORNE CAMPBELL, JEFFRY A. SIMPSON, AND MINDA ORINA

INTRODUCTION

Few topics in the emerging field of evolutionary psychology have piqued greater interest and generated more heated debate than the interlocking issues of sex and mating in human beings. The reason for this intense focus is understandable. Successful reproduction is one of the three major "life tasks" that individuals must successfully complete in order to enhance their inclusive fitness. Along with surviving the perils of childhood and providing adequate parental care to one's own offspring, successful sexual reproduction lies at the core of our evolutionary heritage.

Early models of human mating were heavily influenced by observations and theories of mating patterns in non-human animals. As we shall see, these models—especially the groundbreaking work of Trivers (1972)—greatly clarified the major barriers that males and females in most sexually reproducing species frequently face en route to successful reproduction. In recent years, some of this early work has been criticized for being androcentric and for either oversimplifying or not fully appreciating the highly complex nature of human mating. The main objective of this chapter is to elucidate how different models grounded in evolutionary principles—ranging from Trivers's (1972) Parental Investment and Sexual Selection Theory, to Buss and Schmitt's (1993) Sexual Strategies Theory, to female-focused models of mating proposed by scholars such as Hrdy (1997) and Gowaty (1992a), to Gangestad and Simpson's (1997) Strategic Pluralism Theory—try to explain the different mating strategies witnessed in men and women.

The chapter is divided into four major sections. In the first section, we review the basic ideas from which Trivers developed Parental Investment and Sexual Selection Theory. Some scholars have ignored or misunderstood critical, qualifying components of Trivers's theory. Thus, we discuss Trivers's ideas and principles, highlight some of the important and frequently overlooked nuances in his theory, and then briefly critique his approach to human mating.

In the second section, we review Buss and Schmitt's (1993) Sexual Strategies Theory (SST). SST directly extends some of Trivers's original predictions about sex differences in mating. Moreover, it tries to account for some of the variation in mating strategies that exists within women and men. As we shall see, Buss and Schmitt have marshaled a considerable amount of empirical support for many of SST's major propositions. We review and then briefly critique this perspective.

The third section reviews evolutionary-based theory and research guided by a "female-centered" perspective of sex and mating. We first present and synthesize mating models advanced by Hrdy (1997), Gowaty (1992a), and Waage (1997), all of which have criticized the work of Trivers and/or Buss and his colleagues. We then review the merits of these alternative models.

In the final section, we summarize Gangestad and Simpson's (1997) Strategic Pluralism Theory, which extends their earlier conceptualizing on within-sex variation in mating (see Gangestad & Simpson, 1990). Melding ideas from good-provider and good-genes models of sexual selection, Strategic Pluralism Theory (SPT) attempts to explain why so much within-sex variation exists in human mating. The theory suggests that both sexes make "trade-offs" when choosing and trying to acquire mates. We critique this theory and conclude by suggesting several directions for future theory development and research.

PARENTAL INVESTMENT AND SEXUAL SELECTION THEORY

> Arguments are presented on how one might *expect* natural selection to act on the sexes, and some data are presented to support these arguments. (Trivers, 1972, p. 137)

Trivers's theory of parental investment and sexual selection was proposed as a guideline for interpreting sex differences in mating and sexual behavior; it was *not* intended to be a "sweeping generalization" (Waage, 1997, p. 528) that confined each sex to different and mutually exclusive mating strategies. Nonetheless, Trivers's theory has held up remarkably well in light of what we have learned about sexual and mating behavior in many species. In this section, we outline the basic tenets of Trivers's theory and identify the key concepts he used to explain and elucidate some of the sex differences that have been observed across a wide spectrum of different species.

Differential Reproductive Success

From an evolutionary perspective, one of the most important life tasks that individuals must solve is how to propagate their genes (or their biological relatives' genes) to future generations. The most direct way to achieve this goal is through sexual reproduction with a member of the opposite sex (at least in species that reproduce sexually). In species with a 50:50 sex ratio (such as humans), Trivers noted that there should be enough individuals of each sex to accommodate the reproductive needs of all individuals of the other sex. Hence, nearly every individual should have a chance to mate. Following this logic, it might be assumed that both males and females would be equally variable with respect to their reproductive success (defined as the number of direct biological descendants they leave). If there are enough members of each sex to meet the reproductive needs of every individual within a given species, one might expect that every individual's needs are being met.

In most species, however, this does not hold true. Even when the sex ratio in a species is balanced, some males mate a great deal, and others mate rarely or not at all. Bateman's (1948) classic experiments with *Drosophila melanogaster* first illustrated this fact. Bateman documented that, in Drosophila, (1) male reproductive success was much more variable than female reproductive success (only 4% of the females failed to reproduce over time, whereas 21% of the males failed to reproduce), (2) male reproductive success was severely constrained by their ability to attract females, whereas female reproductive success was not hampered by their ability to attract males (of the 21% of males who failed to reproduce, all of them showed an interest in mating but could not attract a mate), and (3) male reproductive success was positively associated with the number of copulations, whereas female reproductive success did not increase after two copulations. Research investigating several other species has confirmed that, on average, male reproductive success is more variable than female reproductive success (see Trivers, 1985, for a review). The only exceptions are found in species in which males invest more in offspring than females during the earliest stages of offspring development (e.g., phalaropes and some shorebirds: see Trivers, 1985). These observations led Trivers to develop a general theory explaining how and why the sexual and mating behavior of males and females in most species should be influenced by the different "roles" they assume in sexual reproduction.

Relative Parental Investment

Bateman (1948) tried to explain the differential reproductive success of Drosophila using the lowest common denominator—their sex cells. Male Drosophila invest very little metabolic energy in the production of their sex cells compared to females. As a result, female reproductive success is limited by their ability to produce eggs, not by their ability to get their eggs fertilized. Male reproductive success, on the other hand, is limited by their ability to fertilize female eggs, not by their ability to produce sperm. Therefore, most sex differences in sexual behavior should be driven by this fundamental asymmetry in sex cell investment. In addition, because a large difference exists in the size of male versus female sex cells in most species (and, hence, their investment in metabolic production), the results obtained for Drosophila ought to generalize across all species with similar initial inequities in investment.

Trivers (1972) used Bateman's principle as a basis for his theory of parental investment and sexual selection. In most species, however, parental investment involves much more than just metabolic investment in sex cells, and Trivers clearly recognized this fact. He defined parental investment as "any investment by the parent in an individual offspring that increases the offspring's chance of surviving (and hence reproductive success) at the cost of the parent's ability to invest in other offspring" (p. 139). According to Trivers, parental investment includes metabolic investment in sex cells as well as any behavior (e.g., feeding, guarding the young) that benefits an offspring while reducing the parent's ability to invest in other offspring. Each offspring represents an individual investment, and investment in one offspring limits the amount of investment that can be given to other current or future offspring. The magnitude of investment is indexed by the amount a particular investment "act" precludes the parent from investing in other offspring. Assuming that natural selection has produced relatively optimal levels of parental investment designed to enhance the reproductive success of both parents, both intersexual and intrasexual behavior should be affected by the patterns of parental investment exhibited by each sex.

After illustrating how parental investment could serve as a catalyst for intersexual and intrasexual behaviors, Trivers predicted what kinds of behaviors each sex typically should exhibit, given their different levels of initial parental investment. According to Trivers (1972),

Since the total number of offspring produced by one sex of a sexually reproducing species must equal the total number produced by the other (and assuming the sexes differ in no other way than in their typical parental investment per offspring), then the sex whose typical parental investment is greater than that of the opposite sex will become a limiting resource for that sex. Individuals of the sex investing less will compete among themselves to breed with members of the sex investing more, since an individual of the former can increase its reproductive success by investing successively in the offspring of several members of the limiting sex. (pp. 140–141)

Because the sex that initially invests less in offspring usually produces sex cells very rapidly and in larger number, members of the less-investing sex should be able to increase their reproductive fitness simply by reproducing with more different mates. Conversely, the sex that tends to invest more initially cannot increase their reproductive fitness by mating with more mates. In humans, for example, women cannot enhance their reproductive fitness by having sex with more partners once they become pregnant. There is an upper limit, therefore, to the number of "productive" copulations (i.e., copulations that lead to fertilization of an egg) that human females can have. In contrast, males' reproductive success can be heavily influenced by the number of "productive" copulations that can be obtained. As a result, competition among males to maximize the number of "productive" copulations should be fierce. In essence, females are a limiting resource to males. They do not have to worry about getting their eggs fertilized, just about who they want to fertilize them. With respect to the small number of species in which males initially invest more than females, parental investment theory predicts sex differences in the *opposite* direction. According to the theory, the amount of parental investment (not biological sex per se) is the critical variable that should govern mating strategies (Trivers, 1972). In these "sex role-reversed" species, males are a limiting resource for females. Thus, females compete fiercely with each other to obtain male investment in their offspring.

Investment Decisions

> Sexual selection, then, is both controlled by the parental investment pattern
> and a force that tends to mold that pattern. (Trivers, 1972, p. 144)

According to Trivers, relative parental investment in humans also should shape patterns of mating in particular directions. To illustrate, once a woman becomes pregnant and begins experiencing greater initial "costs" relative to her mate, she should become relatively more committed to making further investments (e.g., carrying the child full-term, giving birth, lactating, providing protection postpartum). A man, however, should not be as committed to making further investments (at least initially) because he has not experienced many up-front costs. In fact, he may feel compelled to desert his mate and seek out other mates to increase his reproductive success. Guided by this logic, Trivers argued that males in most species should not be inclined to remain committed to a single female. Rather, selection pressures should have led most males to increase their reproductive fitness by mating with multiple partners, investing a minimal amount in each offspring.

A population in which every male attempted to maximize the number of mates and minimize parental investment could have evolved if a number of mitigating factors were *not* present in evolutionary history. However, they probably were. Due to internal fertilization, women are certain of their maternity, whereas men cannot be completely certain of their paternity. Such uncertainty raises a major problem for philandering males—are his matings resulting in his own offspring? In many instances, they may not be, and the "maximize number of copulations with various women" strategy actually may result in *lower* reproductive success over time (Gangestad & Simpson, 1997). Paternity uncertainty should have led males to weigh the costs and benefits of investing heavily in children with one woman versus investing minimally in the children of many women. If investing heavily in the children of one woman increased the probability of paternity, some men should have been willing to invest more in offspring. Investing in such a fashion should have been a "safer" way to increase the likelihood of paternity and, thus, increase reproductive fitness. Other men could have benefited even more by investing fairly heavily in the offspring of one woman while, at the same time, occasionally pursuing short-term matings with other women (what Trivers called a "mixed strategy"). According to Trivers's theory, therefore, several factors (e.g., internal fertilization, fear of desertion, fear of cuckoldry) should moderate the effects of parental investment on patterns of mating in both sexes. Unfortunately, this facet of Trivers's theory—though not fully developed in his 1972 article—tends to be overlooked or underappreciated by many critics. Despite the fact that differential parental investment is thought to be the force that drives sexual selection, several important factors can alter the way in which parental investment relates to different patterns of mating in men and women.

Summary and Critique

In summary, Trivers's (1972) theory of parental investment and sexual selection proposes that the sex that initially invests more in offspring (usually females, in humans) is a limiting resource for the less-investing sex (usually men). Across different species, disparities in behavior between the two sexes should increase as the asymmetry between parental investment increases. Specifically, members of the less-investing sex should compete more intensely among themselves to mate with members of the more-investing sex, whereas members of the more-investing sex should display less intrasexual competition. However, the more-investing sex should be choosier about the characteristics of potential mates because, once their eggs are fertilized, they must make larger initial minimal investments in offspring. Nevertheless, Trivers clearly acknowledges that many factors (such as paternity uncertainty, fear of desertion, and the potential for cuckoldry) can moderate associations between parental investment and mating patterns.

As we shall see, one limitation of Trivers's theory is that it does not explicitly consider the role of individuals other than mates who can and often do invest in offspring. In introducing Inclusive Fitness Theory, Hamilton (1964) outlined two routes by which individuals can propagate their genes: (1) have their own children and/or (2) help raise their biological relatives. Because individuals share a portion of their genes with relatives (i.e., on average, 50% with their full siblings, 25% with their half siblings, 12.5% with their first cousins), judiciously helping relatives increase their reproductive success should increase an individual's own inclusive fitness. Mating decisions, therefore, may not always be based strictly on the investment that a potential mate has to offer. For instance, a woman who lives with extended family may be able to obtain investment from her kin and, consequently, may have less need to find a high-investing mate. In contrast, a woman who lives alone, has few kin, or has resource-poor kin may require extensive investment, causing her to place greater importance on a mate's investment potential. In the first case, parental investment potential should not be a deciding factor in mate selection. In fact, given her adequate resources, the first woman may not want investment from a mate but only his sperm, behaving like the "prototypical" male in Trivers's model. Thus, while women are, on average, more discriminating than men about whom they mate with, their mating behavior should be contingent on the quantity and quality of resources or promises of future investment offered by people other than potential or current mates.

Trivers's theory also is cryptic and incomplete in its treatment of female sexual strategies. While gains in reproductive success should reach their apex for women after mating with a relatively smaller number of men, subsequent copulations with different men could allow women to obtain or maintain valued resources (see later). That is, females may not always engage in sex for reproductive purposes. If a woman knows that a man will provide food or other resources in exchange for sex, it could benefit her to be sexually receptive to resource-bearing males, even if sex does not result in offspring (see Hill, 1982; Ridley, 1996; Symons, 1979). Sex also may be used to avoid physical harm from aggressive males (Hrdy, 1979, 1981), to facilitate the maintenance of orderly social relationships, or to build social coalitions (Jay, 1973; Lancaster, 1975). Thus, females—especially human females—may not be as sexually coy as Trivers suggested, particularly when they are not ovulating (Hrdy, 1997; Udry & Morris, 1968).

Finally, Trivers probably places too much emphasis on the "ideal" or prototypic mating strategy within each sex, especially in the case of humans. Given keen intrasexual competition and individual differences in mate value, some men and women simply cannot successfully enact the prototypic (modal) mating strategy for their sex. For species in which males invest little in offspring, Trivers proposed that the ideal male mating strategy should be to maximize matings with a variety of females. In most species, however, a sizable minority of males never reproduce. Among those who do reproduce, there is substantial variability in reproductive success. Although not as extreme, these same patterns of differential mating also hold for human males in relation to human females (Jaffe, Urribarri, Chacon, & Diaz, 1993; Mace, 1996). Natural selection should have shaped ecologically contingent, alternate mating strategies, permitting individuals who could not achieve reproductive success using sex-prototypic strategies to take advantage of alternate ones.

SEXUAL STRATEGIES THEORY

Influenced by Trivers, Buss and Schmitt (1993) developed Sexual Strategies Theory (SST) to provide a more complete and systematic evolutionary account of why different sexual strategies exist between and within men and women.

Buss and Schmitt identify several shortcomings of past theories of mating, especially those that do not consider how selection pressures might have shaped human sexual behavior. They highlight five limitations of past theories. First, most theories fail to explain *why* humans should seek mates based on principles such as similarity, equity, complementariness, and proximity. Second, most theories tend to be overly simplistic in that only one process is presumed to govern who mates with whom. Third, past theories have been too general and often do not generate specific predictions. Fourth, many theories start with the assumption that male and female mating strategies should be virtually identical, implying that no sex differences should be found. Finally, most theories predict that people should display the same mating strategy in most, if not all, social contexts.

To address these limitations, SST tries to explain why men and women should exhibit particular mating strategies in different contexts. According to Buss and Schmitt, human mating is strategic in that people seek out mates to solve specific adaptive problems that their ancestors recurrently faced in evolutionary history. Thus, mate preferences and mating strategies (which are *not* necessarily consciously planned or articulated) are conjectured to be the result of specific selection pressures that occurred in the environment of evolutionary adaptedness (the EEA). Mating strategies, therefore, ought to be highly context-dependent, yielding both short-term and long-term strategies and tactics within each sex. To the extent that men and women recurrently faced different adaptive problems in the EEA, different principles should govern when and how often men and women should adopt different mating strategies.

Many of SST's underlying assumptions are based on Trivers's (1972) theory of parental investment and sexual selection. Sexual selection (Darwin, 1871) refers to characteristics that have evolved to give organisms reproductive advantage. Reproductive advantage can be achieved in two ways: (1) through success at intrasexual competition and (2) through success at intersexual attraction. Characteristics that lead to success in either domain should have evolved because they conferred reproductive advantage on their bearers. As noted earlier, the major force behind sexual selection should be the amount of parental investment each sex devotes to its offspring. According to SST, since women tend to be the more-investing sex (due to fertilization, internal gestation, placentation, and lactation) and can produce only a small number of offspring (compared to men) during their lives, women should be more selective and discriminating when choosing mates. Conversely, because men are not obliged to provide high initial parental investment and can sire almost a limitless number of offspring (at least theoretically), men should be less discriminating but more competitive in attracting mates.

Advantages, Problems, and Costs Associated with Different Mating Strategies

Short-Term Strategies: Men. According to SST, the advantage of short-term mating for men is straightforward: on average, the reproductive fitness of males should increase with each new mating. Theoretically, men can achieve greater reproductive success by mating with many partners (assuming that some of these matings produce children) than by having children with a single mate (Betzig, 1986; Dawkins, 1986). Although this strategy can be successful, it has some costs. First, short-term strategies increase the risk of contracting sexually transmitted diseases, many of which can lower or negate an individual's ability to reproduce. Second, the ability to attract mates for long-term relationships might be damaged if men become known as womanizers (Schmitt & Buss, 1996). Third, men who recklessly pursue short-term strategies may risk physical harm from jealous husbands or boyfriends (Daly & Wilson, 1988).

According to SST, short-term strategies solve four basic "problems" that men recurrently faced in evolutionary history. The first problem involves how to increase the number of sexual partners. It has been suggested that men's powerful desire to mate with many women (Symons, 1979), their lower standards for "acceptable" attributes in short-term mates (Kenrick, Sadalla, Groth, & Trost,1990), and the shorter acquaintance time they require before having sex (Clark & Hatfield, 1989) are partial solutions to the problem of partner number. The second problem centers on how to obtain sexual access, given that women should be more discriminating when choosing mates. In response to this problem, men should desire women who are not overly conservative or prudish, not sexually inexperienced, and slightly promiscuous, at least when pursuing short-term mates. The third problem involves how to identify fertile women, given that men must mate with fertile women to increase their own reproductive fitness. Cues of fertility should be provided by a woman's age and health, which may be evident in physical appearance (e.g., clear skin, lustrous hair, symmetrical face and body, good muscle tone: see Buss, 1989; Hamilton & Zuk, 1982; Trivers, 1985), observable behavior (e.g., high activity level: Orians & Heerwagen, 1992), and social reputation (Schmitt & Buss, 1996). The fourth problem focuses on finding ways to avoid excessive investment in a mate. This problem can be solved by pursuing women who do not demand long-term commitment and large investments of time and resources before mating.

Long-Term Strategies: Men. Although short-term strategies have many advantages for men, long-term strategies provide different advantages. First, men who adopt long-term strategies can gain greater control over a woman's lifetime reproduction. Second, if men invest in a single mate, more resources and better social alliances might be developed with the cooperation of her extended family. Third, to attract women of higher mate value, long-term commitment and investment may be necessary. Finally, long-term strategies may allow men to avert the costs of unsuccessfully pursuing short-term mates, solve the problem of concealed ovulation (see Alexander & Noonan, 1979), and secure better cooperation from one's mate. However, the potential advantages associated with short-term strategies are lost.

According to SST, long-term strategies also have evolved to solve certain problems faced by men in the EEA. One of the most pressing problems should have been paternal uncertainty. Because women give birth, they know their children are their own descendants; for men, however, paternity is less certain. Increasing the probability of paternity should be a particularly important objective for men who adopt long-term strategies because the costs of cuckoldry (raising another man's offspring) should be severe when paternal investment is exclusive and high (see Buss & Schmitt, 1993). Male sexual jealousy may be an evolved adaptation in response to this problem (Buss, 1988; Buss, Larsen, Westen, & Semmelroth, 1992; Daly, Wilson, & Weghorst, 1982; Wilson & Daly, 1992). Intense jealousy tends to trigger mate-guarding in men (Buss, 1988), and mate-guarding should be more successful if males devote all of their time and attention to a single female. Furthermore, cuckoldry should be reduced by preferring mates who are chaste and sexually faithful. The second problem involves female reproductive value. Thus, men should place more emphasis on physical attractiveness (Buss, 1989; Buss & Barnes, 1986; Hill, 1945; Hudson & Henze, 1969) and youth (Buss, 1989; Kenrick & Keefe, 1992) when selecting mates than should women, especially for long-term relationships.

Short-Term Strategies: Women. According to SST, the potential costs of short-term strategies should be greater for women. Although women share some of the same costs as men, the damage of engaging in short-term mating should be greater on women's long-term mate value. Promiscuity may be considered a sign that women have relatively low mate value because they are less selective. Moreover, the fear of paternity uncertainty should keep many men from wanting promiscuous women as long-term mates. Short-term women also may be at greater risk for physical or sexual abuse from men in the form of harassment (Studd & Gattiker, 1991) or rape (Thornhill & Thornhill, 1983, 1992). There are, however, some potential benefits available to women who adopt short-term strategies. Such women might be able to attract better mates and, perhaps, better genes that might be passed on to their children. Other benefits might include gaining more resources or better protection from more than one male. Short-term mating also may give women an opportunity to evaluate the long-term prospects of a prospective mate.

When deployed by women, short-term strategies can solve some important problems. First, short-term strategies might expedite the extraction of resources from some men. Second, they might allow women to gauge a man's prospect as a long-term mate more fully. Third, they might help women to assess their own mate value better (e.g., by determining how many high-quality men they can attract), to assess a potential mate's true intentions about the relationship, to evaluate a mate's personal characteristics, or to evaluate his mate value. In some contexts, short-term mating also might afford greater protection, especially for women who are not involved in long-term relationships. Consequently, women should tend to value physical strength in short-term mates as much, if not more, than in long-term mates. However, according to SST, women primarily use short-term strategies to identify men who might be good long-term mates.

Long-Term Strategies: Women. It should be beneficial for some—perhaps most—women to engage in long-term mating strategies, particularly if doing so would ensure greater male parental investment in terms of food, protection, and the transfer of status, power, or resources (Buss, 1989). In addition to obtaining more material benefits for themselves and their children, women who adopt long-term strategies also might be able to garner more or better long-term social and economic benefits. Accordingly, a man's "attractiveness" should be based, at least in part, on his potential to amass and provide resources, either immediately or in the future (Buss, 1989). According to SST, the costs of pursuing long-term strategies should not be as severe for women as they are for men. However, women may be less likely to extract resources from men immediately if they demand high levels of commitment and investment before mating.

The main problem with long-term strategies for women involves gaining and maintaining long-term parental investment from men. In response to this problem, women who adopt long-term strategies should be attracted to men who (1) can obtain, defend, and monopolize valued resources, (2) maintain control over these resources, and (3) are willing to invest these resources in them and their children.

Summary and Critique

In summary, Buss and Schmitt draw three conclusions about men's mating preferences: (1) compared to women, men should invest more effort in short-term mating than in long-term mating, (2) men should have evolved preferences designed to solve the ancestral problem of obtaining many short-term mates, and (3) men should have evolved preferences designed to solve the problem of monopolizing a woman's lifetime reproductive potential. Women also engage in both short-term and long-term mating strategies, but short-term strategies are principally used to assess the viability of long-term mates. This is one of the most controversial claims of SST (see Gangestad & Simpson, 1997). In addition, women should have higher standards for their mates (particularly their short-term mates), require more time before consenting to sex, and desire a smaller number of sexual partners. Two strengths of SST are the large number and the specificity of the hypotheses it generates.

Sexual Strategies Theory integrates much of what we currently know about normative patterns of mating in women and men. In fact, it may account for what we know better than any other single theory. Nonetheless, as Buss and Schmitt (1993) have acknowledged, SST has two primary drawbacks. First, it does not identify all of the variables that lead individuals to adopt short-term versus long-term strategies. According to SST, both men and women should display what Trivers called "mixed" sexual strategies. However, SST says little about how an individual's personal attributes and local environment systematically elicit or promote different sexual strategies. Second, SST does not fully explain why *more* variation in mating-related behaviors exists within men and women than between them (see Gangestad & Simpson, 1997; Gowaty, 1992b; Simpson & Gangestad, 1991). If short-term strategies are so well suited to enhancing reproductive fitness, given how males reproduce, and if long-term strategies are better suited to enhancing reproductive fitness, given how females reproduce, why do a sizable minority women adopt short-term strategies, and why do so many men adopt long-term ones? SST does not fully address why, from an *evolutionary* standpoint, so much variation exists within each sex.

SEXUAL SELECTION AND MATING BEHAVIOR: A FEMALE PERSPECTIVE

> The points that I am stressing are twofold: (a) there should be strong selection on males to control females over and above all other sexually selected behavior, because females limit males' reproduction; and (b) in response to male efforts to control females' reproduction, *females should be selected to resist male control.* (Gowaty, 1992a, p. 231)

> I am convinced that male control over productive resources needed by women to reproduce lies at the heart of the transformation from male-dominated male-philopatric primate societies to full-fledged patriarchy. (Hrdy, 1997, p. 5)

In the last decade, several alternative models of mating reflecting a more "female-centered" perspective have arisen. Virtually all of these models have questioned or criticized the basic premises of Sexual Selection Theory and/or Sexual Strategies Theory. As both quotations imply, males are vulnerable to the power females have in the process of reproduction, and they may have evolved behaviors to gain and maintain greater control. In most species, females select whom they mate with, given their higher initial levels of investment. Males, on the other hand, put on their best displays in the hope of being chosen as a mate (Bateman, 1948; Kirkpatrick, 1987; Small, 1992; Theissen, 1994; Trivers, 1972). Indeed, Waage (1997) suggests that females in most species control multiple factors related to reproduction, such as making mating decisions, affecting the likelihood of fertilization, exerting extra DNA influence on offspring, and influencing the amount of investment given to each offspring.

One might expect that a reasonable amount of theory and research would have focused on the greater control that females seem to have in reproduction. Existing theories, however, rarely elaborate on "female choice," usually focusing more on male intersexual and intrasexual behavior (e.g., Buss & Schmitt, 1993; Trivers, 1972). Theoretical models of sexual selection that address female control in reproduction are starting to emerge. These models devote more attention to how male and female sexual and mating behaviors may have coevolved in response to both sex differences in initial minimal investment and greater female control over reproduction. These models, which are a culmination of theory and research conducted by several individuals, constitute the emerging female perspective (see, e.g., Gowaty, 1992a; Hrdy, 1997; Lancaster, 1991; Smuts, 1995; Waage, 1997).

All theories of sexual selection must acknowledge and address one basic difference between the sexes: females tend to invest more in their offspring than males do, at least initially (Trivers, 1972). Consequently, selection pressures should have produced slightly different behaviors and cognitive mechanisms geared to enhance the reproductive fitness of both men and women (Dawkins, 1978; Lancaster, 1991; Trivers, 1972). In addition, the evolution of certain sex-differentiated behaviors and mechanisms should have been affected by the fact that females should have benefited from receiving assistance in rearing their offspring, and male mates could have provided such assistance. Whereas Trivers (1972) and Buss and Schmitt (1993) have used these principles to develop theories that focus mostly on the role of male behavior in sexual selection, the female perspective highlights the importance of female behavior. The female perspective takes issue with the notions that (1) females have evolved to choose males who will provide maximal resources and (2) females are usually coy and discriminating about granting sexual access. Though the female perspective acknowledges that sex differences do exist, it suggests that they have evolved in response to different selection pressures than previous theories have posited. According to this perspective, males have evolved to control the reproductive capacities of females to improve their own reproductive success.

Male Resources

Sexual Strategies Theory implies that a fairly linear relationship should exist between the amount of male investment and the long-term viability of offspring. Although most women should require some resources from their mates to raise their children, women are likely to differ in how many resources they need, depending on the possessions of their kin and extended family. Women must also consider what they have to "trade" in exchange for male parental investment and whether these trade-offs are in their best interest. Proponents of the female perspective suggest that these issues must be considered before it is assumed that obtaining resources from men was the principal means by which women increased their reproductive fitness in the EEA.

The first major issue involves the ability of women to care for themselves and their offspring independently. Although men compete with each other to mate with women, females of many species also compete with one another for access to food territories (Daly & Wilson, 1983). In nearly all tribal societies, women probably were responsible for the daily collection of food through gathering, while men engaged in the riskier activity of hunting (see Ridley, 1996; Wright, 1994). Even though food obtained from gathering probably did not contain all of the essential nutrients or proteins needed for a balanced diet, individuals who gathered food every day were assured a meal. Gathering also allowed women to bring their young with them, permitting continuous protection. Thus, in some environments, a single woman could have provided for her offspring.

The second issue concerns whether people other than the mate (such as kin) were able and willing to provide resources. The evolution of the human body and brain occurred in social contexts, with individuals living and evolving in relatively small groups (see Wright, 1994). In all likelihood, the members of most groups were biologically related to some degree (see Tooby & Cosmides, 1992). Therefore, when a woman had a child, she often had several relatives in close proximity who should have had a vested interest in helping her care for, and raise, her young (cf. Hamilton, 1964). Furthermore, relatives should have been more willing to invest in the offspring of a female relative than a male relative because of maternity certainty (especially in the case of grandmothers, who could be certain that their daughter's child was, in fact, their biological grandchild). Certain women, therefore, may have required few resources from their mates, especially if they were proficient at obtaining their own food. According to Gowaty (1992a), women may not have evolved to covet and acquire males' resources.

Although the resources that women received from their mates could have augmented their own reproductive success (Lancaster, 1991), heavy investment might not enhance—and could actually undermine—the reproductive success of men, especially if they were cuckolded (Daly & Wilson, 1983; Trivers, 1972). If men could be confident that certain children were, in fact, their own, they could have increased their reproductive success by investing more in these offspring. Judicious investments might allow men to retain sufficient surplus resources necessary to attract new mates while ensuring that their current offspring received adequate care. In the EEA, however, men could not be completely certain of their paternity, particularly if they did not engage in mate-guarding.

Paternity uncertainty should have left men with two choices: (1) do not invest much in children or (2) be as certain as possible that the children in whom you invest are yours. The first choice might have been alluring but should have been feasible for only a small subset of males. Because reproductive success tends to be so variable in males, some men in the EEA should have had few opportunities to mate. Accordingly, these men should have been motivated to maximize paternity certainty before investing heavily, given that misplaced investment would have seriously damaged their reproductive fitness. Since women were a limiting resource, these men should have been particularly motivated to do what it took to find a mate (see Gowaty, 1992a; Hrdy, 1997). To achieve the dual goals of mating and increasing paternity certainty, most men should have demanded that their mates not have sex with other men and remain in close proximity. Women who needed less investment from their mates should have tried to retain the option of increasing their reproductive success by selectively mating with certain males, especially those who exhibited evidence of high genetic viability (see Gangestad & Simpson, 1997). Conversely, their mates should have wanted these women to be monogamous in order to increase their own reproductive success.

To ensure that women remained loyal, adherents of the female perspective propose that men evolved to control and regulate the resources that women needed for reproduction, making it more difficult for them to obtain these resources on their own or from other people. In other words,

the combination of this paternal investment with an asymmetrical risk of cuckoldry (misattribution of parenthood) produces a powerful selective force favoring the evolution of motives that effectively guarantee one's paternity of one's putative offspring as opposed to merely maximizing the number of young sired. . . . We propose that these selection pressures have been responsible for the evolution of psychological mechanisms whose adaptive functions are success in sexual competition and cuckoldry avoidance and that men's attitudes, emotions, and actions indicative of sexual proprietariness and the commoditization of women are products of these evolved mechanisms in the context of particular historical and cultural circumstances. (Wilson & Daly, 1992, p. 290)

These selection pressures should have produced a "male sexual psychology effective in deterring rivals and in limiting female sexual and reproductive autonomy" (Wilson & Daly, 1992, p. 292). Male investment, then, may not reflect a sacrifice on the part of men as much as it reflects a sacrifice made by females— women must relinquish reproductive freedom in return for help in raising their offspring (Lancaster, 1991; Strassman, 1992, 1996).

Female Coyness

The prevailing interpretation of female sexual coyness has recently been challenged (Hrdy, 1997). Hrdy suggests that women also evolved to seek multiple mates. Several lines of evidence support this thesis. For example, unlike most other primates, human females are receptive to sex during their entire menstrual cycle, with sexual arousal peaking at midcycle (Stainslaw & Rice, 1988; for alternate views, see Meuwissen & Over, 1992; Slob, Ernste, & Bosch, 1991). Female sexual activity also increases at midcycle (Bellis & Baker, 1990; Udry & Morris, 1968). Moreover, women engage in extramarital sex at a rate nearly commensurate with men. For instance, it is estimated that approximately 30% of women have had extramarital sex at least once (Thompson, 1983). It has also been conjectured that the female orgasm may allow women to retain a larger amount of sperm from the most desirable mates, thereby increasing the chances of being impregnated by such men (Baker & Bellis, 1993a, 1993b). Given these facts, women may not be as coy as Darwin and other theorists have surmised. Similar to men, women should have evolved to use different mating strategies to their own reproductive advantage.

Recent evidence supports this contention. Bellis and Baker (1990), for example, have found that women are more likely to engage in extra-pair sex (i.e., sex outside an existing, long-term relationship) at a point in their menstrual cycle when pregnancy was most likely to occur. These women continue to maintain a healthy sex life with their long-term partners, which has led Bellis and Baker to surmise that extra-pair sex may be a way for women to have more viable offspring while retaining investment from long-term mates. As discussed earlier, women may also use sex to extract immediate resources from men. Ridley (1996) has speculated that the purpose of hunting by men in tribal societies was not only to secure food but to procure matings as well. Successful hunters may have offered choice pieces of meat in exchange for sex. In the modern world, expensive and valuable gifts may serve the same function. Highly coy women might not receive such gifts, whereas women who used "mixed" sexual strategies could.

Men should have had more reasons to worry about promiscuous women than coy ones. Almost by definition, less coy women were more likely to mate concurrently with other men, decreasing the certainty of paternity. Adherents of the female perspective propose that men evolved to coerce women to become coy so paternity certainty would be increased (Hrdy, 1997; Lancaster, 1991; Wilson & Daly, 1992). As a result, men should have provided abundant resources to women only when they remained monogamous. Women, therefore, are not "naturally" coy; like men, women are sexual opportunists who should also shift their mating strategies to increase their reproductive success. According to this perspective, men try to prevent women from exploring other sexual opportunities.

Summary and Critique

The female perspective explains sex differences in mating by focusing on the control that women have in deciding whether, when, and with whom to mate. This approach assumes that, like men, women evolved to use sex in flexible ways to enhance their reproductive fitness and that mates probably played a less important role in providing resources needed for raising offspring than has previously been suggested. Men, on the other hand, had relatively less control over the process of reproduction. They often had to wait to be chosen as a mate, which resulted in reproductive success being more variable in men than in women. Further, because men could never be fully certain of their paternity, they were exposed to the risk of being cuckolded. To attain greater reproductive control, men should have evolved to acquire and control the resources that women needed to raise their offspring. For women to obtain these resources, however, men should have expected sexual loyalty and fidelity. According to the female perspective, women should have been motivated to resist being controlled by men, whereas men should have tried to monopolize a woman's reproductive capacities. This presumably explains why the sexes are viewed as being antagonistic.

The female perspective offers some cogent, alternative explanations for sex differences in mating behavior, and some of its major premises have been supported by recent research. However, similar to SST, this perspective pays insufficient attention to within-sex variation in mating strategies. It also does not specify the conditions under which men and women should shift from short-term to long-term strategies, and vice versa. We now turn to a recent model that was developed to do so.

STRATEGIC PLURALISM THEORY

Strategic Pluralism Theory (SPT: Gangestad & Simpson, 1997) melds principles from "good-provider" and "good-genes" models of sexual selection to explain variation in mating behavior within and between the sexes. SPT proposes that women have evolved to evaluate men on two basic dimensions: (1) the extent to which a potential mate is likely to be a good provider and investor in offspring and (2) the extent to which a potential mate shows evidence of having good genetic quality. The theory contends that most women had to make "trade-offs" between these two dimensions when selecting mates throughout evolutionary history. The way in which trade-offs were made should have depended on both the attributes that a woman possessed (e.g., her health, physical attractiveness, ability to acquire resources) and the nature of the local environment (e.g., whether it was harsh with scarce resources versus benign with plentiful resources). The theory also posits that men who had higher genetic viability should have been able to reproduce without investing as much time and resources in their mates as men who were less viable. In other words, men with higher viability should have been more successful at using short-term sexual strategies. Conversely, men with less genetic viability should have offered greater investment (indicated by devoting more time, energy, and exclusive commitment to one mate), effectively shifting to long-term mating strategies. Thus, similar to female-centered models, SPT hypothesizes that the sexual strategies men adopt should be strongly influenced by female choice.

Trade-offs

One major limitation of past theories is that most have not used evolutionary functional analysis to assess the nature of trade-offs in mating. As Tooby and Cosmides (1992) have noted, evolutionary functional analysis involves identifying adaptive targets, that is, biologically successful behavioral outcomes. To identify such targets, one must conduct cost-benefit analyses (see Parker & Maynard Smith, 1991). Traits or behaviors are costly when the time or energy that went into developing them results in lower reproductive fitness than would have occurred if time and energy had been allocated differently. To perform cost-benefit analyses, one must first identify the basic criteria that individuals actually use when evaluating potential mates. According to SPT, individuals—particularly women—should make trade-offs on two dimensions: (1) attributes that reflect a potential mate's genetic viability and (2) attributes that signal his willingness to be a good provider/investor.

Consider two examples that run counter to prototypical sex stereotypes: one involving a man who cannot successfully enact a short-term strategy and one involving a woman who does not need additional resources to raise her children. If a man who does *not* possess the attributes that most women desire in short-term mates spends all of his time pursuing short-term mating strategies and fails, he has incurred considerable ''costs'' by not allocating his time and energy to a ''less risky'' solution—offering and providing parental investment in a single relationship. In this case, his ''best'' strategy would have been to waste little or no time and effort in short-term mating, opting to invest heavily in a single woman and her children from the outset. Since short-term mating does not require extensive time and investment, only the most desirable men are likely to mate with women who are looking for short-term mates. Men who do not have these characteristics would be shut out of reproduction entirely unless they *shifted* to long-term sexual strategies in a cost-effective manner, attempting to enhance the phenotypic quality of their offspring through greater parental investment.

Now consider a woman who has abundant resources and support from kin and, therefore, does not need a mate to invest heavily in her children. This woman cannot increase her reproductive fitness simply by having sex with many men and producing more children. However, she can mate with men who possess features that most women find highly attractive without demanding investment from them. If her offspring (especially her sons: see Weatherhead & Robertson, 1979) inherit these desirable attributes, they also should be sought after as mates once they mature, eventually conferring greater reproductive success to their mother by producing either more or higher-quality offspring in future generations. In this case, a woman with sufficient resources would miss out on the benefits associated with adopting a short-term mating strategy at opportune times.

Mate Dimensions, Trade-offs, and Fluctuating Asymmetry

According to SPT, women should choose mates based on the degree to which they are able and willing to invest time and resources into a relationship (including offspring) and the degree to which they show evidence of genetic viability (i.e., fitness-enhancing traits or characteristics that might be passed on to children, including good health or future mate-attracting potential: see Kirkpatrick, 1996). Good-provider models explain variability on the first dimension, whereas good-genes models explain variability on the second one (see Gangestad & Thornhill, 1997c, for a review). To increase their inclusive fitness, men and women ideally should prefer mates who are high on both dimensions, that is, partners who can and will invest heavily *and* who have high viability. Few people, however, can acquire such ideal partners. Most people simply do not have the constellation of stellar attributes necessary to attract and retain partners who are high on both dimensions. In addition, partners with high viability are less likely to invest in a single relationship (Gangestad & Thornhill, 1997a), primarily because many opposite-sex people find them attractive, and, thus, they tend to have more or better alternatives. As a result, the two mate choice dimensions correlate negatively (Gangestad & Simpson, 1997), forcing most individuals to make trade-offs between the two when selecting mates.

Fluctuating asymmetry (FA) should be a good indicator of an individual's genetic viability (see Gangestad, 1993; Gangestad & Simpson, 1997; Gangestad & Thornhill, 1997a, 1997b, 1997c, in press; Gangestad, Thornhill, & Yeo, 1994; Thornhill & Gangestad, 1993, 1994). FA reflects the degree to which individuals deviate from perfect bilateral symmetry at different points of the body (Van Valen, 1962). It is a phenotypic marker of the extent to which individuals have experienced disruptions or perturbations during their physical development. Several factors can affect the degree to which adults are asymmetrical, such as the negative effects of deleterious recessive genes (Lerner, 1954; Parsons, 1990), excessive homozygosity (Lerner, 1954), exposure to environmental toxins or pollutants (Parsons, 1990), and exposure to parasites during development (Møller, 1992b). Individuals who endure or resist these developmental perturbations are more symmetrical as adults. In particular, the size of features on the left side of their body (e.g., ankles, wrists, ear lobes) are more similar to the size of features on the right side (see Møller & Swaddle, 1997, for a review).

According to good-genes models, people with symmetrical features—particularly men—should have fared well in intersexual and intrasexual competitions in evolutionary history (Gangestad & Thornhill, 1997c). FA should be a good marker of genetic viability for three reasons. First, greater asymmetry is associated with lower survival rates, slower growth rates, and lower rates of reproduction in many species. Over 100 studies examining the relationship between FA and fitness traits have now been conducted, and both meta-analytic and qualitative reviews reveal highly reliable effects (on longevity and fecundity, see Leung & Forbes, 1996; Møller, 1997; on disease and health status, see Thornhill & Møller, 1997; on mating success, see Møller & Thornhill, 1998). Experimental studies in which the feathers of male barn swallows (Møller, 1990, 1992a) and the bodies of male scorpionflies (Thornhill, 1992a, 1992b) have been altered to be less symmetrical have found that greater asymmetry *causes* males to be less attractive to females and to have less reproductive success over time (also see Møller & Thornhill, in press). Second, FA is partly heritable. Thus, some of its variance is due to genetic variability, which is likely to be associated with greater fitness and genetic viability (Møller & Thornhill, 1997). Third, the development of symmetry cannot occur unless individuals have efficient immune systems that can ward off pathogens (M;øller & Swaddle, 1997). Individuals who continue to funnel somatic resources to symmetrical growth when they are exposed to parasites and pathogens risk taxing their immune systems to the point of depletion. For this reason, symmetry should be a fairly direct and valid sign that an individual has a well-functioning immune system because it should be an "honest" cue of viability (i.e., it should be difficult to "fake" without incurring substantial costs, including death; see Zahavi, 1975).

Trivers (1972) implies that selection for FA should have operated more strongly on men than on women. Specifically, the initial disparity in minimal parental investment between the sexes should have led women to be more discriminating than men when selecting mates. Since women are a limiting reproductive resource, competition among men for mates should be more intense than competition among women (Daly & Wilson, 1988; Trivers, 1972). Thus, indicators of genetic viability in men should have been exposed to stronger selection pressures during evolutionary history than indicators of viability in women. Men who showed little evidence of viability ran the risk of not reproducing at all, whereas nearly all fertile women had children in evolutionary history (for data on current traditional groups that probably live in environments similar to ancestral humans, see Chagnon, 1968; Hill & Hurtado, 1996). Although men should have preferred women whose positive genetic qualities could have been passed on to their children, selection pressures operating on viability in women should have been less intense. For women, therefore, links between FA and sexually selected attributes should be weaker.

Research Testing SPT

The basic propositions of SPT are just beginning to be tested. Although most research on FA has focused on non-human animals, a handful of studies have examined humans. With regard to physical attractiveness, studies have found that men (but not women) with more symmetrical bodies are rated as more physically attractive than less symmetrical men, even when several potential confounds are controlled for statistically (Gangestad et al., 1994; Thornhill & Gangestad, 1994; also see Furlow, Gangestad, & Armijo-Prewitt, 1998; Gangestad & Thornhill, 1997b). Similarly, men and women who have more symmetrical faces are rated by opposite-sex individuals as more attractive, dominant, sexier, and healthier (Grammar & Thornhill, 1994; Shackelford & Larsen, 1997).

With regard to intersexual and intrasexual behavior, more symmetrical men and women report more lifetime sex partners and engage in first intercourse earlier in development, even when the effects of age, marital status, body height, ethnicity, minor physical anomalies, and rated physical attractiveness are statistically controlled (Thornhill & Gangestad, 1994; Gangestad & Thornhill, 1997b). Recently, Gangestad and Thornhill (1997c) have found that more symmetrical men tend to be larger, more physical, and more socially dominant than less symmetrical men, and these three variables mediate the relation between FA and the number of lifetime sex partners men report. More symmetrical men also are more likely to engage in direct competition tactics when competing for a dating partner by directly comparing themselves with, claiming they are superior to, rival men (Simpson, Gangestad, Christensen, & Leck, 1999). They also are more likely to have physical fights with other men (Furlow et al., in press). This evidence suggests that symmetrical men may be more willing to enter the costly fray of direct intrasexual competition.

In terms of trade-offs, symmetrical men provide fewer material benefits to their romantic partners, and they give them less exclusive time and attention (Gangestad & Thornhill, 1997c). More symmetrical men tend to have more sexual affairs while being involved in established, long-term relationships, and they are chosen more often as extra-pair mates by women. They also are rated as being less honest and less giving of their time in relationships (Gangestad & Thornhill, 1997b). Viewed together, women who mate with symmetrical men appear to be making two trade-offs. First, they seem to be willing to trade time, honesty, and exclusive attention for their mate's viability and intrasexual competitiveness. Second, they appear to trade time, honesty, and attention for their mate's protection (Hrdy, 1981; Smuts, 1985). Both of these trade-offs should have been important in the EEA. More research, however, is needed to document the precise conditions under which women "exchange" genetic viability for investment.

Conditions That Promote Different Sexual Strategies

SPT suggests that mating strategies reflect how men and women make trade-offs. The specific sexual strategies that women adopt, for instance, reflect how they exchange genetic viability and investment. Largely in response to the choices women make, the mating strategies of men should vary according to whether it is cost-effective to adopt short-term versus long-term strategies, given the local mating environment. Although the "default strategy" for men might be short-term strategies, most men should be willing to shift to long-term, highly investing strategies if necessary.

SPT also predicts that certain environmental conditions should influence when different mating strategies are witnessed in each sex. For instance, in ancestral environments in which biparental care was crucial for infant survival, male parenting qualities should have had particularly beneficial effects. Conversely, in ancestral environments with prevalent pathogens, male genetic fitness should have been more important in mate selection. If, over time, women in the EEA were exposed to both kinds of environments, they should have evolved to make adaptive trade-off decisions when weighing a potential mate's investment qualities versus his genetic viability, contingent on the nature of the local environment. If this is true, women's choice of mating strategies should be sensitive to cues (valid in the EEA) that signal the parenting qualities and heritable viability of prospective mates.

What kinds of environmental factors might produce differences between populations? According to SPT, the major factor affecting assessments of male genetic quality should have been the presence and severity of pathogens and disease in the local environment (see Hamilton, 1982). When pathogens were prevalent, women should have placed more emphasis on male genetic qualities.

Three sets of findings support this premise. First, besides conveying information about fertility in women, physical attractiveness also may convey cues concerning an individual's health and perhaps his or her degree of pathogen resistance (Symons, 1979). Examining data from 29 cultures, Gangestad and Buss (1993) have found that individuals who live in regions where pathogens are more prevalent place greater importance on attractiveness when selecting mates. Second, parasite prevalence correlates negatively with the ranked importance of mate attributes associated with direct and exclusive parental care (e.g., dependable character, emotional stability and maturity, desire for home and children: see Buss, 1989). Third, in environments with more pathogens, polygyny is greater (i.e., women are more likely to adopt short-term mating strategies: see Low, 1990a).

Several factors should influence the value of male parenting effort. For example, in environments where the primary cause of infant mortality was the lack of biparental care, women should have valued paternal investment more highly. If, however, the main cause of infant mortality involved diseases, paternal investment should have played a more minor role in women's mate choice decisions. As discussed earlier, the relative value of paternal investment also should have depended on whether women had access to resources. Consistent with this reasoning, Low (1990b) has found that polygyny is greater in cultures in which women have more control over their labor and subsequent resources (see also Gangestad, 1993). Moreover, across 37 cultures, Buss (1989) has found that women's preference for attractiveness in men correlates positively with the proportion of women who participate in the economy.

These factors should, in turn, affect the mating strategies that men adopt. In environments where biparental care is necessary to ensure infant survival, a larger proportion of men should devote more time and effort to parental investment. Over time, this should reduce the variance in men's reproductive success (see Gangestad & Simpson, 1997). However, in environments where pathogens have particularly strong effects on infant mortality, a larger proportion of men should put more time and effort into short-term mating, thereby increasing the variance in men's reproductive success (since more men who are less viable may not mate: see Low 1990a, 1990b).

Summary and Critique

In summary, Strategic Pluralism Theory attempts to explain how and why both men and women adopt different mating strategies from an evolutionary perspective. More specifically, SPT tries to explain (1) how an individual's personal attributes and local environment should elicit or promote different mating strategies, and (2) why *more* variation in mating-related behaviors exists within men and women than between them. The theory contends that, even though women typically should want more investment from men than most men want to provide, women should shift their mating strategies in facultative, cost-effective ways, depending on specific environmental circumstances. When bi-parental care is needed to ensure infant survival, women should place greater weight on paternal investment; when pathogens account for the bulk of infant mortality, women should place more weight on genetic viability. Men, in turn, should adjust their mating behavior in response to women. Although short-term strategies might be the "optimal" way for men to increase their reproductive fitness, few males should have been able to engage in short-term mating suc-cessfully. Thus, a substantial proportion of men (those who displayed less via-bility) should have shifted to long-term strategies. In short, women should track environmental factors when calibrating their mating decisions, and men ought to track the desires and demands of women.

SPT, of course, has some drawbacks. First, research demonstrating precisely how women make trade-offs in mating contexts is still incomplete. We do not know, for example, how women differentially "weight" investment versus ge-netic quality as a function of their own personal attributes, the quality or quantity of resources they can obtain from friends or kin, the perceived quality of "avail-able" mates, or the quality and stability of the local environment. In a statistical sense, some of these variables might interact in unique and unanticipated ways. Second, sexual selection for good parenting could explain some of the findings reported earlier. For example, pathogen-resistant or mutation-free individuals not only may have better genes but, given their superior health, may also be better providers and, for that reason, preferable mates (see Hamilton, 1990; Kirkpatrick & Ryan, 1991). Third, direct selection (i.e., nonsexual selection) on mate pref-erences could explain some of these results. For instance, if pathogen-resistant individuals are less likely to transmit diseases to their mates, they could gain an advantage in mate selection (see Kirkpatrick & Ryan, 1991).

CONCLUSIONS

Theories and models of human mating based on evolutionary principles must acknowledge the different biological roles that women and men assume in re-production. Women gestate for approximately nine months, endure childbirth, and then lactate for weeks, months, or sometimes years postpartum; men do not. Before modern medicine, many women died in childbirth (for data, see Ziegel & Cranley, 1984); men did not. These undisputed facts led Trivers (1972) to conclude that females in most species invest more in offspring than males do, *at least initially*. What many evolutionary theorists have not fully appreciated is that, in most evolutionary environments, biparental care and investment prob-ably were needed until offspring reached at least puberty. This should have reduced the initial imbalance in investment between the sexes. Models of mating developed from species in which biparental care is less important than is true of humans have underestimated the importance of variation in mating apparent within each sex.

In addition to explaining sex differences, complete evolutionary models also must fully account for within-sex variation in mating strategies. When one considers the myriad of adaptations that might have been selected to enhance inclusive fitness, gender is a necessary, but not sufficient, explanatory variable. Many other important factors can influence within-sex variation in mating, which probably accounts for why within-sex variation in mating is substantially greater than between-sex variation. Mating and sexual behavior in humans are extremely complex. The only way to disentangle this Gordian knot is to consider all of the relevant variables instead of focusing mainly on gender. Theorists must use evolutionary functional analyses involving cost-benefit calculations in order to identify and disentangle the various strands underlying human mating.

REFERENCES

Alexander, R. D., & Noonan, K. M. (1979). Concealment of ovulation, parental care, and human social evolution. In N. A. Chagnon & W. Irons (Eds.), *Evolutionary biology and human social behavior: An anthropological perspective* (pp. 402–435). North Scituate, MA: Duxbury.

Baker, R. R., & Bellis, M. A. (1993a). Human sperm competition: Ejaculate adjustment by males and the function of masturbation. *Animal Behaviour, 46,* 861–885.

Baker, R. R., & Bellis, M. A. (1993b). Human sperm competition: Ejaculate manipulation by females and a function for the female orgasm. *Animal Behaviour, 46,* 887–909.

Bateman, A. J. (1948). Intrasexual selection in Drosophila. *Heredity, 2,* 349–368.

Bellis, M. A., & Baker, R. R. (1990). Do females promote sperm competition? Data for humans. *Animal Behaviour, 40,* 997–999.

Betzig. L. (1986). *Despotism and differential reproduction: A Darwinian view of history.* Hawthorne, NY: Aldine de Gruyter.

Buss, D. M. (1988). From vigilance to violence: Mate-guarding tactics. *Ethology and Sociobiology, 9,* 291–317.

Buss, D. M. (1989). Sex differences in human mate preferences: Evolutionary hypotheses tested in 37 cultures. *Behavioral and Brain Sciences, 12,* 1–14.

Buss, D. M., & Barnes, M. (1986). Preferences in human mate selection. *Journal of Personality and Social Psychology, 50,* 559–570.

Buss, D. M., Larsen, R. J., Westen, D., & Semmelroth, J. (1992). Sex differences in jealousy: Evolution, physiology, and psychology. *Psychological Science, 3,* 251–255.

Buss, D. M., & Schmitt, D. P. (1993). Sexual Strategies Theory: A contextual evolutionary analysis of human mating. *Psychological Review, 100,* 204–232.

Chagnon, N. (1968). *Yanomamo, the fierce people.* New York: Holt, Rinehart, & Winston.

Clark, R. D., & Hatfield, E. (1989). Gender differences in receptivity to sexual offers. *Annual Review of Psychology, 39,* 609–672.

Daly, M., & Wilson, M. (1983). *Sex, evolution, and behavior.* Boston: Willard Grant.

Daly, M., & Wilson, M. (1988). *Homicide.* New York: Aldine de Gruyter.

Daly, M., Wilson, M., & Weghorst, S. J. (1982). Male sexual jealousy. *Ethology and Sociobiology, 3,* 11–27.

Darwin, C. (1871). *The descent of man, and selection in relation to sex*. New York: Appleton.

Dawkins, R. (1978). *The extended phenotype*. Oxford: Oxford University Press.

Dawkins, R. (1986). *The blind watchmaker*. London: Penguin Books.

Furlow, B., Gangestad, S. W., & Armijo-Prewitt, T. (1998). Developmental stability and human violence. *Proceedings of the Royal Society of London, 265*, 1–60.

Gangestad, S. W. (1993). Sexual selection and physical attractiveness: Implications for mating dynamics. *Human Nature, 4*, 205–235.

Gangestad, S. W., & Buss, D. M. (1993). Pathogen prevalence and human mate preferences. *Ethology and Sociobiology, 14*, 89–96.

Gangestad, S. W., & Simpson, J. A. (1990). Toward an evolutionary history of female sociosexual variation. *Journal of Personality, 58*, 69–96.

Gangestad, S. W., & Simpson, J. A. (1997). *On the evolutionary psychology of human mating: Trade-offs and strategic pluralism*. Unpublished manuscript, University of New Mexico, Albuquerque.

Gangestad, S. W., & Thornhill, R. (1997a). *An evolutionary psychological analysis of human sexual selection: Developmental stability, male sexual behavior, and mediating features*. Unpublished manuscript, University of New Mexico, Albuquerque.

Gangestad, S. W., & Thornhill, R. (1997b). The evolutionary psychology of extrapair sex: The role of fluctuating asymmetry. *Evolution and Human Behaviour, 18*, 69–88.

Gangestad, S. W., & Thornhill, R. (1997c). Human sexual selection and developmental instability. In J. A. Simpson & D. T. Kenrick (Eds.), *Evolutionary social psychology* (pp. 169–195). Mahwah, NJ: Lawrence Erlbaum.

Gangestad, S. W., & Thornhill, R. (in press). Individual differences in developmental precision and fluctuating asymmetry: A model and its implications. *Journal of Evolutionary Biology*.

Gangestad, S. W., Thornhill, R., & Yeo, R. A. (1994). Facial attractiveness, developmental stability, and fluctuating asymmetry. *Ethology and Sociobiology, 15*, 73–85.

Gowaty, P. A. (1992a). Evolutionary biology and feminism. *Human Nature, 3*, 217–249.

Gowaty, P. A. (1992b). What if within-sex variation is greater than between-sex variation? *Behavioral and Brain Sciences, 15*, 389–390.

Grammar, K., & Thornhill, R. (1994). Human facial attractiveness and sexual selection: The role of symmetry and averageness. *Journal of Comparative Psychology, 108*, 233–242.

Hamilton, W. D. (1964). The genetical theory of social behaviour, I, II. *Journal of Theoretical Biology, 7*, 1–52.

Hamilton, W. D. (1982). Pathogens as causes of genetic diversity in their host populations. In R. M. Anderson & R. M. May (Eds.), *Population biology of infectious diseases*. New York: Springer-Verlag.

Hamilton, W. D. (1990). Mate choice near and far. *American Zoologist, 30*, 341–352.

Hamilton, W. D., & Zuk, M. (1982). Heritable true fitness and bright birds: A role for parasites. *Science, 218*, 384–387.

Hill, K. (1982). Hunting and human evolution. *Journal of Human Evolution, 11*, 521–544.

Hill, K., & Hurtado, A. M. (1996). *Ache life history*. New York: Aldine de Gruyter.

Hill, R. (1945). Campus values in mate selection. *Journal of Home Economics, 37*, 554–558.

Hrdy, S. B. (1979). Infanticide among animals. *Ethology and Sociobiology, 1*, 13–40.

Hrdy, S. B. (1981). *The woman that never evolved.* Cambridge: Harvard University Press.

Hrdy, S. B. (1997). Raising Darwin's consciousness: Female sexuality and the prehominid origins of patriarchy. *Human Nature, 8*, 1–49.

Hudson, J. W., & Henze, L. F. (1969). Campus values in mate selection: A replication. *Journal of Marriage and the Family, 31*, 772–775.

Jaffe, K., Urribarri, D., Chacon, G. C., & Diaz, G. (1993). Sex-linked strategies of human reproductive behavior. *Social Biology, 40*, 61–73.

Jay, P. (1973). Primate field studies and human evolution. In A. Montague (Ed.), *The origins and evolution of man: Readings in physical anthropology.* New York: Thomas Y. Crowell.

Kenrick, D. T., & Keefe, R. C. (1992). Age preferences in mates reflect sex differences in reproductive strategies. *Behavioral and Brain Sciences, 15*, 75–91.

Kenrick, D. T., Sadalla, E. K., Groth, G. E., & Trost, M. R. (1990). Evolution, traits, and the stages in human courtship: Qualifying the parental investment model. *Journal of Personality, 58*, 97–117.

Kirkpatrick, M. (1987). Sexual selection by female choice in polygynous animals. *Annual Review of Ecological Systematics, 18*, 43–70.

Kirkpatrick, M. (1996). Good genes and direct selection in the evolution of mating preferences. *Evolution, 50*, 2125–2140.

Kirkpatrick, M., & Ryan, M. J. (1991). The evolution of mating preferences and the paradox of the lek. *Nature, 350*, 33–38.

Lancaster, J. (1975). *Primate behavior and the emergence of human culture.* New York: Holt, Rinehart, & Winston.

Lancaster, J. (1991). A feminist and evolutionary biologist looks at women. *Yearbook of Physical Anthropology, 34*, 1–11.

Lerner, I. M. (1954). *Genetic homeostasis.* Edinburgh, Scotland: Oliver & Boyd.

Leung, B., & Forbes, M. R. (1996). Fluctuating asymmetry in relation to stress and fitness: Effects of trait type as revealed by meta-analysis. *Ecoscience, 3*, 400–413.

Low, B. S. (1990a). Marriage systems and pathogen stress in human societies. *American Zoologist, 30*, 325–340.

Low, B. S. (1990b). Sex, power, and resources: Male and female strategies of resource acquisition. *International Journal of Contemporary Sociology, 27*, 49–73.

Mace, R. (1996). Biased parental investment and reproductive success in Gabbra pastoralists. *Behavioral Ecology and Sociobiology, 38*, 75–81.

Meuwissen, I., & Over, R. (1992). Sexual arousal across phases of the human menstrual cycle. *Archives of Sexual Behavior, 21*, 101–119.

Møller, A. P. (1990). Male tail length and female mate choice in the monogamous swallow *Hirundo rustica. Animal Behaviour, 39*, 458–465.

Møller, A. P. (1992a). Female swallow preference for symmetrical male sexual ornaments? *Nature, 357*, 238–240.

Møller, A. P. (1992b). Parasites differentially increase the degree of fluctuating asymmetry in secondary sexual characteristics. *Journal of Evolutionary Biology, 5*, 691–700.

Møller, A. P. (1997). Developmental stability and fitness: A review. *American Naturalist, 149*, 916–932.

Møller, A. P., & Swaddle, J. P. (1997). *Developmental stability and evolution*. Oxford: Oxford University Press.

Møller, A. P. & Thornhill, R. (1997). A meta-analysis of the heritability of developmental stability. *Journal of Evolutionary Biology, 10*, 1–16.

Møller, A. P. & Thornhill, R. (1998). Bilateral symmetry and sexual selection: A meta-analysis. *American Naturalist, 151*, 174–193.

Orians, G. H., & Heerwagen, J. H. (1992). Evolved responses to landscapes. In J. Barkow, L. Cosmides, & J. Tooby (Eds.), *The adapted mind: Evolutionary psychology and the generation of culture* (pp. 555–579). New York: Oxford University Press.

Parker, G. A., & Maynard Smith, J. (1991). Optimality theory in evolutionary biology. *Nature, 348*, 27–33.

Parsons, P. A. (1990). Fluctuating asymmetry: An epigenetic measure of stress. *Biological Review, 65*, 131–145.

Ridley, M. (1996). *The origins of virtue: Human instincts and the evolution of cooperation*. New York: Penguin Books.

Schmitt, D. P., & Buss, D. M. (1996). Strategic self-promotion and competitor derogation: Sex and context effects on the perceived effectiveness of mate attraction tactics. *Journal of Personality and Social Psychology, 70*, 1185–1204.

Shackelford, T. K., & Larsen, R. J. (1997). Facial asymmetry as an indicator of psychological, emotional, and physiological distress. *Journal of Personality and Social Psychology, 72*, 456–466.

Simpson, J. A., & Gangestad, S. W. (1991). Individual differences in sociosexuality: Evidence for convergent and discriminant validity. *Journal of Personality and Social Psychology, 60*, 870–883.

Simpson, J. A., Gangestad, S. W., Christensen, P. N., & Leck, K. (1999). Fluctuating asymmetry, sociosexuality, and intrasexual competition tactics. *Journal of Personality and Social Psychology*.

Slob, A. K., Ernste, M., & Bosch, J. J. (1991). Menstrual cycle phase and sexual arousability in women. *Archives of Sexual Behavior, 20*, 567–577.

Small, M. F. (1992). Female choice in mating: The evolutionary significance of female choice depends on why the female chooses her reproductive partner. *American Scientist, 80*, 142–151.

Smuts, B. B. (1985). *Sex and friendship in baboons*. New York: Aldine de Gruyter.

Smuts, B. B. (1995). The evolutionary origins of patriarchy. *Human Nature, 6*, 1–32.

Stainslaw, H., & Rice, F. J. (1988). Correlation between sexual desire and menstrual cycle characteristics. *Archives of Sexual Behavior, 17*, 499–508.

Strassman, B. I. (1992). The function of menstrual taboos among the Dogon: Defense against cuckoldry? *Human Nature, 3*, 89–131.

Strassman, B. I. (1996). Menstrual hut visits by Dogon women: A hormonal test distinguishes deceit from honest signaling. *Behavioral Ecology, 7*, 304–315.

Studd, M. V., & Gattiker, U. E. (1991). The evolutionary psychology of sexual harassment in organizations. *Ethology and Sociobiology, 12*, 249–290.

Symons, D. (1979). *The evolution of human sexuality*. Oxford: Oxford University Press.

Theissen, D. (1994). Environmental tracking by females: Sexual lability. *Human Nature, 5*, 167–202.

Thompson, A. P. (1983). Extramarital sex: A review of literature. *Journal of Sex Research, 19*, 1–22.

Thornhill, R. (1992a). Fluctuating asymmetry and the mating system of the Japanese scorpionfly. *Behavioral Ecology, 3*, 277–283.

Thornhill, R. (1992b). Fluctuating asymmetry, interspecific aggression, and male mating tactics in two species of Japanese scorpionflies. *Behavioral Ecology and Sociobiology, 30*, 357–363.

Thornhill, R., & Gangestad, S. W. (1993). Human facial beauty: Averageness, symmetry, and parasite resistance. *Human Nature, 4*, 237–269.

Thornhill, R., & Gangestad, S. W. (1994). Fluctuating asymmetry and human sexual behavior. *Psychological Science, 5*, 297–302.

Thornhill, R., & Møller, A. P. (1997). Developmental stability, disease, and medicine. *Biological Reviews, 72*, 497–548.

Thornhill, R., & Møller, A. P. (in press). Developmental stability, disease and medicine. *Biological Reviews.*

Thornhill, R., & Thornhill, N. W. (1983). Human rape: An evolutionary analysis. *Ethology and Sociobiology, 4*, 137–173.

Thornhill, R., & Thornhill, N. W. (1992). The evolutionary psychology of men's coercive sexuality. *Behavioral and Brain Sciences, 15*, 363–421.

Tooby, J., & Cosmides, L. (1992). The psychological foundations of culture. In J. Barkow, L. Cosmides, & J. Tooby (Eds.), *The adapted mind: Evolutionary psychology and the generation of culture* (pp. 19–136). New York: Oxford University Press.

Trivers, R. (1972). Parental investment and sexual selection. In B. Campbell (Ed.), *Sexual selection and the descent of man, 1871–1971* (pp. 136–179). Chicago: Aldine.

Trivers, R. (1985). *Social evolution.* Menlo Park, CA: Benjamin/Cummings.

Udry, J. R., & Morris, N. M. (1968). Distribution of coitus in the menstrual cycle. *Nature, 220*, 593–596.

Van Valen, L. (1962). A study of fluctuating asymmetry. *Evolution, 16*, 125–142.

Waage, J. K. (1997). Parental investment—Minding the kids or keeping control? In P. A. Gowaty (Ed.), *Feminism and evolutionary biology* (pp. 527–553). New York: International Thomson.

Weatherhead, P. J., & Robertson, R. J. (1979). Offspring quality and the polygyny threshold: The "sexy son" hypothesis. *American Naturalist, 113*, 201–208.

Wilson, M., & Daly, M. (1992). The man who mistook his wife for a chattel. In J. Barkow, L. Cosmides, & J. Tooby (Eds.), *The adapted mind: Evolutionary psychology and the generation of culture* (pp. 289–322). New York: Oxford University Press.

Wright, R. (1994). *The moral animal.* New York: Vintage.

Zahavi, A. (1975). Mate selection—a selection for a handicap. *Journal of Theoretical Biology, 53*, 205–214.

Ziegel, E. E., & Cranley, M. S. (1984). *Obstetric nursing* (8th ed.). New York: Macmillan.

3

Historicity and the Evolution of the Individual Psyche

WILLIAM G. GRAZIANO and RENÉE M. TOBIN

This chapter begins with two stories. Both are true and potentially enlightening about the constraint of history on psychology, but in different ways. The first story is about a father and a four-year-old child's interpretation of an incident in a book. Like many parents throughout the world, the first author reads stories to his daughter, Claudia. Reading projects of this sort often begin with lofty (and perhaps naive) goals. Surely, reading great classics to a child must be better than having her watch violent and stultifying American network television! Like many parents, the father had an agenda and selected material alert to that agenda. He wanted to implant an appreciation for cultural diversity and a resistance to fundamentalism, the notion that all important ideas can be found in only one book. This agenda-driven, education-oriented reading is an important aspect of "socialization." The intent is to provide directed experiences to children with the goal of building one kind of psychological structure (Bugental & Goodnow, 1997; Tooby & Cosmides, 1992). The agent of socialization hopes that the child's experience and history will influence her developmental trajectory.

Here, his hope was to impart some knowledge of classical Greek culture. Peter Connolly's (1986) children's book, *The Legend of Odysseus*, is an excellent vehicle for readers with such an agenda. The exposition is in the form of a story, complete with background information and drawings of characters who resemble real people. The narrative is backed with maps, archaeological scholarship, and historical details. This is the kind of book a professor (and hopefully his four-year-old daughter) could love.

As background for his main narrative, Connolly (1986) describes the famous battle between Ajax and Hector (Book VII, *The Iliad*). In this exchange, the Greek Ajax and the Trojan Hector trade insults, spears, and finally in frustration, boulders. This event is portrayed vividly in Connolly's book, complete with a detailed drawing (p. 23) (see Figure 3.1). With great satisfaction the reader watched the four-year-old listen to the story with increasingly wide-eyed astonishment. She asked for a pause to examine the drawing of Ajax and Hector with care. Seeing this reaction, her father asked the four-year-old what she thought of this part of the story. With some agitation, she said, "These boys are throwing rocks! They need to be in time-out!" Ajax and Hector are boys throwing rocks? Would "time-out" have stopped the Trojan War?

A second, less homey story comes from personality psychology, the field par excellence for the study of psychological structure. Specifically, it comes from longitudinal work (Veroff, Depner, Kulka, & Douvan, 1980) on need for achievement, or *nAch*. Data collected in 1957 showed a statistically significant correlation between *nAch* and satisfaction with work. The direction of the correlation was negative: the higher the need for achievement, the less the satisfaction with work. The explanation was that *nAch* causes people to have an unslacking desire to set higher and higher standards. Each advance is merely a stepping-stone to a still higher level of achievement.

Data collected in a comparable survey in 1976 also showed a statistically significant correlation. This time, however, the direction of the correlation was *positive*. Few researchers expect the directions of their correlations involving psychological structure to reverse across 20 years. To their credit, Veroff et al. did not pretend to explain the reversal with a single variable or set of variables. They noted, however, a remarkable increase in women's *nAch* from 1957 to 1976 and suggested that an increasing number of women in the workforce were probably contributing to the reversed result.[1]

The two stories offered here appear to be very different, but they carry some common implications for the present volume on the evolution of the psyche. First, for persons of all ages, meaning must be forged on the anvil of existing psychological structures and life experiences. Greeks of the fourth century B.C.E. would probably attribute meanings to the actions of Ajax and Hector different from those of contemporary Greeks, much less contemporary, North American preschoolers. Furthermore, preschool girls have more salient experiences with boys' throwing rocks than with shield-and-spear-bearing warriors (even granting the popularity of televised episodes of Xena, Warrior Princess). More to the point, perhaps, are the levels of meaning that different individuals can extract from narratives involving conflict (e.g., Graziano, Jensen-Campbell, & Hair, 1996; Nisbett & Cohen, 1996). In the second story, the meaning of achievement to North American adults in 1976 probably changed following the social realignments of the 1960s. The meaning would not be filtered passively through existing structure but created in concert with existing structure. From a developmental perspective, experiences of the sort encountered in the 1960s by North American women can even shape and alter psychological structure.

Granting these points, why do some characters of antiquity still speak to us? Not all of them do, of course. Still, the arrogance of Agamemnon and Ramses strikes a chord, as do the miseries of Priam and Job. These characters may be

Figure 3.1
Ajax and Hector as Boys Throwing Rocks

speaking to us not as individual persons but to the evolved psychological structures within us that are prepared to produce a specific meaning with small provocation (Cosmides & Tooby, 1992; Rosen, Smith, Huston, & Gonzalez, 1991). We face a serious intellectual question: How can we reconcile historical accounts that assign a high priority to the powerful role of individual experience (Elder, Modell, & Parke, 1993; Feigl, 1970; Lewis, 1997; Nisbett & Cohen, 1996) with evolutionary accounts of psychological structure that give meaning to persons and events, presumably transcending time and place? How do history and individual experience constrain evolved psychological structure, and vice versa?

On one hand, Clio has a seductive charm, offering comprehensive explanations for events in terms of basic processes. The charm is misleading because there is an asymmetrical relation between a historical account and a theoretical account; a theoretical account is expressly intended to generalize across time and place, whereas a historical account is not. Philosophers of science have noted repeatedly that a historical description falls far short of a theoretical explanation (Feyerabend, 1970; Hiebert, 1970; Schaffner, 1970). A theoretical account is falsifiable, at least in principle. Precisely what do we know after reading even the most apparently penetrating analysis of the German Reformation or the French Revolution? What would have happened to the process if individual elements (e.g., the unique persons of Johann Tetzel or Denis Diderot) were removed from the account? From the historical analyses, would we have predicted with precision the antecedents and pattern for Elizabethan Reformation in England or the Russian Revolution of 1917 (e.g., Slovic & Fischhoff, 1977; Gurr, 1970)?

Historical accounts are even more seductive when the goal is to understand individual humans. Most contemporary psychologists assume that psychological structure underlying each individual's behavior and cognition is related to prior experience/conditions. What would have happened to persons like, say, Beethoven or Brahms if individual elements (e.g., barbaric treatment by drunken, irresponsible fathers) were removed from the account? Would they have produced different psychological structures and less revolutionary music (more like, say, Mendelssohn's) (see Cross & Ewen, 1953, p. 481; cf. Tesser, 1980)?

Yet we cannot dismiss history and individual experience so readily. In the language of the evolutionary biologist George C. Williams (1992), an organism is a ''historical document.'' Historical antecedents in the form of individual experiences can have a vast impact on human psychological structures. It is a commonplace that the mother who is loving or cold, supportive or dismissive lives in the psychological structure of her child, perchance indelibly, long after the mother has passed on. Exposure to concentration camps, combat, sexual assaults, and divorce may also leave effects on individual structures long after the event has passed (e.g., Elder, 1986).

It may be less obvious, perhaps, that historical events constrain the kinds of models of mind we build, test, and teach. Ward (1994, 1995) showed that creative cognition is very conservative and constrained by experience. When asked to draw space aliens, college students generated a narrow range of exemplars, nearly all of which were erect, bilaterally symmetric, binocular organisms with eyes at the top of their single heads. Presumably, the hypothetical aliens' similarity to humans was constrained by students' exposure to intelligent vertebrate organisms on this unique planet. For professional psychologists, the creative cognition that generates theoretical explanations may be similarly constrained. Theoretical accounts of psychological structure may be dependent on historical contexts in ways unrecognized in the theory or by the theorist. Meehl's (1970) writing on nuisance variables in psychology discusses the distinction between "accidental universals" and nomologicals. Historical accidents can have unrecognized influence on the causal models we build and our identification of variables as causal or nuisance.

For Darwin, historical description was not in conflict with theoretical explanation because he was a Lamarckian. For us in the last years of the twentieth century, a potential conflict is present (see Buss, Haselton, Shackelford, Bleske, & Wakefield, 1998). Most contemporary scientists do not believe that when the father eats sour grapes, the son's teeth are literally placed on edge, or that giraffes have long necks because of the stretching behavior of their ancestors.

We grant these points but suggest several larger issues. Some phenomena are intrinsically tied to temporal sequences and can be made sensical only through careful attention to historical antecedents. Other phenomena are explicable without a historical analysis. Both kinds of phenomena (and analyses) have their place at the table of science. Gould (1986) talks of Science A (experimental-predictive) and Science B (historical). Science A includes physics and chemistry, in which laws are not contingent on history. The trajectory of photons can be altered by gravitational fields, and it does not matter that the photons originated at Alpha Centauri or at our own sun. Science B includes geology and biology, in which laws are contingent on historical antecedents. The biobehavioral responses to photons in evolved visual systems, at least for organisms on this planet, are dependent on historical accidents of ancestry; light-sensitive cells in horseshoe crabs respond to photons in ways quite different from those in birds and horses (see Williams, 1992, pp. 72–73; Budiansky, 1997, pp. 111–117). On other planets, where history may have taken a different course in shaping organic evolution, biobehavioral systems for photon responses probably would be very different from ours.

HISTORICITY AND EVOLUTION

Along with the notions of mechanism and natural selection, the concept of *historicity* has been important to biological research, at least in the last century (Williams, 1992). In his book *Growth of Biological Thought*, Ernst Mayr (1982) observes that the notion of the directionality in life (e.g., "higher vs. lower") goes back at least to Aristotle. Mayr notes that it took many more years to gain "the crucial insight of the importance of history (in contrast to the timelessness of physical laws)." Nevertheless, it ultimately "led to a recognition of the process of development"(p. 129).

Mayr (1982) offers the following definition of historicism: "the belief that the adequate understanding of the nature of any phenomenon and an adequate assessment of its value are to be gained through considering it in terms of the place that it occupied and the role that it played within the process of development" (p. 130). Historicity is a term referring to the sequential, causal contingency among relations. If the sequence among the variables is altered, the relation itself is altered. In the present case, historicity refers to the historical contingency that determined the properties of all living things on this planet. The formation of organisms on this planet was a unique event. If we rewound the evolutionary tape of our planet, the outcome would almost certainly be different from the one we see now (Gould, 1989; for an interesting discussion of historicity in equine evolution, see Budiansky, 1997, pp. 17–21).

Williams (1992) offers the anatomical illustration of historicity for the vertebrate eye. The processes of human vision are very precise and highly structured. Vision has been used as a model for understanding physiological functioning, structure of the senses, and even cognition. Nevertheless, the human eye carries a historical legacy that makes it a poor design. Williams notes that the human eye originated in small, transparent organisms with no blood corpuscles. A small group of light-sensitive cells arose on the dorsal side of the anterior region of the nervous system. With evolution from a flat to a tubular nervous system and the related evolution of a circulatory system with blood vessels, the visual system became internalized. Through history, the photosensitive layers of the visual system have retained their position beneath other layers of the retina. Williams notes that if the human eye were really designed intelligently (i.e., on purely functional considerations), then there would be no blind spot. The mammalian blind spot is one manifestation of a historical contingency that yields a working system, but not necessarily an optimal or efficient one. (Other vertebrates like horses also have retinal blind spots, but due to their particular evolutionary history, the structure is different; see Budiansky, 1997, pp. 112–117).

Moving from the anatomical to the psychological, the best-known advocate of historicity in modern psychology is Kenneth Gergen, who concentrates on social psychology. We use Gergen's (1984) discussion here to illustrate the power of assumptions about psychological structure and process. His claim is that social psychology is a time-contingent history, not the ahistorical, nomothetic science presented in textbooks. According to Gergen, three "romances" have dominated recent social psychology, and all three have blocked the development of a social psychology that recognizes temporal contingencies. They are relevant to our discussion of the evolution of psychological structures. The first romance is for *mechanistic* explanations, which make human action intelligible by positing stable psychological structures or mechanisms. Attitudes, schemas, and traits are examples.

The second romance involves the preference for the analysis of *punctate* phenomena. Mechanistic explanations are most useful when they focus on temporally truncated sequences of events, such as onetime attitude change, or single-occasion attraction. The third romance, *phenomenal immutability*, may be a consequence of the other two. According to Gergen (1984), social psychology proceeded as though psychological structure and processes stood outside time and were inherent in the natural order. This belief in a fundamental, unchanging human nature represents a vestige of the early faith in a Platonic human soul, a basic essence beyond time and historical contingency (Verhave & Hoorn, 1984).

Gergen's (1984) historical approach rankles many psychologists. Basic, invariant principles and essences transcending time and place are the hallmarks of modern science, are they not? The sheer power of classic ahistorical analyses in other sciences is overwhelming. Let us return to Gould's (1986) distinction between Science A and Science B and consider the Classic Gas Laws of Charles and Boyle: PV=nRT. Whatever a gas's previous history, the relations among pressure, volume, and temperature remain the same. They are ahistorical in that it does not matter whether a given gas had been liquid or solid before its gaseous phase. The gases still will display the same relations among these measures. Further, physics and chemistry laws are said to hold universally; whether the gas is on Mars, Earth, or Alpha Cedi Five, the relations are unaltered by context or history. Similarly, Boltzmann's constant does not change over time or by context.

In contrast, prior states in evolution not only matter but are critical to the understanding of what Gould called Science B. Darwin's critics allegedly described his new theory as the "Law of Higgledy Piggledy" precisely because it did not offer the same kind of ahistorical analysis as the gas laws. It was "historical." According to his theory, events in the Pleistocene were causally formative of human anatomy and physical structure, including behavior and cognition. As a Lamarckian, Darwin believed in historical events with a vengeance. Without awareness of Mendel's informing work, Darwin held that experience shaped structure. Supposedly, giraffes stretching their necks gave birth to giraffes with longer necks. Timothy Perper (personal communication, 1996) phrases this well: "Lamarckian inheritance of acquired characteristics implies that events in the life of an individual are inscribed into the substance of inheritance, as if human history had a recording angel who not merely noticed what had happened to a person, but also wrote it down for all who came later."

In one sense, Mendel's work removed the historical element of Darwin's theory. Lamarck's position on inheritance was replaced: genotypes affect phenotypes but are themselves unaffected by history and experience. History, however, can influence genotype *frequency*, but not genotypes per se, as demonstrated later at the population level by the Hardy-Weinberg Law. Without any selection process, closed breeding populations are apparently immune to history (i.e., gene frequencies do not change from generation to generation). At the individual level—the level we study in psychology—experience seems to matter, but at the population level in evolutionary processes, experience and history matter largely because frequencies of the genes may be altered.

INTEGRATING HISTORY AND EXPERIENCE INTO STRUCTURE

In psychology, the modern connection of historical experience to individual psychological structure did not begin with Thorndike (1911) but was strongly influenced by his analysis. Thorndike suggested that natural selection operated not only on anatomy of organisms across the eons but also on the behavior of individual organisms in much shorter periods. Experiences leave residues and ultimately affect the psychological structure of individual organisms. From the perspective of the present chapter, a critical issue is how some experiences leave residue and affect structure, and other experiences do not. For Thorndike, the key was in hedonic consequences. Experiences associated with "satisfying" and "discomforting" outcomes leave structural residues; those without hedonic consequences do not. Connections among neurons produce psychological structure through the "natural selection" of pleasing and annoying outcomes. This is a cognitive rephrasing of Thorndike's well-known Law of Effect.

WHAT IS THE STRUCTURE OF THE PSYCHE?

If a first critical question involves differential impact of experiences, then a second critical issue involves the nature of the psychological structure itself. Let us return to Thorndike (1911), who made several assumptions that were not stated explicitly in his writing. He apparently believed that animals possessed great behavioral plasticity but could form specific structures quickly (in evolutionary time). In keeping with his zeitgeist, Thorndike described the emerging structure in terms of a hierarchy of habits. Experiences associated with hedonic outcomes, causing the hierarchy of potential responses to change. Experiences shape psychological structure because they alter the habit hierarchy.

Missing from Thorndike's (1911) analysis was the possibility that experiences can serve different functions and have different effects on the psychological structure. With the advantage of 85 more years of research, we can see that there is more to experience than reinforcement and habit. The developmental biologist Gottlieb (1983) provides a valuable organizational scheme for conceptualizing advances in thinking about experience. In particular, Gottlieb suggested three major functions for experience. The first function was *maintenance*: experience may preserve an already developed state or end point, no matter how the state was achieved. An example is sensory deprivation. Lacking sensory input, visual systems can deteriorate. Similarly, attention from preschool teachers and peers may help maintain aggressive behavior in a preschool bully. Maintenance is the weakest role for experience, but it is certainly not trivial for the operation of diverse biobehavioral systems. Gottlieb notes that much of the operant literature is about maintenance of behavioral repertories and sensory responsiveness. This class of experience seems to resemble the Skinnerian S-d/ S-delta system.

A second class of experience involved *facilitation*: experience may act as a temporal regulator of developmental achievement, which nonetheless eventually will be reached even if the organism were deprived of this experience. Here experiences act to "accelerate" development. An example might be reading stories like *The Iliad* to children to promote verbal facility. With or without parental reading, most middle-class, North American children eventually will learn to read, albeit with varying degrees of competence. The Geneva-based Piagetians describe this as the "American problem," because Americans seem to be very interested in speeding up development.

The third class of experience involved *induction*: this class of experience exerts the strongest effect on the development of psychological structure. At least in theory, without this class of experiences, required to occur within a narrow developmental window, the organism will never develop the relevant structure. Work on the issue was initiated by T. C. Schneirla in the 1960s but was restricted largely to sensory systems in altricial species. As Klopfer (1996) correctly notes, cross-species generalizations are extremely hazardous, even in closely related species, much less from birds to humans. Theorists have speculated on the kinds of experiences that might be inductive for humans and have suggested experiences as diverse as maternal nurturance during infancy, peer contact in middle childhood, and even carpentered housing sometime during the life course. The scientific evidence so far is limited but suggests that inductive experiences are rare for any human developmental system (and may be non-existent for personality and social development). Exposure to certain gonadal hormones may be inductive.

Now let us turn the tables and ask about structure. Whatever label we assign it, the structure of the psyche is an abstract, hypothetical construct. It is a verbal, summary description of schematically organized systems within individuals. It includes residues of experience. For humans, the structure is influenced by the ways specific cultures organize experiences for individuals. How does individual experience shape psychological structure through maintenance, facilitation, or induction?

Wagner's (1978) work on memory illustrates this phenomenon. Wagner noted that literacy was associated with direct religious instruction of the Koran in Islamic cultures. Thus, literacy is associated with knowledge of religious texts, so skills in recall of prose are associated with both literacy and knowledge of classic Islam. One might conclude that memory skills and metamemory skills can be influenced by education, but a basic part of the pan-human structure of the psyche involves language. When Wagner pitted literate, well-educated Moroccan Islamic scholars against illiterate rug merchants on a memory-for-a-prose test, he was not surprised to learn that the Islamic scholars fared better. When the task shifted to memory for rug patterns, however, the results were exactly reversed. For rug merchants, the structure of memory was not connected to literacy, at least in the same way that it was for the Islamic scholars.

What do these outcomes say about the structure of the psyche? These results point to both cognitive plasticity and an experience-based approach to its structure. One might make the case that the individual educational experiences of Islamic scholars in Morocco facilitated the development of cognitive structures and that regular reading of verbal material from the Koran maintained those structures. Rug merchants in Morocco had a different educational experience and developed adaptive cognitive skills that were missing in the Islamic scholars. Presumably, skills in rug pattern identification might still be latent (and open to experience-based development) in the Islamic scholars. It is not plausible that experiences with rugs are inductive in shaping psychological structure for memory of rugs.

How can we use this information to enhance our understanding of the evolution of psychological structure? We agree with Buss (1995) that we must identify psychological mechanisms that link antecedents with behavior and cognition. We also agree with Tooby and Cosmides (1990) that mechanisms should be dedicated and narrow in scope. We, too, envision a Swiss army knife, not an all-purpose Pentium processor. With these considerations in mind, we took a model originally presented by the Laboratory of Comparative Human Cognition (LCHC, 1983).

According to the model presented by LCHC (1983) (see Figure 3.2), we should consider the possibility that psychological structure resembles a distributed process system (DPS), rather than a single, monolithic, unified psychological structure (SUS). The traditional model of mind, of course, is the SUS. The IQ and the Piagetian concrete-operational child are two different examples of single, central, unified processors. It is literally true that the same head that solves math problems also solves interpersonal problems, but it may not be literally true that the same psychological structures are involved in both sets of problems. What if we did not make the SUS assumptions that all experience must be filtered through a single structure or that a single, central structure shapes each experience or that a single, unified structure is the entity with which experiences interact? In the DPS approach, psychological structure may include several functionally distinct, cognitive, adaptive specializations (Graziano & Waschull, 1995, pp. 250–252). Let us think of them as "dedicated modules." The modules may generally operate in a concerted way but in certain situations may perform their specific work relatively independently of each other, just as the heart pumps blood, and the liver detoxifies poisons (Tooby & Cosmides, 1990). In some contexts, the modules may not connect at all. The head that solves math problems will not necessarily show the same analytic competence with interpersonal problems. There will be similarities in structure of the psyche among subsets of individuals, to be sure. We expect these similarities when

Figure 3.2
Central and Distributed Processor Models

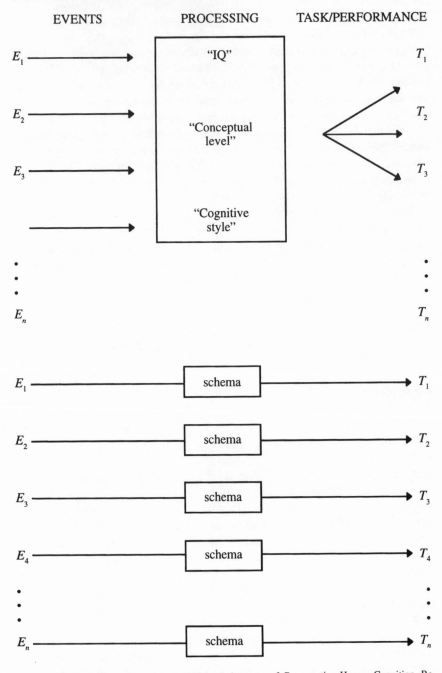

people share patterned experiences and when tasks can be expected to be associated, as in the cases of the Islamic scholars and the rug merchants.

At this point, even a friendly critic might wonder how our approach is appreciably different from Thorndike's (1911) or from any radical empiricist's. We believe that our approach to psychological structure shares common concerns with the classic empiricists but is also different. We suggest that the number of distributed processing systems is not infinitely large, at least for modules associated with personality and social behavior. If psychological structure has evolved, it has evolved as a patterned reaction to recurrent problems (Buss, 1995; Tooby & Cosmides, 1990). In the case of personality, dedicated modules may be tied to motives for coping with the recurring problems of group living (Hogan, 1983; Wiggins, 1991; Wiggins & Trapnell, 1997).

Hogan (1983), in particular, argues that humans needed to evolve characteristics that allowed them to capitalize on the advantages of group living. In particular, to survive and reproduce, humans had to evolve procedures for cooperating, negotiating, and exchanging resources. Individuals who were unable to make social adjustments may have been excluded from social groups, presumably to their personal and reproductive detriment. Wiggins (1991) suggested a way to link this theorizing to personality. He marshals evidence that two major (and apparently orthogonal) motivational systems, agency and communion, underlie many kinds of interpersonal behaviors. Agency is the motive to be effective against the environment, to stand out compared with others, to be an origin, not a pawn. The other motive system, communion, is independent of agency. It involves the striving for intimacy, union, and solidarity with others. In the language of the five-factor approach to personality structure (Wiggins & Trapnell, 1997), agency can be mapped onto the dimension of surgency/extraversion and is linked conceptually to dominance, traditional masculine sex roles, and achievement. Communion can be mapped onto the dimension of agreeableness and is linked conceptually to cooperation (Graziano, Hair, & Finch, 1997), efforts to reduce conflicts (Graziano, et al., 1996), traditional feminine sex roles, and prosocial behavior (Graziano & Eisenberg, 1997).

The evolved psychological structure proposed here for personality and social behavior is a distributed processing system. Two dedicated modules, largely operating independently of each other, form the core of evolved psychological structure. The two dedicated modules deal with the agentic and communal aspect of group living, respectively. The motivational systems underlying agency and communion are not necessarily in opposition; they are independent of each other, at least in theory (e.g., Wiggins, 1991; but see Jensen-Campbell, Graziano, & West, 1995). Consistent with the idea of a loosely federated distributed processing system, an individual in some settings may be simultaneously highly agentic and highly communal, whereas in other settings the motive modules may operate independently of each other (Graziano, Jensen-Campbell, Todd, & Finch, 1997). Individual experience and personal history may shape the structure of these modules (e.g., Graziano, Jensen-Campbell, & Finch, 1997; see Graziano

& Eisenberg, 1997, "Is there an altruistic personality?"), but the modules are preadapted psychological structures within us that are prepared to produce a specific meaning with small provocation (Cosmides & Tooby, 1992; Rosen et al., 1991). Achilles and Jesus speak to us across the ages because we have experience with them but also because we are prepared to hear them.

SOME PASSING THOUGHTS ON NARRATIVES IN THE STRUCTURE OF PSYCHE

We began with a story about *The Iliad* and promised to say more. There is something special about narratives and stories as vehicles for describing and explaining psychological structure (McAdams, 1995). Those of us who read stories to children or who teach courses know that a good story can swamp truckloads of more objective information. (One of our colleagues once claimed that the undergraduate psychology course he taught was ruined one term when he was asked for a narrative illustration and could not provide one.) Some critics pooh-pooh stories as the vehicles necessary for teaching preliterate persons. These critics may be right in that narratives speak to a part of us that may be older and less accessible, but this may also explain the potency of narratives. We do not have romantic illusions about such narratives. Beyond the issue of interpretation, there is an issue of content. Even in versions designed for children, *The Iliad* is appallingly barbaric, and a modern reader wonders about the deep structure of the behavior. This is an *alternative* to violence on television? Has social evolution progressed to modern civilization so that a return to Bronze Age "heroic" codes is impossible? We think not (see Nisbett & Cohen, 1996).

If we were forced to bet on any single aspect of dedicated modules in the structure of the psyche, we would bet on a procedure, not on specific content. Our hunch is that evolution has prepared humans to extract some of our most important experiences and our own individual history from narratives. All of us like a good story.

NOTES

This work was supported in part by an NIMH grant to William G. Graziano. Portions of this chapter were presented at a conference entitled "Evolution of the Psyche," chaired by David Rosen, held at Texas A&M University, College Station, Texas. The authors are grateful for the constructive criticisms provided by other conference participants. Special appreciation is expressed to David M. Buss, Timothy Perper, and Constantine Sedikides for advice.

1. One point warrants comment here. Veroff et al.'s general explanation involves changing historical relations, with which we are in sympathy (Veroff et al., 1980). They are being true to the historical origins of this literature. After all, achievement motivation is presumed to have its origins in the historical antecedent of changes in child socialization following the Protestant Reformation, with its emphasis on training individual efforts to earn salvation (Byrne, 1966; McClelland, 1961). Nevertheless, we do not be-

lieve that change in women's level of achievement motivation is a plausible explanation for the historical reversal. Even in the earliest achievement work, the research evidence has shown that women often showed *higher* achievement motivation and showed less variation in it across experimental manipulation than did men (e.g., Veroff, 1950).

REFERENCES

Budiansky, S. (1997). *The nature of horses: Exploring equine evolution, intelligence, and behavior.* New York: Free Press.

Bugental, D. B., & Goodnow, J. J. (1997). Socialization processes. In W. Damon (Series Ed.) & N. Eisenberg (Vol. Ed.), *Handbook of child psychology: Vol. 3. Social, emotional, and personality development* (5th ed.) (pp. 389–462). New York: Wiley.

Buss, D. M. (1995). Evolutionary psychology: A new paradigm for psychological science. *Psychological Inquiry, 6,* 1–30.

Buss, D. M., Haselton, M. G., Shackelford, T. K., Bleske, A., & Wakefield, J. C. (1998). Adaptations, exaptations, and spandrels. *American Psychologist, 53,* 533–548.

Byrne, D. (1966). *An introduction to personality: A research approach.* Englewood Cliffs, NJ: Prentice-Hall.

Connolly, P. (1986). *The legend of Odysseus.* Oxford: Oxford University Press.

Cosmides, L., & Tooby, J. (1992). Cognitive adaptations for social exchange. In J. H. Barkow, L. Cosmides, & J. Tooby (Eds.), *The adapted mind: Evolutionary psychology and the generation of culture* (pp. 163–228). Oxford: Oxford University Press.

Cross, M., & Ewen, D. (1953). Felix Mendelssohn. In *Milton Cross' encyclopedia of the great composers and their music* (pp. 471–488). Garden City, NY: Doubleday.

Elder, G. H., Jr. (1986). Military times and turning points in men's lives. *Developmental Psychology, 22,* 233–245.

Elder, G. H., Jr., Modell, J., & Parke, R. D. (1993). *Children in time and place: Developmental and historical insights.* Cambridge: Cambridge University Press.

Feigl, H. (1970). Beyond peaceful coexistence. In H. Feigl & G. Maxwell (Gen. Eds.) & R. H. Stuewer (Vol. Ed.), *Minnesota Studies in the Philosophy of Science: Vol. 5. Historical and philosophical perspectives of science* (pp. 3–11). Minneapolis: University of Minnesota Press.

Feyerabend, P. K. (1970). Philosophy of science: A subject with a great past. In H. Feigl & G. Maxwell (Gen. Eds.) & R. H. Stuewer (Vol. Ed.), *Minnesota Studies in the Philosophy of Science: Vol. 5. Historical and philosophical perspectives of science* (pp. 172–183). Minneapolis: University of Minnesota Press.

Gergen, K. H. (1984). *Historical social psychology.* Hillsdale, NJ: Lawrence Erlbaum.

Gottlieb, G. (1983). The psychobiological approach to developmental issues. In P. Mussen (Series Ed.) & M. M. Haith and J. J. Campos (Vol. Eds.), *Handbook of child psychology: Vol. 2. Infancy and developmental psychobiology* (4th ed., pp. 1–26). New York: Wiley.

Gould, S. J. (1986). Evolution and the triumph of homology, or why history matters. *American Scientist, 74,* 60–69.

Gould, S. J. (1989). *Wonderful life.* New York: Norton.

Graziano, W. G., & Eisenberg, N. (1997). Agreeableness: A dimension of personality.

In R. Hogan, J. Johnson, & S. Briggs (Eds.), *Handbook of personality psychology* (pp. 795–824). San Diego: Academic Press.

Graziano, W. G., Hair, E. C., & Finch, J. F. (1997). Competitiveness mediates the link between personality and group performance. *Journal of Personality and Social Psychology, 73 (6)*, 1394–1408.

Graziano, W. G., Jensen-Campbell, L. A., & Finch, J. F. (1997). The self mediates the link between personality and adjustment. *Journal of Personality and Social Psychology, 73*, 392–404.

Graziano, W. G., Jensen-Campbell, L. A., & Hair, E. C. (1996). Perceiving interpersonal conflict and reacting to it: The case for agreeableness. *Journal of Personality and Social Psychology, 70*, 820–835.

Graziano, W. G., Jensen-Campbell, L. A., Todd, M., & Finch, J. F. (1997). Interpersonal attraction from an evolutionary psychology perspective. In J. A. Simpson & D. Kenrick (Eds.), *Evolutionary social psychology* (pp. 141–167). Hillsdale, NJ: Lawrence Erlbaum.

Graziano, W. G., & Waschull, S. (1995). Social development and self-monitoring. *Review of Personality and Social Psychology, 15*, 233–260.

Gurr, T. R. (1970). *Why men rebel.* Princeton, NJ: Princeton University Press.

Heibert, E. N. (1970). Mach's philosophical use of the history of science. In H. Feigl & G. Maxwell (Gen. Eds.) & R. H. Stuewer (Vol. Ed.), *Minnesota Studies in the Philosophy of Science: Vol. 5. Historical and philosophical perspectives of science* (pp. 184–203). Minneapolis: University of Minnesota Press.

Hogan, R. (1983). A socioanalytic theory of personality. In M. Page (Ed.), *1982 Nebraska symposium on motivation* (pp. 55–89). Lincoln: University of Nebraska Press.

Jensen-Campbell, L. A., Graziano, W. G., & West, S. G. (1995). Dominance, prosocial orientation, and female preferences: Do nice guys really finish last? *Journal of Personality and Social Psychology, 68*, 427–440.

Klopfer, P. R. (1996). ''Mother love'' revisited: On the use of animal models. *American Scientist, 84*, 319–321.

Laboratory of Comparative Human Cognition (1983). Culture and cognitive development. In P. H. Mussen (Series Ed.) & W. Kessen (Vol. Ed.), *Handbook of child psychology: Vol. 1. History, theory, and methods* (pp. 295–356). New York: Wiley.

Lewis, M. (1997). *Altering fate: Why the past does not predict the future.* New York: Guilford.

Mayr, E. (1982). *The growth of biological thought: Diversity, evolution, and inheritance.* Cambridge: Harvard University Press.

McAdams, D. P. (1995). What do we know when we know a person? Special issue: Levels and domains in personality. *Journal of Personality, 63*, 365–396.

McClelland, D. C. (1961). *The achieving society.* New York: Free Press.

Meehl, P. E. (1970). Nuisance variables and the ex post facto design. In H. Feigl & G. Maxwell (Gen. Eds.) & M. Radner & S. Winokur (Vol. Eds.), *Minnesota studies in the philosophy of science: Vol. 4. Analyses of theories and methods of physics and psychology* (pp. 373–402). Minneapolis: University of Minnesota Press.

Nisbett, R. E., & Cohen, D. (1996). *Culture of honor: The psychology of violence in the South.* Boulder, CO: Westview.

Rosen, D. H., Smith, S. M., Huston, H. L., & Gonzalez, G. (1991). Empirical studies of associations between symbols and their meanings: Evidence of collective unconscious (archetypal) memory. *Journal of Analytical Psychology, 36*, 211–228.

Schaffner, K. F. (1970). Outline of a logic of comparative theory evaluation with special attention to pre- and post-relativistic electrodynamics. In H. Feigl & G. Maxwell (Gen. Eds.) & R. H. Stuewer (Vol. Ed.), *Minnesota Studies in the Philosophy of Science: Vol. 5. Historical and philosophical perspectives of science* (pp. 311–353). Minneapolis: University of Minnesota Press.

Slovic, P., & Fischhoff, B. (1977). On the psychology of experimental surprises. *Journal of Experimental Psychology: Human Perception and Performance, 3*, 544–551.

Tesser, A. (1980). Self-esteem maintenance in family dynamics. *Journal of Personality and Social Psychology, 39*, 77–91.

Thorndike, E. L. (1911). *Animal intelligence*. New York: Macmillan.

Tooby, J., & Cosmides, L. (1990). On the universality of human nature and the uniqueness of the individual: The role of genetics and adaptation. *Journal of Personality, 58*, 17–68.

Tooby, J., & Cosmides, L. (1992). The psychological foundations of culture. In J. H. Barkow, L. Cosmides, & J. Tooby (Eds.), *The adapted mind: Evolutionary psychology and the generation of culture* (pp. 19–136). Oxford: Oxford University Press.

Verhave, T., & Hoorn, W. (1984). The temporalization of the self. In K. J. Gergen & M. M. Gergen (Eds.), *Historical social psychology*. Hillsdale, NJ: Lawrence Erlbaum.

Veroff, J. (1950). *A projective measure of the achievement motivation of adolescent males and females*. Unpublished honors thesis, Wesleyan University, Middletown, CT.

Veroff, J., Depner, C., Kulka, R., & Douvan, E. (1980). Comparison of American motives: 1957 versus 1976. *Journal of Personality and Social Psychology, 39*, 1249–1262.

Wagner, D. A. (1978). Memories of Morocco: The influence of age, schooling, and environment on memory. *Cognitive Psychology, 10*, 1–28.

Ward, T. B. (1994). Structured imagination: The role of category structure in exemplar generation. *Cognitive Psychology, 27*, 1–40.

Ward, T. B. (1995). What's old about new ideas? In S. M. Smith, T. B. Ward, & R. A. Finke (Eds.), *The creative cognition approach* (pp. 157–178). Cambridge: MIT Press.

Wiggins, J. S. (1991). Agency and communion as conceptual coordinates for understanding and measurement of interpersonal behavior. In W. Grove & D. Cicchetti (Eds.), *Thinking clearly about psychology: Essays in honor of Paul E. Meehl* (pp. 89–113). Minneapolis: University of Minnesota Press.

Wiggins, J. S., & Trapnell, P. D. (1997). Personality structures: The return of the Big Five. In R. Hogan, J. Johnson, & S. Briggs, (Eds.), *Handbook of personality psychology* (pp. 737–765). San Diego: Academic Press.

Williams, G. C. (1992). *Natural selection: Domains, levels, and challenges*. New York: Oxford University Press.

4

Evolution of the Symbolic Self

JOHN J. SKOWRONSKI
and CONSTANTINE SEDIKIDES

Folk wisdom suggests that our lives are strongly influenced by a sense of personal identity, often referred to as the "sense of self." For example, it is common to note that a developmental milestone occurs when an individual "finds herself." Similarly, radical behavior changes in response to self-initiated challenges to personal identity are often referred to as a "midlife crisis." Finally, observers will sometimes report admiration of another for being "at peace with himself."

This fascination with the self has also characterized research and theory in psychology. The self has been a topic of scientific scrutiny for as long as psychology has adopted the methods of science (James, 1890/1950), and it continues to be an intensively investigated area. Although the theoretical and empirical approaches to the study of the self vary widely, these approaches share with folk wisdom the notion that the self plays a central role in human psychological functioning (for overviews, see Banaji & Prentice, 1994; Baumeister, 1993; Sedikides & Strube, 1997; Symons & Johnson, 1997).

The centrality that has been accorded to the concept of the self in psychology leads naturally to the question of the origins of the self—where does the self come from? In the present chapter, we offer an answer to this question that is derived from principles of evolution. The central thesis of this chapter is that the human capacity to construct a sense of self (which we term the *symbolic self*) is an evolutionary adaptation. We argue that the symbolic self is a trait that was selected and distributed in the human population because of its considerable adaptive value. We further argue that this trait evolved from a more primitive form of self-concept, and we support this argument by discussing evidence documenting the presence of such rudimentary self-concepts in non-human species. Finally, we paint a more complete picture of the symbolic self by discussing several factors related to its evolution: (1) the temporal origins of the symbolic self; (2) the ecologically important problems that have spurred the evolution of the symbolic self; and (3) some of the adaptive functions of the symbolic self (for a more detailed exposition, see Sedikides & Skowronski, 1997).

Before proceeding, however, we need to be more specific about the *symbolic self*. We wish to draw a distinction between symbolic self-awareness, on one hand, and subjective and objective self-awareness, on the other. Symbolic self-awareness requires several capacities, many of which are unique to the human organism: (1) the formation of an abstract, cognitive representation of the self through language; (2) the communication of the symbolic self to other organisms; (3) negotiation of the content of the symbolic self with other organisms in an effort to establish personal and social relationships; (4) the setting of social or achievement goals that are prompted by the symbolic self far into the future; (5) the performance of goal-guided behaviors; (6) the evaluation of the outcome of these behaviors (i.e., judging whether the behaviors have fulfilled the relevant goals); (7) the linking of the behavioral outcome to feelings toward the symbolic self (e.g., high self-esteem or pride when goals are met and shame or embarrassment when goals are not met); and (8) the defense of the symbolic self against threatening events and ideas through several strategies, such as avoidance and rejection of negative feedback, derogation of negative evaluators, and even self-deception. In sum, the symbolic self refers to both the language-based and abstract representation of one's own attributes and the use of this representation for effective functioning in affective, motivational, and behavioral domains.

We distinguish the notion of symbolic self-awareness from two other aspects of the self: *subjective self-awareness* and *objective self-awareness*. Subjective self-awareness is a property of all living organisms that refers to an organism's cognitive capacity to discriminate between itself and physical or social aspects of the environment. This crude self-other differentiation provides at least two benefits to the organism: (1) self-regulation (a process where systemic parts of the organism coordinate the action of each other) and (2) the ability to perceive, respond to, and alter the environment. Note that this differentiation between the self and the environment does not require the presence of a cognitive representation of the self in memory. Instead, these crude self-other differentiations can be made in a relatively "thoughtless," reflexive, or automatic fashion.

By comparison, an organism possessing objective self-awareness must have a self-representation stored in the memory system. Objective self-awareness is defined as the organism's cognitive capacity to "become the object of its own attention" (Gallup, 1992, p. 117), to be aware of its "own state of mind" (Cheney & Seyfarth, 1992, p. 240), and (3) "to know it knows, to remember it remembers" (Lewis, 1992, p. 124). A major distinguishing characteristic of objective self-awareness is that it allows for self-referential behavior. That is, it allows the use of one's own knowledge to model the knowledge of other organisms. Objective self-awareness occurs at a substantially more explicit or conscious level than subjective self-awareness.

Objective self-awareness is a necessary precursor to symbolic self-awareness, and two sources of evidence suggest that objective self-awareness precedes subjective self-awareness. Certainly, the human developmental evidence is consistent with the idea that the initial self-concept is fairly primitive, developing increasing complexity with life experience (Damon & Hart, 1986; Higgins, 1991; Lewis, 1990). More important for purposes of the present chapter is the possibility that, in terms of the evolution of the human species, the capacity for objective self-awareness preceded the capacity for symbolic self-awareness. This possibility is important because evolution does not create traits and attributes out of thin air; instead, it often modifies or amplifies existing attributes to cope with new environmental pressures. The implication of this notion is that one should find evidence of objective self-awareness in other species, especially in species that are closely related to humans on the bush of evolution.

OBJECTIVE SELF-AWARENESS IS POSSESSED BY OTHER SPECIES

Current evidence from investigations of other species suggests that some of the great apes (in particular, chimpanzees, orangutans, and bonobos) possess the capacity for objective self-awareness. For example, the *rouge test* is often thought to be an indicator of self-awareness in human children. A human child is thought to possess a self-concept when she moves to wipe a spot of rouge off her own face instead of attempting to wipe the spot off the face of the image of herself that she sees reflected in a mirror (Lewis, 1990, 1994). Gallup (1970, 1977) and Suarez and Gallup (1981) have observed this behavior in chimpanzees and orangutans.

Additional evidence that some animals possess objective self-awareness comes from consideration of other abilities thought to be related to the self. For example, Gallup (1983, 1985; Gallup & Suarez, 1986) reasoned that if the presence of objective self-awareness necessarily involves the capacity to use the self referentially, then organisms ought to possess several advanced capacities: (1) the ability to reflect on their own knowledge state in a situation and reason inferentially about another organism's knowledge state in the same or similar situation; (2) the ability to anticipate what other organisms might do (i.e., by attributing intentions to other organisms); and (3) the ability to influence other organisms (e.g., by intervening in their behavior). Organisms without objective self-awareness should not exhibit such capabilities.

Empirical evidence suggests that such abilities exist in the higher primates. Chimpanzees are capable of understanding the relation between perceiving and the resulting cognitive state of knowing (Povinelli, Nelson, & Boysen, 1992b), and they are capable of role-taking (Povinelli, Nelson, & Boysen, 1992a; Povinelli, Parks, & Novak, 1992). Furthermore, behaviors such as the attribution of knowledge states in others (Premack & Premack, 1983; see also Seyfarth & Cheney, 1989), responsibility-taking (Goodall, 1986; Premack & Woodruff, 1978), concealment (Savage-Rumbaugh & McDonald, 1988), distraction, lying (Menzel, 1971; Premack & Woodruff, 1978), creation of a social image (de Waal, 1982), and intentional intraspecies deception (de Waal, 1982, 1986) have been conclusively documented in chimpanzees, orangutans, and bonobos. Such behaviors would be impossible without the use of a self-concept.

SPECULATIONS ON THE EVOLUTION OF THE SYMBOLIC SELF

The existing evidence, then, strongly suggests that non-human species can possess objective self-awareness and that this trait exists in organisms that are closely related to humans. The evidence also supports our hypothesis that objective self-awareness was present in the early ancestors of humans but was altered and amplified in response to evolutionary pressures. Given the paucity and uncertainty of anthropological evidence, exactly when, how, and why this selection occurred is obviously a matter of much speculation. However, we believe that the existing evidence allows the formation of reasonable hypotheses about both the causes of the evolution of the symbolic self in humans and the time course of this evolution.

The Time Course of Human Evolution: Speculations on the Temporal Emergence of the Symbolic Self

There are several different credible scenarios for the time course and progress of human evolution. The details of this evolution are continuously debated, especially in the face of new anthropological discoveries. The evolutionary time line that we describe later is meant to convey only one of these plausible scenarios.

DNA-RNA hybridization experiments (Sibley & Ahlquist, 1984) suggest that hominids split from the common ancestor of chimpanzees, bonobos, and humans approximately 6.3–7.7 million years ago. The immediate precursors of the human family may be the australopithecines, who are thought to have appeared about 5.5 million years ago. The oldest confirmed fossils of *Australopithecus* are approximately 3.8 million years old (Day, 1986). The date of the exact transition from the australopithecines to early humans is unclear. An early human, *Homo habilis*, may have coexisted with the australopithecines (Leakey, 1966). Alternatively, early humans may have been direct descendants of the early australopithecines. However, regardless of the exact origin, it is clear that rapid changes in the size and organization of the human brain coincided with the appearance of *Homo habilis* (Falk, 1987; Holloway, 1975; Tobias, 1971). The data suggest that this trend continued through time. The next human species in the time line, *Homo erectus*, had a relatively large and differentiated brain (McHenry, 1992).

Homo erectus appeared by at least 1.8 million years ago. *Homo erectus* is thought to have given rise to *Homo sapiens*, who appeared approximately 300,000 years ago (and maybe as early as 800,000 years ago). *Homo sapiens* likely spread from Africa (perhaps in several waves) and replaced archaic hominids (e.g., Neanderthals) elsewhere—a scenario supported by several sources of evidence (i.e., fossil and archaeological records, data on the genetic associations and diversity of present-day humans; see Klein, 1992). *Homo sapiens sapiens* appeared by at least 100,000 years ago and is the human species found on the Earth today.

Given the anthropological and biological evidence, we speculate that the capacity for a symbolic self appeared as early as *Homo erectus*. The existing evidence suggests that, by this period, humans had evolved the capacity for abstract symbolic thought, a capacity that is essential for the emergence of a symbolic self. However, this placement is obviously a rough guess. One cannot exclude the possibility that the symbolic self may have appeared earlier, especially given that some of the behaviors that we use to make our case may predate *Homo erectus*.

Nonetheless, despite these difficulties, we argue that *Homo erectus* had the capacity to form and use a symbolic self. In the following sections, we review two explanations for the emergence of the symbolic self during this time period. The first of these explanations is that the symbolic self is a consequence of the enhanced cognitive capacities that emerged in response to ecological pressures. The second explanation is that the symbolic self is a consequence of the problems associated with the social lifestyle of early humans. In the course of evaluating these two explanations, we review some of the evidence that links the symbolic self to *Homo erectus*.

Ecological Pressures and the Evolution of Cognitive Capacity

One explanation for the evolution of the symbolic self is that the symbolic self is a consequence of an increase in the human ability to engage in symbolic thought. There is substantial evidence lending plausibility to this notion. For example, anthropological data suggest that there is a trend (although an admittedly imperfect one) toward increasing encephalization in more recent *Homo* species. That is, as speciation progressed, the brains of early hominids tended to increase in size at a faster rate than their body size. Furthermore, braincase casts suggest that with developing speciation, the outward appearance of the brains increasingly resembles the appearance of the brains of members of the *Homo sapiens sapiens* subspecies. Such increases in brain size (relative to body size) and the increasing resemblance to modern brains have been thought to reflect the increasingly sophisticated mental capabilities of the early *Homo* species members. Those increasing capabilities are also thought to be reflected in other evidence, such as the fact that tools and artifacts appear to become more sophisticated in more recent *Homo* species.

However, there is some question as to why this increase in cognitive capacity occurred. Some theorists have speculated that this increase in cognitive capacity was related to food procurement. Several lines of thought support this speculation. First, humans' omnivorous lifestyle may be a contributor to large brain capacity. Omnivorous extractive foragers (the category to which humans belong) have the largest brain/body ratios among primates (Gibson, 1986; Parker & Gibson, 1979).

Second, there is speculation that human evolution was spurred by climatic changes that produced challenges to food procurement. More specifically, the evolution from *Homo habilis* to *Homo erectus* may have been a consequence of the challenges posed by climatic changes. Early humans were primarily forest dwellers, but climatic changes caused a relative increase in open savanna. Some hominids were probably forced into this climatic zone, which likely caused problems in food procurement. Such problems could have helped to spur the cognitive development of hominid species. This proposition is supported by several observations. For example, data suggest that problems in foraging are associated with increased encephalization, and the irregular distribution of food supplies in time or space is associated with larger brain/body ratios among frugivore primates (Milton, 1981, 1988).

Other speculations have focused on how changes in the environment might have affected specific feeding behaviors. One change in behavior that appeared as evolution proceeded was a transition from a fruit-eating to an omnivorous lifestyle. For *Homo erectus*, hunting appears to have been an important source of food, and this hunting activity possibly involved the pursuit of big game (i.e., more than fifteen kilograms; Isaac, 1978). In retrospect, hunting was an extraordinarily difficult task for an animal that was not well equipped for survival and reproduction on the open savanna. Given its arboreal background, early *Homo erectus* was probably a terrible hunter. As Fox (1980) noted, very little about these species members would inspire confidence in their hunting ability: "not the stature, the speed, the strength, the ferocity, or even the mental equipment" (p. 175).

If early hominids were poor hunters, the demands of hunting could have spurred the evolution of their cognitive capabilities. For example, consider a description of hunting provided by Laughlin (1968):

The hunter is concerned with the freshness of the track and the direction in which he is moving. He wants all possible information on the quarry's condition: its age, sex, size, rate of travel, and a working estimate of the distance by which the animal leads him. In the final stages, when he is closing with the animal, the hunter employs his knowledge of animal behavior and situational factors relevant to that behavior in crucial fashion. For all birds, animals, and fish the hunter must estimate flight distance, the point at which they will take flight or run away. Conversely, with animals that are aggressive, he needs

to interpret any signs, raising or lowering of tail, flexing of muscles, blowing, or sali-
vation, etc., that indicate an attack rather than a flight. (pp. 308–309)

It is clear from this description that hunting requires several cognitive skills: the
better a hominid could perform these skills, the better hunter the hominid would
be.

It is probable that the frugivore hominids had already developed capacities
for recognizing food, finding food, and handling/processing food, and these ca-
pabilites would be modified or enhanced by evolution. This could have happened
simultaneously along several dimensions. First, for early humans to cope with
disparate and fast-changing pieces of information, perceptual and imaging capabilities needed to improve (Kaplan & Kaplan, 1978). Prey often attempts to
hide in cover, and the ability to detect prey in the perceptual confusion provided
by the cover can be quite helpful. Prey also attempts to escape, and enhanced
mental orientation and mental rotation skills can help hunters to anticipate and
thwart such escape attempts.

Hunting also probably placed demands on the memory system used by early
hominid hunters. For example, in many cases it is beneficial if prey recognition
occurs rapidly. Such recognition requires the ability to form abstract categories
"remote in time and space from the immediate flux of sensations" (Griffin,
1976, p. 5) and the speedy placement of objects into those categories. To accomplish this, several memory capabilities must operate at a high level. Because
of the need to store information about a large number of possible food sources,
a large memory capacity is needed. Because an efficient cognitive taxonomy of
prey facilitates recognition, a complex memory organization also is required.

Finally, hominid food procurement efforts would be augmented by good cognitive mapping skills. Early hominids covered a territory of 100 square miles or
more from a home base (Kaplan, 1992). The efficient use of such a territory
requires a vast repertoire of environmental knowledge regarding distribution of
food, patterns of prey movement, and shortcuts that could speed food procurement (Peters & Mech, 1975). Also, detailed and accurate cognitive maps would
facilitate adroit escape from predators (Kaplan, 1976).

In summary, the evidence is consistent with the notion that the evolution of
cognitive faculties in humans, including the capacity for symbolic and abstract
thought, was a consequence of environmental pressures that led to problems in
food procurement and to the evolution of a lifestyle that included hunting.
However, even if the food procurement hypothesis does explain cognitive evolution in humans, it does not necessarily represent the only factor affecting evolution. Moreover, it is not clear that the mere emergence of cognitive
capacities naturally and automatically leads to the evolution of the capacity for
a symbolic self-concept. Instead, such sophisticated cognitive evolution may be
a necessary, but insufficient, contributor to the evolution of the capacity for a
symbolic self.

Social Pressures and the Evolution of the Symbolic Self

Indeed, in the context of the growth of the human intellect, we speculate that the rise of relatively large and stable social groups may also have contributed to the evolution of a symbolic self in humans. Central to this perspective is the idea that the symbolic self is formed, in large part, by internalizing the way members of a social group perceive and evaluate an individual—a process that is called *reflected appraisal*. This type of thinking about the self is possible only given the prior development of sophisticated cognitive abilities. Once those abilities have been achieved, social interaction can lead to the construction of a symbolic self.

The social pressures perspective is based on the assumption that social problems posed powerful selection pressures for *Homo erectus*, and the symbolic self was an evolutionary response to these social problems. More specifically, this perspective embodies two assumptions. First, ecological factors (i.e., predation and predator pressures) played a deterministic role in shaping human social systems. Second and most importantly, social pressures deriving from a group lifestyle and from these social systems led directly to the evolution of the symbolic self (for related proposals, see Brewer & Caporael, 1990; Caporael & Brewer, 1991; Wilson & Sober, 1994).

Ecological Factors and Social Systems. Let us consider the first assumption, that ecological factors played a role in shaping social systems. From an evolutionary perspective, group living is associated with several benefits. The first of these benefits is that group living is highly advantageous when it comes to predation. Group living improves hunting efficiency, for individual group members can pool and coordinate their resources for increased hunting success. Group hunting efforts would seem to be particularly important when the individuals in the group have relatively poor hunting capabilities, as was likely the case for early humans. A second potential benefit of group living is that it can enhance survival and reproductive success of individual group members through food sharing. For example, successful hunting of big game can produce surplus meat, which can be shared among group members (McGrew & Feistner, 1992). Safety concerns also enter into the equation, for early humans were themselves apparently prey for various carnivores. A third advantage of group living is that it can reduce predator pressures, and it can do so in several ways (Alexander, 1974): (1) group living can increase overall environmental vigilance and, thus, provides earlier detection of, and warnings about, predators (Crook & Gartlan, 1966; Eisenberg, Muchenhirn, & Rudran, 1972; Van Schaik, 1983); (2) group living can reduce the risk of any given group member's being preyed upon by predators (Clutton-Brock & Harvey, 1977; Crook, Ellis, & Goss-Custard, 1976); and (3) group living can provide protection against predators through various forms of predator mobbing (Chan, 1992). A final benefit of group living is related to competition with other groups. Group living affords cooperative defense of key resources, such as food sources and mates, against rival groups of conspecifics (Alexander, 1974; Wrangham, 1979).

Given the natural capabilities and weaknesses of early humans and the advantages of group living, it is not surprising that early *Homo erectus* probably lived in social groups in which hunting parties ranged from stable home bases. These groups appear to have had two crucial characteristics. First, the social groups apparently were relatively large in numbers. This fact makes sense when evaluated in terms of the data. Group size is likely to be larger the higher the predation risk, and terrestrial species living in an open-country savanna environment, as has been suggested for *Homo erectus*, are at high predation risk (Alexander, 1974; Crook & Gartlan, 1966; Eisenberg et al., 1972; Kummer, 1971).

A second characteristic of these groups was the presence of some form of organization (Eisenberg et al., 1972). Such organization is typically exemplified by status differentiation. However, we suggest that status differentiation did not take the form of a strict and simple dominance hierarchy of the type observed in many animal species. Such strict group structures simplify social relationships—one simply responds to others based on memory of their fixed social rank. Instead, early humans probably maintained a relatively loose and flexible social structure in which status was often quite changeable from moment to moment and from situation to situation. In such structures, one does not know automatically where one stands in the group. Instead, one's position or status changes with altered circumstances and shifting alliances. Such a flexible structure places heavy cognitive demands on the individual. That is, to be successful, the individual must constantly monitor other group members and the current situation. In addition, foresight and planning become useful attributes, especially if one attempts to acquire or solidify power in the social hierarchy. Thus, we suggest that the relatively loose and flexible group structure of humans was important to the evolution of a symbolic self. In theory, such a loose structure made social organization and coordination a complex affair, producing selection pressures that led to the evolution of the capacity for a symbolic self.

Social Problems Pressuring the Evolution of a Symbolic Self. Let us examine these social pressures more closely. A high level of social complexity brings the opportunity for several types of social interactions (Galdikas & Vasey, 1992; Hinde & Stevenson-Hinde, 1976). First, interactions occur among individuals. Examples of such interactions are feeding, grooming, playing, traveling, mating, and fighting. Second, relationships exist among individuals. Relationships that are long-term and multigenerational place constraints on the nature of interactions (i.e., who does what to whom, how often, and under what conditions) and can be based on several factors, including kinship, sex, age, and individual history. Third, these interactions and relationships may be constrained by the system of rules that govern a group. Such systems may place constraints on individual status and on the short-term alliances and the long-term relationships that can be formed. Given that *Homo erectus* used stable home bases—a qualitatively unique attribute of humans—one might also expect these rules to be relatively stable.

One such social rule is cooperation (Guisinger & Blatt, 1994; Simon, 1990). Cooperation is beneficial to both the giver and the recipient. The giver may incur short-run costs, but, because the recipient often reciprocates, in the long run the benefits outweigh the costs. Furthermore, cooperative behavior can lead to the formation of reciprocal dyadic alliances or friendships (Trivers, 1971). Of course, triadic relationships are also possible, and such relationships can lead to new social complexities, such as coalition building and maintenance.

Indeed, individuals are often induced to enter cooperative alliances because of external threat from others. In entering alliances to counter such threats, the organism must assess several important factors: (1) the type of relationship between the potential allies and opponents; (2) the competitive ability of the opponent and the opponent's allies; (3) kin relationship to the opponent; (4) risk of injury to self or to the solicited party from opponents if support is denied; and (5) whether joining the alliance is more beneficial overall than abandoning it (Harcourt, 1988).

Of course, cooperating with others in these alliances presents its own challenges. A working group needs to fulfill several functions. Such functions include role differentiation, coordination of individual effort, conformity with rules, group loyalty, and fear of social exclusion. However, not every group member cooperates at either the dyadic or the group level. Placing immediate personal benefit over long-term group benefit through nonreciprocity or cheating can be lucrative if the members of the group continue to respond cooperatively toward the cheater. This allows the cheater to maintain a consistent advantage. Of course, obvious deviance from reciprocity is not well tolerated, so that a successful deviant or cheater is one who needs *Machiavellian intelligence* (Byrne & Whiten, 1988). To be successful at cheating, individuals with this trait need to possess a relatively high level of social intelligence. That is, they need to be capable of monitoring the behavior of same-group conspecifics, changing their own behavior as a function of the social situation, and engaging in such behavior in a nonobvious fashion.

From the group's perspective, it is advantageous for rule-abiding group members to be able to prevent deviance or detect cheating. In fact, humans may have a specialized ''detection of cheaters'' cognitive algorithm that affects the way in which they approach social exchange situations (Cosmides, 1989; Cosmides & Tooby, 1989). Such detection would presumably ensure that an individual's noncooperative behavior was not detrimental to the success of a group.

Nonetheless, there are circumstances in which noncooperative interaction strategies (e.g., individualism or competition) can be advantageous. Obviously, if one can overwhelm others and garner resources for oneself at relatively low cost, competition can be effective in resource acquisition. This competition can take two major forms. The first form is intergroup competition, that is, competition against other groups of conspecifics. Note that there is a paradox in this competitive strategy: successful intergroup competition is often made possible through intragroup cooperation. More specifically, this intergroup competition strategy has the best chance of being successful if the group members cooperate in attempting to achieve several goals at the possible expense of other groups. These goals might include the following: (1) recruitment of multiple new females to the group, (2) induction of the males to breed with the females, (3) taking steps to assure that the territorial resources enhance the chances that the offspring reach reproductive maturity, (4) maintenance of in-group solidarity and mutual support, (5) defense of the territory against adversaries, and (6) retention of the male offspring in the natal group (Ghiglieri, 1989).

A second form of competition is intragroup competition (Axelrod, 1984). This intragroup competition can take several forms. A very important form is intrasexual competition for suitable mates and its natural accompaniment, epigamic selection (i.e., interactions between the sexes, such as mate attraction, mate selection, and mate retention; Huxley, 1938). Intrasexual competition places many cognitive demands on the individual: (1) each individual may need to remember his or her relationships with other adults in the group (e.g., rank, kinship); (2) each individual may need to monitor the rank and physical condition of potential competitors (e.g., to stay away from conflict with higher-rank group members and to try to control the access of others to potential mates); (3) each individual may need to be capable of deceiving higher-ranked competitors; (4) each individual may need to monitor the spatial distribution, sexual receptivity, and fitness of potential mates; and (5) each individual may need to exhibit physical and social prowess in order to attract potential mates (Galdikas & Vasey, 1992; Parker, 1987). In addition to these tasks, adult females must also safeguard against forced copulation attempts on the part of males.

All of the aforementioned social factors suggest that groups can become complicated. We speculate that in *Homo erectus*, individuals who had the capacity to form and use a symbolic self could excel at these group functions. Thus, they would have had a reproductive advantage, gaining access to food, mates, and protection from predators. Individuals who could not form and use a symbolic self were not good at group functions and, hence, were at a competitive disadvantage. These individuals were likely to be ostracized and, therefore, were more vulnerable to predators and/or the consequences of low resource allocation (Baumeister & Leary, 1995; Buss, 1990).

ADDITIONAL ADAPTIVE CONSEQUENCES OF THE EVOLUTION OF THE SYMBOLIC SELF

Once the capacity to form a symbolic self had emerged, it could be adaptive in ways that go beyond the solving of social problems. For example, a self-system can be adaptive to the extent that it can serve as a useful guide to increasing the effectiveness of behavior. This can happen in several ways. For example, the symbolic self can directly serve as an aid to decision making.

Awareness of the content of the symbolic self can aid in the decision to join bands that provide the best match to one's personal goals.

Furthermore, one of the consequences of having a symbolic self is that one can consider oneself in alternative times and circumstances (Markus & Nurius, 1986), often producing the expectation of positive emotions (Staats & Skowronski, 1992). Research indicates that such reflection facilitates both short-term and long-term goal setting (Rosenberg, 1988) and motivation to pursue various life tasks (Cantor, Markus, Niedenthal, & Nurius, 1986). In addition, thinking about oneself in a variety of future contexts and situations can lead to behaviors that are adaptive in those contexts and circumstances.

A focus on the adaptive nature of the symbolic self may have implications for the topic of self-esteem. One way to engage in self-evaluation is to match self-ideals or plans against the outcomes obtained. If such an evaluation indicates a reasonable match, then positive self-evaluation (or self-esteem) and pride will result. On the other hand, if the match indicates that behavior was unsuccessful, it will result in negative self-esteem and shame. These emotional responses can serve to enhance the adaptiveness of the symbolic self. First, they can provide immediate feedback with regard to the current state of goal achievement and, thus, help to redirect action accordingly (i.e., persist along the same lines or take corrective action). Second, emotional responses may provide crucial feedback regarding the efficiency of effort allocation. Experiencing positive self-esteem in the face of challenge is informative with respect to the appropriateness of an approach response. Experiencing negative self-esteem in the face of challenge is informative with respect to the appropriateness of an avoidance response. In short, self-esteem can serve as a gauge for goal attainment.

SUMMARY AND CONCLUSIONS

Evolutionary accounts posit that to perpetuate the ability for reproductive survival, many human traits evolved in response to environmental pressures. We have included the symbolic self among those traits and have attempted to present a coherent case for this position. In making our case, we noted that the rudiments of a symbolic self appear elsewhere in the animal kingdom, especially in those species that are closely related to humans on the bush of evolution. Furthermore, we argued that although the evolution of brainpower and the capacity for symbolic thought could have come from several sources (such as food procurement pressures), the evolution of a symbolic self seems to have arisen from the selection pressures derived from the early humans' social interactions. We reviewed both theory and data on early humans' social circumstances and noted the advantages that would be conferred if an individual possessed a symbolic self in such a social environment. In particular, we argued that the evolution of a symbolic self would have been advantageous in social circumstances similar to those of early human societies in which no strict social hierarchies existed.

We recognize that many of our arguments are highly speculative and contain many potential pitfalls. For example, although the symbolic self certainly seems to be a trait that is widely held among humans, we certainly do not wish to maintain that any trait that is widespread in a population is necessarily adaptive, a logical error known as the *naturalistic fallacy*. Indeed, though natural selection suggests that widely held traits in a population *may, at one time*, have facilitated reproductive survival *in a particular environment*, the fact that a trait is currently widely held does not necessarily imply that it is (or was) adaptive. Clearly, not all widely held traits are adaptive; some traits appear to have no bearing on reproductive fitness.

A somewhat more insidious problem is that a trait may have originally evolved to serve a different function from the one it currently serves. That is, the environmental pressures that led to the initial spread of a trait may no longer be important, but the trait itself may continue to be maintained because it is responsive to alternative environmental pressures. Hence, we acknowledge that the symbolic self may have originally had different functions from those currently served.

Nonetheless, the fact that a trait is widely held in a population and is currently adaptive constitutes a legitimate basis for exploring the possibility that the trait evolved in response to environmental pressures. In the present chapter, we have attempted just such an exploration. However, we strongly emphasize that these speculations are only the beginning. Being empiricists at heart, we hope that the analyses and speculations that we offer in this chapter will lead researchers to develop testable hypotheses about the possible evolutionary origins of the self.

REFERENCES

Alexander, R. D. (1974). The evolution of social behavior. *Annual Review of Ecology and Systematics, 5*, 324–382.

Axelrod, R. (1984). *The evolution of cooperation.* New York: Basic.

Banaji, M. R., & Prentice, D. A. (1994). The self in social contexts. *Annual Review of Psychology, 45*, 297–332.

Baumeister, R. (1993). *Self-esteem: The puzzle of low self-regard.* New York: Plenum.

Baumeister, R. F., & Leary, M. R. (1995). The need to belong: Desire for interpersonal attachments as a fundamental human motivation. *Psychological Bulletin, 117*, 497–529.

Brewer, M. B., & Caporael, L. R. (1990). Selfish genes versus selfish people: Sociobiology as origin myth. *Motivation and Emotion, 14*, 237–243.

Buss, D. M. (1990). Evolutionary social psychology: Prospects and pitfalls. *Motivation and Emotion, 14*, 265–286.

Byrne, R. W., & Whiten, A. (Eds.). (1988). *Machiavellian intelligence: Social expertise and the evolution of intellect in monkeys, apes, and humans.* Oxford: Clarendon Press.

Cantor, N., Markus, H., Niedenthal, P., & Nurius, P. (1986). On motivation and the self-concept. In R. M. Sorrentino & E. T. Higgins (Eds.), *Motivation and cognition: Foundations of social behavior* (pp. 96–127). New York: Guilford Press.

Caporael, L. R., & Brewer, M. B. (1991). Reviving evolutionary psychology: Biology meets society. *Journal of Social Issues, 47*, 187–195.

Chan, L. K. W. (1992). Problems with socioecological explanations of primate social diversity. In F. D. Burton (Ed.), *Social processes and mental abilities in non-human primates* (pp. 1–30). Lewiston, NY: Edwin Mellen Press.

Cheney, D. L., & Seyfarth, R. M. (1992). Precis of *How monkeys see the world. Behavioral and Brain Sciences, 15*, 135–182.

Clutton-Brock, T. H., & Harvey, P. H. (1977). Primate ecology and social organization. *Journal of Zoology, 183*, 1–39.

Cosmides, L. (1989). The logic of social exchange: Has natural selection shaped how humans reason? *Cognition, 31*, 187–276.

Cosmides, L., & Tooby, J. (1989). Evolutionary psychology and the generation of culture, Part II: Case study: A computational theory of social exchange. *Ethology and Sociobiology, 10*, 51–98.

Crook, J. H., Ellis, J. E., & Goss-Custard, J. D. (1976). Mammalian social system: Structure and function. *Animal Behavior, 24*, 261–274.

Crook, J. H., & Gartlan, J. S. (1966). Evolution of primate societies. *Nature, 210*, 1200–1203.

Damon, W., & Hart, D. (1986). Stability and change in children's self-understanding. *Social Cognition, 4*, 102–118.

Day, M. H. (1986). *Guide to fossil man.* Chicago: University of Chicago Press.

Eisenberg, J. F., Muchenhirn, N. A., & Rudran, R. (1972). The relation between ecology and social structure in primates. *Science, 176*, 863–874.

Falk, D. (1987). Hominid paleoneurology. *Annual Review of Anthropology, 16*, 13–30.

Fox, R. (1980). *The red lamp of incest.* New York: E. P. Dutton.

Galdikas, B. F., & Vasey, P. (1992). Why are orangutans so smart? Ecological and social hypotheses. In F. D. Burton (Ed.), *Social processes and mental abilities in non-human primates: Evidence from longitudinal field studies* (pp. 183–224). Lewiston, NY: Edwin Mellen Press.

Gallup, G. G., Jr. (1970). Chimpanzees: Self-recognition. *Science, 167*, 86–87.

Gallup, G. G., Jr. (1977). Self-recognition in primates: A comparative approach to the bidirectional properties of consciousness. *American Psychologist, 32*, 329–338.

Gallup, G. G., Jr. (1983). Toward a comparative psychology of mind. In R. E. Mellgren (Ed.), *Animal cognition and behavior* (pp. 473–510). Amsterdam: North-Holland.

Gallup, G. G., Jr. (1985). Do minds exist in species other than our own? *Neuroscience and Biobehavioral Reviews, 9*, 631–641.

Gallup, G. G., Jr. (1992). Levels, limits, and precursors to self-recognition: Does ontogeny recapitulate phylogeny? *Psychological Inquiry, 3*, 117–118.

Gallup, G. G., Jr., & Suarez, S. D. (1986). Self-awareness and the emergence of mind in humans and other primates. In J. Suls & A. G. Greenwald (Eds.), *Psychological perspectives on the self* (Vol. 3, pp. 3–26). Hillsdale, NJ: Lawrence Erlbaum.

Ghiglieri, M. P. (1989). Hominoid sociobiology and hominid social evolution. In P. G. Heltne & L. A. Marquardt (Eds.), *Understanding chimpanzees* (pp. 370–379). Cambridge: Harvard University Press.

Gibson, K. R. (1986). Cognition, brain size, and the extraction of embedded food resources. In J. G. Else & P. C. Lee (Eds.), *Primate ontogeny, cognition and social behavior* (pp. 93–103). Cambridge: Cambridge University Press.

Goodall, J. (1986). *The chimpanzees of Gombe.* Cambridge: Harvard University Press.

Griffin, D. R. (1976). *The question of animal awareness.* New York: Rockefeller University Press.

Guisinger, S., & Blatt, S. J. (1994). Individuality and relatedness: Evolution of fundamental dialectic. *American Psychologist, 49,* 104–111.

Harcourt, A. H. (1988). Alliances in contest and social intelligence. In R. Byrne & A. Whiten (Eds.), *Machiavellian intelligence: Social expertise and the evolution of intellect in monkeys, apes and humans* (pp. 132–152). Oxford: Oxford University Press.

Higgins, E. T. (1991). Development of self-regulatory and self-evaluative processes: Costs, benefits, and tradeoffs. In M. R. Gunnar & L. A. Sroufe (Eds.), *Self-processes and development: The Minnesota symposium on child development* (Vol. 23, pp. 125– 165). Hillsdale, NJ: Lawrence Erlbaum.

Hinde, R. A., & Stevensen-Hinde, J. (1976). Towards understanding relationships: Dynamic stability. In P. P. G. Bateson & R. A. Hinde (Eds.), *Growing points in ethology* (pp. 451–480). Cambridge: Cambridge University Press.

Holloway, R. L. (1975). Early hominid endocasts. In R. H. Tuttle (Ed.), *Primate functional morphology and evolution* (pp. 393–415). The Hague: Mouton.

Huxley, J. S. (1938). The present standing of the theory of sexual selection. In G. R. de Beer (Ed.), *Evolution: Essays on aspects of evolutionary biology presented to Professor E. S. Goodrich on his seventieth birthday* (pp. 11–42). Oxford: Clarendon Press.

Isaac, G. (1978). The food-sharing behavior of proto-human hominids. *Scientific American, 238,* 90–108.

James, W. (1890/1950). *The principles of psychology.* New York: Dover.

Kaplan, S. (1976). Adaptation, structure, and knowledge. In G. T. Moore & R. G. Golledge (Eds.), *Environmental knowing: Theories, research, and methods* (pp. 32– 45). Stroudsberg, PA: Dowden, Hutchinson, & Ross.

Kaplan, S. (1992). Environmental preference in a knowledge-seeking, knowledge-using organism. In J. H. Barkow, L. Cosmides, & J. Tooby (Eds.), *The adapted mind: Evolutionary psychology and the generation of culture* (pp. 581–598). New York: Oxford University Press.

Kaplan, S., & Kaplan, R. (1978). *Humanscape.* North Scituate, MA: Duxbury.

Klein, R. G. (1992). The archeology of modern human origins. *Evolutionary Anthropology, 1,* 5–14.

Kummer, H. (1971). *Primate societies: Group techniques of ecological adaptation.* Chicago: Aldine.

Laughlin, W. S. (1968). Hunting: An integrating biobehavior system and its evolutionary importance. In R. B. Lee & I. DeVore (Eds.), *Man the hunter.* Chicago: Aldine.

Leakey, L. (1966). *Homo habilis, Homo erectus,* and the australopithecines. *Nature, 209,* 1279–1281.

Lewis, M. (1990). Self-knowledge and social development in early life. In L. A. Pervin (Ed.), *Handbook of personality: Theory and research* (pp. 277–300). New York: Guilford Press.

Lewis, M. (1992). Will the real self of selves please stand up? *Psychological Inquiry, 3,* 123–124.

Lewis, M. (1994). Myself and me. In S. T. Parker, R. W. Mitchell, & M. L. Boccia, (Eds.), *Self-awareness in animals and humans: Developmental perspectives* (pp. 20–34). New York: Cambridge University Press.

Markus, H., & Nurius, P. (1986). Possible selves. *American Psychologist, 41*, 954–969.

McGrew, W. C., & Feistner, A. T. C. (1992). Two nonhuman primate models for the evolution of human food sharing: Chimpanzees and Callitrichids. In J. Barkow, L. Cosmides, & J. Tooby (Eds.), *The adapted mind* (pp. 229–243). New York: Oxford University Press.

McHenry, H. M. (1992). How big were early hominids? *Evolutionary Anthropology, 1*, 15–19.

Menzel, E. W. (1971). Communication about the environment in a group of young chimpanzees. *Folia Primatologia, 15*, 220–232.

Milton, K. (1981). Distribution patterns of tropical plant foods as an evolutionary stimulus to primate mental development. *American Anthropologist, 83*, 534–548.

Milton, K. (1988). Foraging behaviour and the evolution of primate intelligence. In R. Byrne & A. Whiten (Eds.), *Machiavellian intelligence: Social expertise and the evolution of intellect in monkeys, apes and humans* (pp. 285–305). Oxford: Oxford University Press.

Parker, S. T. (1987). A sexual selection model for hominid evolution. *Human Evolution, 2*, 235–253.

Parker, S. T., & Gibson, K. R. (1979). A developmental model for the evolution of language and intelligence in early hominids. *Brain and Behaviour Science, 2*, 367–408.

Peters, R., & Mech, L. D. (1975). Behavioral and intellectual adaptations of selected mammalian predators to the problem of hunting large animals. In R. H. Tuttle (Ed.), *Socioecology and psychology of primates* (pp. 279–300). Chicago: Aldine.

Povinelli, D. J., Nelson, K. E., & Boysen, S. T. (1992a). Comprehension of social role reversal by chimpanzees: Evidence of empathy? *Animal Behaviour, 43*, 633–640.

Povinelli, D. J., Nelson, K. E., & Boysen, S. T. (1992b). Inferences about guessing and knowing by chimpanzees *(Pan troglodytes)*. *Journal of Comparative Psychology, 104*, 203–210.

Povinelli, D. J., Parks, K. A., & Novak, M. A. (1992). Role reversal by rhesus monkeys, but no evidence of empathy. *Animal Behaviour, 44*, 269–281.

Premack, D., & Premack, A. G. (1983). *The mind of an ape*. New York: Norton.

Premack, D., & Woodruff, G. (1978). Does the chimpanzee have a theory of mind? *Behavior and Brain Sciences, 1*, 515–526.

Rosenberg, M. (1988). Self-objectification: Relevance for the species and society. *Sociological Forum, 3*, 548–565.

Savage-Rumbaugh, E. S., & McDonald, K. (1988). Deception and social manipulation in symbol-using apes. In R. W. Byrne & A. Whiten (Eds.), *Machiavellian intelligence* (pp. 224–237). Oxford: Oxford University Press.

Sedikides, C., & Skowronski, J. A. (1997). The symbolic self in evolutionary context. *Personality and Social Psychology Review, 1*, 80–102.

Sedikides, C., & Strube, M. J. (1997). Self-evaluation: To thine own self be good, to thine own self be sure, to thine own self be true, and to thine own self be better. In M. P. Zanna (Ed.), *Advances in Experimental Social Psychology* (Vol. 29, pp. 209–269). New York: Academic Press.

Seyfarth, R., & Cheney, D. (1989). *How monkeys see the world*. Chicago: University of Chicago Press.

Sibley, C. G., & Ahlquist, J. E. (1984). The phylogeny of the hominoid primates, as indicated by DNA-DNA hybridization. *Journal of Molecular Evolution, 20*, 2–15.

Simon, H. A. (1990). A mechanism for social selection and successful altruism. *Science, 250*, 1665–1668.

Staats, S., & Skowronski, J. J. (1992). Perceptions of self-affect: Now and in the future. *Social Cognition, 10*, 415–431.

Suarez, S. D., & Gallup, G. G., Jr. (1981). Self-recognition in chimpanzees and orang-utans, but not gorillas. *Journal of Human Evolution, 10*, 175–188.

Symons, C. S., & Johnson, B. T. (1997). The self-reference effect in memory: A meta-analysis. *Psychological Bulletin, 121*, 371–394.

Tobias, P. V. (1971). *The brain in hominid evolution.* New York: Columbia University Press.

Trivers, R. L. (1971). The evolution of reciprocal altruism. *Quarterly Review of Biology, 46*, 35–57.

Van Schaik, C. (1983). Why are diurnal primates living in groups? *Behavior, 87*, 120–144.

de Waal, F. B. M. (1982). *Chimpanzee politics.* New York: Harper & Row.

de Waal, F. B. M. (1986). Deception in the natural communication of chimpanzees. In R. W. Mitchell & N. S. Thompson (Eds.), *Deception: Perspectives on human and nonhuman deceit* (pp. 221–266). New York: State University of New York Press.

Wilson, D. S., & Sober, E. (1994). Reintroducing group selection to the human behavioral sciences. *Behavioral and Brain Sciences, 17*, 585–654.

Wrangham, R. W. (1979). On the evolution of ape social systems. *Social Science Information, 18*, 334–368.

5

Evolution and Creativity

STEVEN M. SMITH AND THOMAS B. WARD

The human mind produces novel and useful ideas, adapting to, and even flourishing in, rapidly changing environments. This creative ability uniquely distinguishes humans from other animals. Creative products pervade our lives so much that, although we often take them for granted, these innovations are manifest throughout the artificial environments in which we live, in our foods, medicines, modes of transportation, tools, entertainments, communications, and arts, to name several areas of human creativity. The same cannot be said for any other species. Nonetheless, the component parts that underlie human creativity can be seen in evolutionary terms, throughout the phylogenetic scale. In this chapter we describe some of the important components of the mind that underlie creativity, pointing out the evolutionary relevance of the components. Finally, we speculate about an evolutionary pattern that may be seen in the cognitive processes that produce creative ideas.

Traditional approaches to the topic of creativity have struggled with definitions of the subject matter, alternately defining creativity in terms of the remarkable products that have resulted from creative activities or in terms of the distinguishing characteristics in the personalities of creative and noncreative people, focusing especially on creative geniuses. These approaches to the study of creativity are more scientific than the simple notion that creativity is unpredictably bestowed by divine inspiration. However, they fail to take into account the mental processes that creative individuals go through to construct creative products. Furthermore, these approaches to the study of creativity, which focus on the culturally remarkable products of geniuses, can prevent us from seeing the more commonplace components and antecedents that are evident throughout human evolution.

OUR APPROACH TO CREATIVITY

We consider creativity in terms of the cognitive processes that underlie and support creative thinking, what we term a *creative cognition* approach (e.g., Finke, Ward, & Smith, 1992; Smith, Ward, & Finke, 1995; Ward, Finke, & Smith, 1995). To understand creative cognition and how it differs from other perspectives on creativity, we first consider a *family resemblance* definition of creativity that stems from this creative cognition approach. A family resemblance refers to a set of features that are shared by most of the examples of a concept, even though there are no features that are necessary and sufficient properties of the concept. In terms of creativity, it is impossible to identify any single property of a product or idea that makes it creative. We define something as creative if it exhibits several features of a set that includes novelty, practicality, insightfulness, emergence, combination, originality, playfulness, and metaphoricity, to name a few features of creative ideas.

Likewise, we hold a family resemblance view of the cognitive processes responsible for the development of the creative products that possess those features. No single process is uniquely tied to creative outcomes. Rather, various processes, such as learning, insight, conceptualization, analogical reasoning, abstraction, and visualization, operate in different combinations to instigate new ideas and bring them to creative fruition.

In terms of the cognitive processes that are involved, we see no difference between *personal creativity* and *cultural creativity*. Cultural creativity refers to creative ideas and innovations that are objectively novel in civilized society, such as Edison's invention of the phonograph or Picasso's introduction of cubism to the world of art. Personal creativity, on the other hand, refers to innovation that is novel to an individual, even if someone else in one's culture has already thought of the idea. Finally, although we acknowledge and celebrate the creative genius, we also acknowledge the everyday creativity that is so intrinsically a part of all human experience. Whether creativity is personal or cultural, produced by a genius or a more common member of our species, the same cognitive processes serve as the psychological components that give rise to that creativity.

In this chapter, as we attempt to trace the evolutionary antecedents of creativity, we maintain that creativity is widespread only throughout the world of humanity. Paradoxically, we also claim that components of creativity can be seen in other animals. These two claims are not contradictory, however, because the *combination* of the many components of creativity gives rise to the extraordinary ideas, innovations, and discoveries of humankind.

A FUNCTIONALIST APPROACH TO THE EVOLUTION OF CREATIVITY

Simple observation reveals that humans create far more and far more complexly than any other species. This leads to the inference that humans are ideally suited to create. By this statement we do not necessarily mean that there will never exist a better engine of creativity than the human being. We mean that relative to other species, humans have shown a tremendous capacity to create. Why?

The functionalist approach to explaining the human mind focuses on the adaptive significance of our mental capacities, asking what the function is of the mind. We might identify creative thinking as the single most adaptive feature of our species, granting us far more power over our competitors, our environment, our needs, and ourselves than has been realized by any other species. Our powers of creative thinking serve us at three different levels. At the experiential level, creative thinking can be intrinsically rewarding, providing us with the joy of discovery and understanding or the hedonic pleasure associated with fun. At the personal level, creativity can facilitate an individual's survival and adaptation to the world, serving basic motivational needs. Finally, at the species level, creative solutions to important problems can help ensure not only that the species as a whole will prosper but also that the creative individuals will procreate, preserving the genetic potential for creativity in the human gene pool.

A speculative proposal that we consider here turns this functionalist perspective on creativity around. In its most neutral, least provocative form, this proposal simply states that the mind operates in a manner that supports creativity rather than that creativity operates in a way that supports humankind. A stronger version of the proposal not only posits that a particular directional relation exists but also assumes that an underlying purpose or function of our species is to create. That is, products of human creativity may outlive human creators, having existence and influence far beyond the lives of progenitors. The strongest version of this hypothesis is that the *purpose* of humanity is to create. This teleological proposal is not scientific but rather philosophical, existential, or spiritual. Universal conceptions of God, the ideal, or ultimate all involve creation, recognizing the fundamental importance of creativity. This highly speculative hypothesis views evolution as a gradual progression toward an ultimate purpose.

COMPONENTS OF CREATIVITY

Using our family resemblance definition of creativity, we can identify a set of components that are shared by most examples of creativity. These include both motivational and cognitive components. In this chapter we consider (1) the motivational components of curiosity, play, and exploration, (2) the cognitive components of learning, insight, reasoning, conceptualization, abstraction, visualization, and (3) intentional thought and manipulation of the environment.

Motivational Components

Although Hull's now-outmoded drive reduction theory stated that the motivational goal of an organism is to eliminate drive or arousal by satisfying needs, we now recognize that this rule is useful only for situations in which there are heavy demands upon the organism for coping and survival responses. When needs are satisfied, however, and arousal levels are low, phylogenetically advanced organisms, such as mammals, engage in behavioral patterns that have the effect of increasing arousal, rather than decreasing it. When humans and other animals are idle too long, they become bored. Mammals cope with boredom by becoming curious, by playing, and by exploring, three important components of creativity.

Although purported at times to be lethal for certain felines, curiosity has been a vital adaptive feature of humans and other mammals. Curiosity is a need for knowledge, such as knowledge of one's surrounding territory or understanding of the major forces in one's life. Inquisitiveness provides the impetus for creative thought. Although much of the literature on creative thinking is devoted to problem solving, there is also a general acknowledgment of the need for *problem finding* in the creative process. Problem finding is the process of identifying those situations most in need of resolution or those problems whose solutions might provide the best opportunities for true advancement. When we are busy coping with life's exigencies, we do not look for more problems; we do our best to avoid them. Curiosity, if not habitually inhibited, will arise only when all basic needs are met.

Exploring is an adaptive behavioral response to boredom and curiosity and can be seen commonly in mammals and birds. Exploration introduces an organism to novel stimuli, thereby increasing arousal and demands upon the organism to respond in adaptive ways. The need to explore, therefore, directly contradicts drive-reduction theory. Nonetheless, exploration is adaptive, sometimes leading to new resources that can satisfy basic and higher-order needs. Exploration is also one of the basic components in creative cognition, as exemplified by the *geneplore* theory of creative thinking (Finke et al., 1992), which characterizes the creative process in terms of generative and exploratory phases.

Play is another common behavioral pattern in mammals that has the effect of increasing arousal and demands upon an organism. Like exploration, play is more likely to be seen when the organism is very secure. Play is more frequently seen in immature members of species, although many domesticated animals play throughout their adult lives, as is the case with humans. Play behaviors probably evolved as an adaptive mechanism that helps young organisms practice adult behaviors in relatively nonthreatening settings. The intrinsic rewards of playing (i.e., having fun) motivate an organism to practice adaptive behaviors, such as hunting and fighting, much like the intrinsic rewards of sexual intercourse motivate organisms to procreate their kind. Play is also an important component of the creative process that leads to novel concepts and innovations. In the creative process, as in nature, play requires a very secure, nonthreatening environment. The playful ''misuse'' of knowledge is at the basis of intelligent, creative thinking (Schank & Cleary, 1995).

Cognitive Components

People use all of their cognitive skills and abilities in the course of creative thinking, but we focus on a set of these abilities that are especially relevant to creativity. These cognitive components of creativity include learning, insight, reasoning, conceptual thought, abstraction, visualization, and intentional manipulation of the environment. We briefly discuss the roles of these cognitive components in the creative process and point out evolutionary evidence of these abilities.

Learning. Learning is a change in one's behavioral potential that is brought about by experience. Creating depends on learning, a basic psychological ability found throughout the animal kingdom. From planaria learning to avoid a light, to parrots learning to speak words, to people learning astrophysics, living creatures show this fundamental ability to learn.

To be truly creative, one must use, or at times reject the use of, one's learned knowledge. Even the most serendipitous discoveries must be recognized as being creative, or they will never be implemented as useful ideas, innovations, or products. Creative thinkers usually acknowledge that "we stand on the shoulders of giants," meaning that our own creative achievements depend on what we have learned from the work of our predecessors. Creative thinkers are warned not to try to "reinvent the wheel," which is to strive in futility to create what has already been created; rather, one should learn from the past and move forward with one's own creative efforts.

When most people discover a cigarette ash, the most they are likely to think about it is that it should be cleaned up. When Sherlock Holmes sees it, however, it may supply a host of important clues to the solution of some diabolical crime. His supposed long and detailed study of ash from cigarettes and cigars gave Holmes the knowledge that allowed him to solve difficult problems that the rest of us could not solve. When Joseph Lister found petri dishes in his laboratory with bacteria cultures that had been killed by an invading mold that contaminated the culture, he didn't simply wash the glassware out and start a new bacteria culture; he knew that the event was noteworthy and turned it into the discovery of penicillin. Lister had what Louis Pasteur called a *prepared mind*, that is, a mind prepared with extensive learning to notice and discover solutions to difficult problems. A mind can be prepared only by acquiring enough relevant knowledge to recognize the importance of new discoveries.

It is worth noting here that humans, unlike most other species, are in a position to override their learning experiences. Whereas planaria have little choice as to whether or not they will flinch after being conditioned to associate a light with shock, humans have at least some capacity to temporarily suspend their knowledge in service of solving a problem for which that knowledge might be an impediment. Thus, learning alone, though present throughout evolutionary development, is not the source of creativity, although it clearly is a member of the family of important features.

Insight.[1] Insight refers to a deep or profound understanding that might not be obvious to someone who has a more incomplete comprehension of a subject. Psychologically speaking, however, the term "insight" refers not only to the depth of one's understanding but more specifically to the sudden realization of such understanding (e.g., Smith, 1994). Other descriptive terms that refer to the insight experience include epiphany, illumination, and *aha!* or *eureka!* phenomena. Most noteworthy about the insight experience is that it is experienced as an unexpected surprise, implying mysterious origins. Also noteworthy is that the experience of insight is generally accompanied by a feeling of certainty that one's new idea is true or correct.

Many historically famous examples of insight experiences revolutionized, for example, the worlds of art, science, and technology. For example, after visiting an exhibition of nonrepresentational paintings, Calder invented the abstract mobiles that we are familiar with today when he suddenly realized that his wire sculptures could be composed of likewise abstract forms. Nobel laureate Kary Mullis revolutionized the world of chemistry with an insight that occurred to him on a drive through the country, leading to the polymerase chain reaction, a method for replicating minute amounts of DNA. Edison's insight that produced the phonograph was a similarly sudden realization that worked the first time he tried it. These insight experiences are examples of societally important contributions, yet phenomenologically, they resemble the less earth-shattering insights that all humans experience, such as realizing the solution to a job-related matter or a problem with a personal relationship.

The earliest studies of insight used non-human subjects (see Pierce, this volume). Köhler, the Gestalt psychologist, studied the behavior of chimpanzees on the island of Tenerife early this century (e.g., Köhler, 1927). Köhler observed and described a number of apparently sudden insight experiences in chimpanzees that indicated restructuring of an ape's mental set, leading to the immediate implementation of solutions to problems that had previously stumped the chimps. In one problem, for example, Köhler had bananas suspended from the ceiling of a chimpanzee's cage, beyond the reach of the ape. After jumping and stalking frustratedly about the cage, the chimp momentarily glimpsed a view of some wooden crates in the corner of the cage while also looking at the desired bananas. In a flash of insight, the chimp deliberately went about stacking the crates under the fruit and then climbed directly to the prize. This sudden insight appeared to have been triggered by pattern recognition, in this case, seeing suddenly that the crates could be used to reach the goal. Importantly then, insight may not be the sole province of humans, though the extent to which it pervades the animal kingdom is uncertain.

Pattern recognition refers to the process by which you recognize, for example, that the pattern recorded by your visual system is a person's face or an oncoming truck. Pattern recognition gives you a conscious representation of an automatically encoded sensory stimulus. The process is very rapid and fluid, and we rarely notice its smooth functioning. At times your process of pattern recognition can be surprisingly ingenious, recognizing your cat from a faint curve down a darkened hall or seeing instantly in a child's facial expression that she is worried about an impending storm. Recognizing a familiar pattern is fast and easy, whereas unfamiliar patterns (such as the three-dimensional images in random dot stereograms) take longer and are more difficult to recognize. Pattern recognition resembles the insight experience, that sudden "aha!" that accompanies the recognition of a novel concept.

Pattern recognition, which may be the cognitive basis of insight experiences, is a process that is not limited to humans but rather can be clearly identified in most animals. Although very simple organisms can quickly recognize food, a mate, a predator, or a competitor, computerized robotic systems find this process very difficult to simulate. They may surpass the greatest human chess masters in logical trains of thought, but computerized systems remain far behind simple organisms when it comes to pattern recognition and insight.

Reasoning and Conceptual Thought (Suppression of the Environment). Within the animal kingdom survival depends on sensitivity to one's immediate surroundings. An organism's environment provides sustenance, shelter, and opportunities for mating, in addition to predators, competitors, and natural disasters. Sensory systems that detect stimuli in various sense modalities and the perceptual systems that rapidly interpret sensory signals are clearly adaptive mechanisms that, in concert with closely aligned motor systems, interface organisms with their environments.

Glenberg (1997) has theorized that human memory and conceptual processing evolved from these perceptual systems. The demands of survival, according to this view, are better satisfied by more intelligent perceptual systems that not only can represent an organism's immediate environment but can also represent objects that are not perceptually present. Piaget referred to this ability as object permanence. The cognitive apparatus used to represent nonpresent objects, according to Glenberg, is the same one that is used to represent one's ambient environment. Therefore, to represent nonambient objects, the organism must be able to at least temporarily suppress its processing of its environment to free up the resources needed for this difficult mental activity.

This ability to represent objects cognitively beyond one's immediate environment confers two important capabilities, namely, conscious or explicit memory and conceptual processing. Although most animals can use knowledge acquired through the conditioning of habits and behaviors of various types, explicit remembering allows us to reexperience aspects of previous events in a conscious way. Even more important for creative thinking is conceptual processing, the conscious use and manipulation of abstract knowledge.

Conceptual cognitive processing is what allows us to carry out what we typically think of as intelligent mental activities. These activities include deductive and inductive reasoning, analogical reasoning, and abstraction. Deductive reasoning is the process of reaching conclusions and inferences based on a set of logical operations. Inductive reasoning, another type of logic, is the discovery of general rules or principles that are true for an entire category or set of instances. Inductive reasoning, for example, allows us to mentally represent all of the winged, feathered, flying creatures we have seen as a single category, birds. Abstraction, which is similar to inductive reasoning, refers to the ability to perceive general qualities of concepts, such as birds' ability to fly. Analogical reasoning is the perception and use of similarity between objects, concepts, or even complex systems. For example, a bird's nest might be seen as analogous to a bear's cave or a human's house.

All of these conceptual abilities are critical tools in creative thinking and are possible only for organisms that can suppress processing of their immediate environment, thereby allowing conceptual processing. Of course, in light of our previous discussion of motivational bases of creativity, it should be clear that an organism is free to suppress processing of its immediate environment only when it is secure, safe from immediate harm. Thus, security not only leads to curiosity and exploration but also liberates the organism from immediate environmental demands, thereby allowing conceptual thought as well.

HOW HUMAN MINDS DIFFER

Although evolution has produced species with all of the component elements of creativity, we do not see astounding degrees of creativity in any species except humans. In humans, for the first time in evolutionary history, all of the essential elements are combined, giving members of our species the potential for remarkable levels of creativity. There are some important ways that human minds differ from those of other species; we possess mental abilities that make us, at least relative to other species, ideal creators. One of those abilities is the capacity for symbolic thought, including abstraction, reasoning, and reinterpretation of ambiguous forms. The ability to think symbolically, as discussed previously, may derive from our ability to suppress processing of the immediate environment. Another quality that sets us apart from other species is our ability to produce real-world results from imagined ideas. Whether non-human animals, such as apes or cetaceans, can exercise their imaginations to the extent that humans can is not known. It is clear, however, that if nonhuman animals do have great imaginations, they have not used them as humans have, creatively implementing ideas in real-world contexts. Finally, it is also noteworthy that humans have far more extended neoteny (Morris, 1967) than any other organism. Human maturity, including brain development, is not complete for about the first two decades of life, a duration that exceeds the life spans of most other species. We spend far more time maturing than other animals do. Importantly, this extended neoteny produces adolescents who acquire adult skills before discarding their playful, childlike activities. This combination of childish playfulness with mature skill is exactly the blend of abilities that is needed for the creative process, a playful misuse of knowledge.

Although other organisms may possess one or another of the relevant cognitive or motivational features to some degree, the relative strength of the individual processes, their pervasiveness through the species, their deliberate deployment, and their complex interactive use set humans apart. That is what leads to the striking creativity that humans display.

CREATIVITY RECAPITULATES ONTOGENY AND PHYLOGENY

In this section we consider the similarities and differences between creativity and both ontogenetic and phylogenetic development. Part of this hypothesis, that ontogeny, or development, follows the same stages as phylogenetic evolution, is not new at all. Embryologists have studied the evolutionary relationships among species in terms of the similarity in the development of the embryos of different species. The logic used is that evolutionary change adds something to the genetic code that continues or advances the development of a species, adding a stage to the developmental sequence of the more primitive species to produce the newly evolved species. Thus, as one observes the development of an embryo, one sees the progression of stages that are common to evolutionary ancestors. Although not taken as being literally true today, the idea that ontogeny recapitulates phylogeny is a familiar one in the history of developmental psychology and serves us here in the form of a more abstract principle than a scientific mechanism.

In this chapter we point out three important similarities among evolutionary stages, developmental stages, and stages of creativity. These three stages begin with a union of elements from different domains or an extension of the original elements of a system. The second common stage is a period of protected vulnerability. Finally, the systems reach a stage of secure maturity.

The first of these stages is *generation*, the creation of a new entity. New entities, such as new species, new individual organisms, and new ideas, all can arise from the restructuring of existing entities. In the case of a newly evolved species, the genetic mutation of an original species can produce a resultant species with new, adaptive capabilities. In development, the combination of different genetic codes from sperm and egg produces a new individual. Likewise, in creative thinking, combinations and extensions of existing ideas can result in novel, creative discoveries and products. The generation of new species, individuals, and ideas is an abrupt process relative to the time required at other stages of evolution, development, and creative exploration.

The second stage is *growth*, a period of incremental increase in the progress of the entity. Relative to the time needed for generation, growth tends to be a slow process. As in other processes, such as annealing, crystallization, or cooking, slower progress at this stage may ultimately produce a less flawed product. In development, an extended period of immaturity is called neoteny, a phenomenon seen in some insects, birds, and mammals. This prolonged period of growth can be a great asset to the mature entity that is eventually produced, but it comes at a cost, namely, a time of vulnerability during which the growing entity requires safety and protection. In evolutionary terms, a newly evolved species needs time to become established within a niche or ecosystem. In development, immature organisms need protection, whether from great numbers of others of its kind or from protective parents. In creativity, novel ideas require a period of development during which they are "fleshed out," explored, and improved in incremental ways that expand the originally generated ideas. In this immature phase of creativity, large numbers of ideas are encouraged, and negative judgments are deferred. Like the predators and other environmental threats that are so particularly hazardous for neonates, criticisms are especially threatening for newly formed ideas.

The third stage is *maturity*, when the entity has finally reached its potential stability and effectiveness. In evolutionary terms, a well-adapted species will thrive within its ecosystem. Developmentally speaking, the mature adult of a species is usually the most adaptive and can protect itself and provide for its own needs. Creative ideas become useful and practical as the ideas mature, and we eventually come to rely on products that began as startlingly innovative notions.

THE FUTURE

What will be the future of creativity in our species? We offer a few speculations concerning this question. One possible future is that we will see even more neoteny in individuals, extending far into what we now think of as adulthood. Adult humans, even elderly ones, are clearly capable of immature playfulness throughout the life span. As our civilization matures, a period of stability throughout the world could provide the safety and protection essential to curiosity, creative exploration, and discovery. Another advance could a more deliberate and systematic use of the intrinsic rewards of insight. That is, the joy and inspiration that arise from discovery and creation are personally rewarding experiences, a source of self-actualization. If children learn to seek these intrinsic rewards, the result will be adults whose creative contributions to society will come as a by-product of personally fulfilling activities. Finally, we may see more support for creativity in terms of environmental assistance,[2] as well as in biological enhancement. Given the adaptive value of creativity, we should expect to find humans in the future with more brain development than we now see in our species. We can only hope that our descendants will have the foresight and the means to provide more societal support for creative individuals.

NOTES

1. For a more detailed and in-depth discussion, see Chapter 6, "An Evolutionary Perspective on Insight."

2. A peaceful epoch facilitating social and cultural support of educational and vocational programs that stimulate and enhance creativity.

REFERENCES

Finke, R. A., Ward, T. B., & Smith, S. M. (1992). *Creative cognition: Theory, research, and applications.* Cambridge: MIT Press.

Glenberg, A. M. (1997). Mental models, space, and embodied cognition. In T. B. Ward, S. M. Smith, & J. Vaid. (Eds.), *Creative thought: An investigation of conceptual structures and processes* (pp. 495–522). Washington, DC: American Psychological Association Books.

Köhler, W. (1927). *The mentality of apes.* New York: Liveright.

Morris, D. (1967). *The naked ape.* New York: McGraw-Hill.

Schank, R. C., & Cleary, C. (1995). Making machines creative. In S. M. Smith, T. B. Ward, & R. A. Finke (Eds.), *The creative cognition approach.* (pp. 229–248). Cambridge: MIT Press.

Smith, S. M. (1994). Getting into and out of mental ruts: A theory of fixation, incubation, and insight. In R. Sternberg & J. Davidson (Eds.), *The nature of insight* (pp. 121–149). Cambridge: MIT Press.

Smith, S. M., Ward, T. B., & Finke, R. A. (1995). *The creative cognition approach.* Cambridge: MIT Press.

Ward, T. B., Finke, R. A., & Smith, S. M. (1995). *Creativity and the mind: Discovering the genius within.* New York: Plenum Press.

6

An Evolutionary
Perspective on Insight

BENTON H. PIERCE

No treatise on evolutionary psychology would be complete without reference to thinking, learning, and problem solving. An important aspect of the field of learning and problem solving is the concept of *insight*. The word "insight," derived from the Old Dutch for "seeing inside" (Csikszentmihalyi & Sawyer, 1995), is defined by *Webster's New World Dictionary* as "seeing and understanding the inner nature of things clearly, especially by intuition" (Neufeldt & Guralnik, 1991). Mayer (1995) describes insight as a "process by which a problem solver suddenly moves from a state of not knowing how to solve a problem to a state of knowing how to solve it" (p. 3). The concept of insight itself, like other words referring to mental concepts that are relatively rare and valued, such as wisdom, intuition, and virtue, is likely to have been selected and retained in the vocabulary because of its adaptive significance (Csikszentmihalyi & Rathunde, 1990).

For psychologists, insight has two principal meanings (Gruber, 1995). The first, adopted by cognitive psychologists and students of creativity, refers to one's "seeing" the solution in a surprising and sudden way. A second interpretation is used in the areas of psychoanalysis and personality and refers to insight as a certain knowledge state or understanding, without any emphasis on the way it is attained. In this interpretation, intuition is taken for granted as the underlying cause of insight. In this chapter, I focus primarily on the first interpretation, related to problem solving, learning, and thinking.

The psychologist Graham Wallas proposed something closely akin to insight in a seminal book entitled the *Art of Thought* (1926). He outlined four stages in the discovery of a new idea or problem solution: (1) preparation—a systematic and conscious process of information gathering and analysis; (2) incubation—the problem solver steps away from the problem and does not consciously or intentionally think about it; (3) illumination (i.e., insight)—the solution suddenly appears in consciousness; and (4) verification—the solution is tested for its validity.

There has been considerable controversy among psychologists about the role of insight in problem solving (Dominowski & Dallob, 1995). As Mayer (1995) points out, the nature of insight remains one of the most difficult questions pertaining to the psychology of thinking. Although we lack a deep understanding of the mechanisms underlying insight, it may be enlightening to explore the phenomenon from an evolutionary standpoint. Such a perspective seems especially appropriate because, according to Simonton (1995), one of the keys to Charles Darwin's theory of evolution by natural selection came to him in a joyous, illuminating, or insightful moment (but see Gruber, 1995, for a more tempered account).

This chapter outlines the benefits or selective advantages that insight or insightful learning gives to the learning organism or problem solver. In doing so, I provide a background to the evolution of insight by discussing the origins of the term itself as it is used in the cognitive psychology literature. I next examine the characteristics of insight, explore its possible selective advantages, and take a look at possible examples of insight in the animal kingdom. Finally, I explore some of the processes associated with insight as they relate to hemispheric specialization in the brain.

ORIGINS OF INSIGHT IN PSYCHOLOGICAL THEORY

Theories of insight and psychological research into its characteristics trace back to the work of the German psychologist Wolfgang Köhler in the first part of this century. Köhler, along with Max Wertheimer and Kurt Koffka, founded the school of Gestalt psychology. Gestalt psychology largely rebelled against the atomistic psychology of Wilhem Wundt. Although Gestalt theory was initially interpreted in the United States as a theory of perception, the theory was, in fact, much larger and emphasized in particular the areas of thinking and learning (Benjamin, 1988).

In 1913, Köhler was working on research with Wertheimer and Koffka in Frankfurt, Germany. He was forced to leave, however, to assume directorship of the anthropoid station maintained by the Prussian Academy of Sciences on Tenerife in the Canary Islands. As station director, Köhler studied chimpanzee behavior. Köhler stayed at Tenerife until 1920 and made discoveries that had profound effects on the Gestalt view of thinking, insight learning, in particular.

While at Tenerife, Köhler carried out a series of experiments to test the intelligence of chimpanzees. The simplest set of experiments, termed roundabout or *umweg* problems by Köhler (Köhler, 1925), involved situations in which the direct route to an objective (food) was blocked, although the objective remained in sight. This situation required the chimps to use a detour or roundabout way in order to reach the food. Köhler found that the chimps could easily reach the objective as long as they could survey the possible detours. In a more difficult set of experiments, Köhler tested the chimps in the use of implements or tools, which required the chimps to make a connection to the objective by means of a third object. In one such task, the chimps could use a stick to retrieve food placed beyond normal reach outside their cage. In another test, two tubes that could be fitted together were placed inside the cage. Neither tube by itself was long enough to reach the goal; only by joining them together could an implement of sufficient length be fashioned to reach the objective. Sultan, the chimpanzee tested in this problem situation, eventually connected the tubes and retrieved the food.

Köhler's experiments became progressively more complicated and therefore more difficult for the animals. For example, he placed several boxes in the cage and hung bananas from the ceiling. The chimps were sometimes able to stack the boxes into a crude structure, climb the structure, and retrieve the bananas, but the difficulty of the task resulted in much trial-and-error behavior (Köhler, 1925).

In assessing the rather remarkable success of the animals in solving these problems, Köhler made the following observations:

1. The parts of the problem situation taken separately were meaningless to the chimps but when taken as a whole achieved significance.
2. The "optics" or visual aspects of the situation were critical for the chimps in solving the problems.
3. When the chimp named Sultan connected the two tubes to fashion a longer implement, he clearly assessed the relative thickness of the two tubes, as he never tried to connect two tubes of the same thickness.
4. During the tests, the animals always paused for a period of time, during which they would scrutinize the entire area.
5. In a successful solution, a long pause would often be followed by a sudden, definite, and continuous action in obtaining or reaching the goal (Köhler, 1925).

Köhler concluded from these experiments that the chimps, when successful, exhibited intelligent behavior by seeing how the different parts of the problem situation fitted together. Köhler termed these behaviors insight: the appearance of a complete solution with reference to the whole layout of the field (Köhler, 1925). He concluded that an act that is meaningless or even disadvantageous by itself can become intelligent in connection with another act, but only then. In other words, the whole, taken together, represents the solution.

CHARACTERISTICS OF INSIGHT

Köhler described insightful behavior in his chimpanzees, but what characteristics of insight relate to cognitive functioning? I previously mentioned that insight helps one to understand a situation more fully. In humans, this seems to be an experience that is relatively common in our everyday lives, such as understanding a joke or suddenly "seeing" something that was previously unclear (Dominowski & Dallob, 1995).

Gestalt psychologists proposed that insight could be achieved in several ways. Wertheimer outlined one method that included *grouping, reorganization,* and *structurization.* In it a problem is divided into subwholes, while still seeing how the subwholes fit together. This process involves a grasp of the inner relatedness among the parts of the problem and how they fit together (Wertheimer, 1959). Wertheimer labeled this process *productive thinking,* as opposed to *reproductive thinking,* in which procedures are applied that solved identical or similar problems in the past (Mayer, 1995).

The Gestalt psychologist Karl Duncker expanded Wertheimer's ideas on restructuring as a necessary condition for insight. Duncker's monograph *On Problem-Solving* (1945) may be the most important work ever produced on the concept of insight (Mayer, 1995). Duncker maintained that insight results when one redefines or clarifies the problem, such as reformulating the given parts of the problem or the goals (Mayer, 1995). In redefining the goal, a process Duncker called a *suggestion from above,* the problem solver formulates the general purpose that needs satisfying. This process proceeds from general to specific. In *suggestions from below,* the problem solver seeks ideas about how to reformulate the function of the given parts or elements of the problem. In this process, the given information is reformulated in a new and productive way (Mayer, 1995).

Duncker also proposed that the reformulation of a problem situation is often prevented when one's previous experience serves as a mental block. This mental block or fixation can prevent the discovery of new or novel approaches to solving a problem.

Another defining characteristic of insight is suddenness. One possible explanation for this feature of an insightful solution is that the restructuring process results in an abrupt transition from one problem representation to a different representation (Dominowski & Dallob, 1995). The appropriate representation, therefore, leads quickly to a solution that appears suddenly and separately from prior solution attempts. Köhler (1925) emphasized this sudden characteristic in the chimps' successful problem solutions. Suddenness of insight has also been given empirical support. For example, Metcalfe (1986) and Metcalfe and Wiebe (1987) examined subjects' metacognitive judgments during both insight and noninsight problem solving. Subjects were asked to give subjective warmth ratings at ten-second intervals whereby *warmer* meant being closer to a solution. The results showed that on noninsight problems that usually require an incremental approach (e.g., algebra problems), subjects, indeed, reported gradual, incremental increases in their warmth ratings. On the insight problems, however, subjects' warmth ratings showed a sharp increase only a few seconds prior to solving the problem. When subjects reported an incremental increase in feelings of warmth during the insight problems, they tended to give incorrect solutions, whereas the times in which they suddenly felt they knew the answer were more likely to be those for correct solutions. Metcalfe and Wiebe (1987) concluded that insight problems are solved, at least subjectively, by a sudden flash of illumination rather than by an incremental process.

Insight is also frequently associated with an "aha" or "eureka" experience. Gick and Lockhart (1995) propose that this affective response arises from two sources. According to them, the first component of the "aha" experience is the surprise or unexpectedness that the correct representation is different from those initially attempted. The second component is the realization that the restructuring process leads to an easy or quick solution.

AN EVOLUTIONARY BASIS FOR THE INSIGHT PHENOMENON

To discuss insight from an evolutionary standpoint, one starts with an operational definition of the term itself. One useful view of the term distinguishes *insight* as a type of understanding from the *insight experience*, the sudden emergence of an idea into conscious awareness, or the "aha" experience (Smith, 1995). For the present evolutionary discussion, insight is broadly defined as a state of knowledge that provides a solution to a new or novel problem brought about by a restructuring or recombination of prior experience or knowledge. Furthermore, this state of knowledge will frequently be accompanied by suddenness and surprise (i.e., the insight experience).

An insight experience, however, does not guarantee a correct solution or real insight. One may restructure or recombine certain elements into a unique configuration that provides the experience of suddenness and surprise but is nevertheless an incorrect solution to the problem. An analogy exists in the biological realm. Constant variation in biological organisms results in few stable combinations that ultimately survive the process of natural selection, just as the restructuring or recombining process does not guarantee a correct solution or "insight."

Selective Advantages of Insight

Insight versus Trial-and-Error Learning. Donald Hebb defined insight as the "functioning of mediating processes in the solution of problems" (Hebb, 1966, p. 292). Insight results in a sharp rise in an organism's learning curve when compared to purely random trial-and-error learning, an obvious selective advantage. In this respect, insight represents a mediation of the learning process superior to a process by which every possible permutation (i.e., representation or solution method) of a problem situation must be explored in a random fashion. Random trial-and-error learning is mistake-prone and potentially fatal to an organism. This is not to say that insight totally excludes trial-and-error learning.

In Köhler's studies, the chimpanzees exhibited a certain amount of trial-and-error behavior, but the behavior represented "intelligent groping" in that the trials largely moved in the general direction of the good solutions (Köhler, 1925).

Insight also means something can be learned on the first trial, giving the learner or problem solver a significant advantage. Insight does not arise from nothing, however. It exemplifies something not learned in that it can be accomplished on the first attempt but still depends on learning (Hebb, 1966). Hebb pointed out that the subject must have had some prior experience with a part of the problem or something similar to it. Restructuring or recombination of prior experience leads to the "insightfulness" of the solution.

Insight and Memory. Insight provides greater memory retention if a restructuring process underlying insight leads to a true understanding of the inner structure of a problem or relations among the problem's components and the solution (Dominowski & Dallob, 1995; Scheerer, 1963). This understanding of how the parts of the problem are related to the solution also allows one to solve other, similar problems. Wertheimer (1959) referred to this process as *transposability*. Ability to transfer a solution method to similar problems is especially important in a complex environment containing numerous variations of a specific problem situation. Grasping relationships inherent in a situation or the understanding of organization leads to stronger associations in memory than associations formed by contiguity, habit, or repetition (Köhler, 1947). Therefore, insightful learning ought to be more durable or resistant to forgetting.

Insight in Non-human Species

Already discussed is the insightful behavior in Köhler's chimpanzees. But what can be said about insight in other non-human species? Before attributing insight to animals in general, insight must be distinguished from other forms of intelligent behavior. That is to say, although insight may be a form of intelligence, clearly not all intelligent behavior is insightful. For example, Simon (1981) describes the behavior of an ant as it makes its way home across a wind- and wave-molded beach. The ant's path in traversing the beach represents a rather complex and goal-directed behavior. But is this behavior intelligent or insightful? Simon argues that the complexity of the ant's path can be explained by something outside the ant itself. The apparent complexity of its behavior stems from the complexity of its environment. The ant, he says, is rather simple when viewed as a behaving system. Clearly, then, the ant's behavior would not be labeled as insightful, but possibly as intelligent due to highly adaptive and acute sensory mechanisms.

Another example of noninsightful, yet highly complex and perhaps intelligent, behavior is the dance "language" of bees. In this behavior, a foraging bee that has recently returned to the hive having discovered a good source of food, performs a dance that communicates to the other bees the general location and quality of the food source. This intricate waggle dance represents an abstract and symbolic communication system with few rivals in terms of information capacity and complexity (Gould & Gould, 1986). As Gould and Gould point out, however, this behavior is totally programmed and innate, with prior experience playing no role in the behavior's performance.

On the other hand, if we broadly interpret insight to mean a reorganization of prior experience in accordance with the requirements of a new problem situation (Birch, 1967), insight describes a wide array of animal behavior. Take a dog that is separated from a goal (food) by a wire mesh barrier, for example. The dog displays insight when it turns away from the food and goes around the barrier (i.e., an indirect route) to reach its goal (Hebb, 1966). This problem situation is equivalent to Köhler's *umweg* or roundabout problems in his chimpanzee experiments. When exhibiting such roundabout behavior, the dog shows a clear superiority to animals such as chickens (Hebb, 1966). The role of prior experience, however, should not be ignored in such behavior. Dogs raised in isolation with no opportunity to learn about barriers show significantly inferior capacity for indirect or roundabout behavior compared to normal dogs (Hebb, 1966).

Evidence of insight in other animals is far from definitive. Some theorists, such as Maier and Schneirla (1964), claim that birds, although highly developed in many ways, are largely incapable of reorganizing their prior experiences in order to adapt to a new situation. Yet Epstein, Kirshnit, Lanza, and Rubin (1984) offered an example of apparent insight in a pigeon. In these researchers' experiment, pigeons learned two separate behaviors. One behavior consisted of pushing a box toward a colored spot, and the other involved climbing a box and pecking a banana. Subsequently, the pigeons trained in this fashion were placed in a situation in which the box and banana were both present. After visually surveying the situation, they pushed the box toward the banana, climbed the box, and pecked (Epstein et al., 1984).

Yet another example of behavior that could be termed insightful involves the ability of animals to form a "cognitive map" (Gould & Gould, 1986). For example, a rat can explore each arm of an eight-armed maze in a random order without inspecting any arm twice and can remember the maze after having been removed from it for a time. The rat in this case forms a mental map and behaves appropriately, perhaps by imagining alternative scenarios (Gould & Gould, 1986).

Given these examples of insightful behavior in animals, can we conclude that insight is a direct function of an organism's complexity and intelligence? Do higher organisms exhibit the greatest degree of insight? One way to answer these questions considers the relationship between insight and programmed behavior. If insight directly results from adaptive mechanisms, primarily the reorganization of prior experience, then insight may serve as a compensatory process to innate or programmed behavior. That is to say, when an organism's programmed behavior fails to work, another system (i.e., insight) may compensate, particularly as the organism's environment becomes increasingly complex.

The previously cited examples of insightful behavior reveal the notion of concept formation: separate concepts are united into one complex structure by their referential mechanisms (Csanyi, 1988) (but see Chater & Heyes, 1994, for a dissenting view of concept formation in animals). Csanyi claims that to the extent that an organism's brain is capable of not only forming concepts but also performing mental transformations on them, the organism is capable of thinking. I suggest that insight is closely tied to this ability. More advanced species with more complex brains, therefore, would, indeed, appear more capable of displaying insightful behavior.

In addition, however, the aspect of awareness in insight must be addressed. I have claimed that insight requires reorganization of prior experience, but implicit in the concept of insight is that the organism understands or grasps relationships. Tolman (1951) claimed that insight "was 'conscious' and that it usually involves the appearance of new relations not previously at the 'immediate command' of the organism" (p. 200). Clearly, one may observe behavior in animals that appears insightful or novel. But it is quite another matter to presume that the animal *understands* or is conscious of the insight problem solution. The subject of animal consciousness reaches beyond the scope of this chapter. This topic is extremely controversial; most scientists concerned with animal behavior object (Griffin, 1984). Indeed, using mentalistic vocabulary to describe animal behavior sparks criticism from those who call it overly anthropomorphic and untestable (Allen & Hauser, 1996).

But there are gaps in understanding at all levels of thinking, both in animals and in humans. For example, a person turning on the radio likely has little understanding of the intricacies of the device. To that person, the turning of the knob and the production of sound form a cause-and-effect relationship that is sufficiently understood. Understanding, then, is a matter of approximation (Koestler, 1964). Insight, like consciousness, is not all-or-nothing (Hebb, 1966). But along with consciousness, we more easily attribute insight to higher species. To the extent that true insight implies a deep awareness, a realization that one has "seen the light," we most easily detect its existence in ourselves. Due to the fact that we possess language, we can freely discuss the concept itself, especially its affective component (i.e., the "aha" experience). So the question of whether we are more "insightful" than animals may be unanswerable. What we can say is that we know that we know—we are aware of our own insight experiences.

Neuropsychological Connections to Insight

Discussion of insight up to this point has treated its existence as an inferred phenomenon. In other words, when problem-solving behavior in both humans and animals meets the criteria for insight, that behavior is labeled insightful.

This type of reasoning makes an evolutionary account of the phenomenon difficult. One intriguing avenue for an evolutionary basis for insight explores possible neuropsychological connections. Stephen Fiore and Jonathan Schooler of the University of Pittsburgh have explored such connections with interesting hypotheses (Fiore & Schooler, 1998).

They note there are striking parallels between the characteristics of insight problem solving and cognitive functioning in the right hemisphere (RH) of the brain. The parallels include (1) a reliance on nonverbal processes; (2) an avoidance of fixation or perseveration; (3) access to non-dominant interpretations or meanings; and (4) global pattern recognition and restructuring. A brief overview of these parallels identified by Fiore and Schooler is presented here, along with empirical evidence that points to a possible right hemispheric role for insight problem solving.

Nonverbality of the Right Hemisphere. The left hemisphere (LH) seems predisposed for verbal activities, whereas the right hemisphere (RH) specializes more in visuospatial abilities (Bradshaw & Nettleton, 1981). Split-brain studies show that language is the most salient and profound difference between the two hemispheres (Springer & Deutsch, 1985). Gazzaniga (1983) indeed claimed the RH is non-linguistic (but see Zaidel, 1983).

Fiore and Schooler (1998) state that the right hemisphere's relative lack of linguistic ability may preclude it from performing certain higher-order cognitive functions, such as propositional reasoning. The authors claim, however, that other sophisticated processes may be independent of language or even inhibited by it. One such process may be finding solutions to insight problems that are initially not obvious. Previous studies demonstrated detrimental effects of verbalization on processes such as visual imagery, aesthetic evaluations, and face recognition (Schooler, Fallshore, & Fiore, 1995). This phenomenon, in which subjects who are required to verbalize certain processes do more poorly than subjects who do not verbalize, has been termed *verbal overshadowing* (Fallshore & Schooler, 1995). This phenomenon was extended to insight problem solving (Schooler, Ohlsson, & Brooks, 1993). Experimenters examined for detrimental effects of verbalization on two problem types. One analytical problem type is typically solved by an incremental series of steps. The problem type of the insight variety required a nonobvious alternative solution approach. Specifically, the latter were problems that (1) could be solved by normal subjects, (2) likely caused an impasse in which the subject does not know what to do next, and (3) likely resulted in an "aha" experience once the impasse was broken (Schooler et al., 1993). Results showed that verbalization (i.e., thinking out loud) while working on the problems impaired performance on the insight problems but did not affect the analytical/logic problems. The researchers concluded that verbalization disrupted nonreportable processes associated with insight problem solving. In addition, insight may involve cognitive processes distinct from language (Schooler et al., 1993).

Overcoming Fixation and Perseveration. Second, Fiore and Schooler (1998) suggest that insight processes and RH functioning relate by overcoming fixation and perseveration. A brief description of these phenomena is in order. In seminal work on fixation, the Gestalt psychologist Karl Duncker (1945) used the term *functional fixedness* for when one can envision using an object such as a tool only in a traditional manner, not in a nontraditional or novel way. Analogous to fixation in the use of objects is the idea of a mental set—a particular frame of mind—involving an existing problem representation, problem context, or problem-solving procedure (Sternberg, 1996). This mental set may work well with many problems but may prevent one from solving a new problem that requires a different approach.

Fiore and Schooler point out that perseveration, from literature in cognitive neuroscience, is an analog to fixation. This describes the repetition of an action or the adherence to a certain approach despite its previous ineffectiveness. The authors cite several studies, including Rausch (1977), who examined learning strategies in patients with either left or right anterior temporal lobotomies. Rausch found that right anterior temporal lobectomized patients (i.e., those relying on the LH) perseverated on the same hypotheses. Patients with left anterior temporal lobotomies, on the other hand, continually reformulated problems, although previous hypotheses were appropriate (Rausch, 1977). Fiore and Schooler conclude that these results underline the RH's advantage for maintaining a fresh perspective in approaching problems, an ability critical for solving insight problems.

Nonobvious Interpretations of Problem Elements. Fiore and Schooler's third right hemisphere/insight connection involves the need in insight problems to consider nonobvious approaches, interpretations, or problem elements. For example, some insight word problems require the problem solver to retrieve infrequently used meanings of words with multiple definitions. Neurological studies show that damage to the right hemisphere can impair memory retrieval processes critical to insightlike functions. In a metaphor, for example, the literal and nonliteral interpretations of it must be evaluated in a specific context. Realizing that a nonliteral interpretation of the metaphor fits the present context is a type of insight. Fiore and Schooler cite Foldi, Cicone, and Gardner (1983), who showed that patients with right hemispheric damage (RHD) had trouble matching language with the context in which it was used; they just as likely chose a literal interpretation of a metaphor as the correct nonliteral interpretation.

Fiore and Schooler also found that some RHD patients have difficulty with humor and jokes. The authors liken the "getting" of a joke to an insightlike process that involves shifting from an expected resolution to an unexpected one, in which a nonobvious or non-dominant meaning is crucial in understanding the joke.

But Fiore and Schooler feel that the most direct evidence for the RH's ability to access nondominant meanings results from split-visual field priming studies. In these studies, subjects are asked to identify target words presented unilaterally (i.e., in one visual field) after having seen related word primes presented cen-

trally. The primary variable of interest in these studies is the amount of facilitation in recognizing the target as a function of prior exposure to the primes.
The split-visual field priming technique utilizes the natural split in human visual
pathways. That is, visual stimuli presented briefly to a person's left visual field
are projected first to the right hemisphere, whereas stimuli flashed briefly to the
right visual field are initially projected to the left hemisphere (Springer &
Deutsch, 1985). For example, Beeman et al. (1994) found that the left visual
field-right hemisphere (LVF-RH) benefited more from distantly related primes
followed by a remote target than did the right visual field-left hemisphere (RVF-
LH). On the other hand, direct primes benefited the right visual field-left hemisphere, whereas there was no priming effect in the left visual field-right
hemisphere. Beeman (1993) noted that hemispheric processing may result from
how information is coded in the two hemispheres, suggesting:

The RH may *coarsely code* semantic input, so that one comprehended word activates
many semantic features, but each one only weakly—so that only a vague interpretation
can be made. In contrast, the LH may *finely code* semantic input, so that one comprehended word activates few semantic features, but all so strongly that they are accessible
to consciousness and selected for further processing, such as production. (p. 90)

Or as Taylor (1988) suggests, "the RIGHT (hemisphere) proposes, and the
LEFT (hemisphere) disposes interpretations" (p. 324). Related to the preceding
theories, Gur et al. (1980) found a greater amount of gray matter relative to
white matter in the left hemisphere than in the right. This disparity prompted
Gur et al. to suggest that the left hemispheric organization lends itself to within-
region processing, whereas the right hemisphere is better organized for processing or transfer across regions.

Fiore and Schooler suggest that the apparent advantage of the RH in accessing
distant or remotely related associates may stem from its weaker inhibitory mechanism relative to the LH. They reason that the RH's access of non-dominant
meanings or interpretations may be useful in insight-type contexts but may lead
to confusion in other situations. Therefore, there may be "great adaptive value
to inhibiting non-dominant meanings in many situations" (Fiore & Schooler,
1998, p. 358).

Restructuring and Pattern Recognition. Fiore and Schooler's fourth parallel
between insight and RH functioning involves restructuring and pattern recognition. They highlight the emphasis of the Gestalt psychologists on perceptual
restructuring, in which the identity of an object is suddenly apprehended. This
parallel exists in many modes, including the suggestion by Ellen (1982) that
insight is like a figure-ground reversal. They also cite Ippolito and Tweney
(1995) suggesting that the use of perceptual processes "can affect the self-
defined and problem-defined domain in which the insightful discovering un-
folds" (p. 435).

Evidence for a link between perceptual pattern recognition and insight processes was provided recently by Schooler and Melcher (1995). In this study, a number of possible correlates of success in insight problem solving included such measures as Scholastic Aptitude Test (SAT) scores. Schooler and Melcher found that insight problem solving correlated best with ability to recognize out-of-focus pictures. Fiore and Schooler suggest that recognizing an out-of-focus picture resembles insight problems. At first such pictures may be totally unclear—similar to the initial impasse of many insight problems. An incorrect interpretation of the picture is like fixation, such that when the picture's identity occurs, the experience is typically sudden and includes a complete change of perception (Fiore & Schooler, 1998).

Fiore and Schooler offer several pieces of evidence that the RH may be involved in restructuring processes, including Semmes' (1968) suggestion that the RH is better at tasks that involve global integration, whereas the LH appears to be superior at more fine-grained analyses. They also offer strong evidence that the RH has an advantage in global pattern recognition, including the highly reliable advantage in recognizing faces at low visual-spatial frequencies, for faces perceptually degraded (Hellige, 1993; Sergent, 1988), and via detecting configural relations among features. Conversely, the LH demonstrates superiority in face recognition tasks that involve processing specific features (Hillger & Koenig, 1991).

Direct Evidence for a Right Hemisphere/Insight Connection

Fiore and Schooler conducted a preliminary study that directly examined the role of the RH in the insight problem-solving process. The insight problems in this experiment consisted of "verbal riddles." The authors asked if one-word "hints" presented to the subjects' left and right visual fields would lead to differential effects in insight problem solving. If the RH has a special involvement in the process, then Fiore and Schooler reasoned that these hints would benefit problem-solving success more when presented to the LVF-RH than the RVF-LH.

After subjects read the problems, the experimenters presented hints both immediately and after two-minute delays to examine the possible role of fixation or impasses resulting from an inappropriate problem representation. In other words, if an impasse is a critical component of the insight process, and if the RH is especially important in overcoming the impasse, then a delay in hint presentation might increase the differences in subjects' receptivity to the hints presented through the different visual fields. The results showed that subjects benefited more from hints presented to LVF than RVF. In addition, the effect of delayed hint presentation was significant—the RH advantage for hints was greater in the delay condition.

Fiore and Schooler concluded that this preliminary study provided initial direct support for a critical RH involvement in insight problem solving. Particularly important was the finding that subjects showed a LVF-RH advantage for hints and that this advantage was greater after a delay. The latter supports the notion that the RH functions especially in overcoming fixation or impasses. However, they emphasize that the RH should not be viewed as totally responsible for insight processes and that the LH is also involved, particularly because many insight problems are language-based. They concluded that an integration of LH and RH processes is required for insight problem solving and that "the RH may be involved in processes that are necessary, but probably not sufficient, to lead to insight solutions" (p. 368).

Right Hemisphere Functioning and the Evolution of Insight

This analysis of the parallels that Fiore and Schooler have drawn between RH processes and insight problem solving has important evolutionary implications. As previously discussed, inferring the psychological construct of insight from behavior that appears insightful makes an evolutionary account of the phenomenon problematic. Identifying certain processes that underlie insight problem solving, however, and providing neuropsychological evidence that these processes are associated with hemispheric specialization lead to a plausible evolutionary scenario.

In this scenario, insight-related processes conferred selective advantage or adaptive value. For example, the nonverbal character of insight may have arisen simply because prehuman animals before the acquisition of language required a method of problem solving that short-circuited the extremely inefficient, random, trial-and-error process. Compare this to the use of algorithms and heuristics: although an algorithm certainly and eventually produces problem solutions, the use of a heuristic, if it is a proper one, functions much more efficiently. Insight processes may have evolved before language. Evidence of insightful behavior in lower species also supports its significant selective advantages. Insight's overcoming fixation and perseveration has obvious adaptive value in providing fresh perspectives or new alternative approaches in complex environments. In such situations, what may have worked before may not suffice when adaptive demands change in ways not initially detected. There are obvious adaptive advantages for insight's pattern recognition qualities, particularly in recognizing configural features of faces or faces in visually degraded conditions.

The idea that insight problem solving relies on integrated LH and RH processes can extend to the evolution of thinking more generally. In this respect, we must realize that most problems involve extensive logical reasoning, punctuated occasionally by need for insight—when one needs an alternative approach (Fiore & Schooler, 1998). This description of problems supports the need for both insight and noninsight processes. Optimum problem solving occurs when each process is utilized at the appropriate time, that is, when the two processes are complementary. This requirement for complementary problem-solving processes fits well with theories of hemispheric specialization and asymmetry. For example, hemispheric asymmetry may allow homologous areas of the two hemispheres to assume primary roles in different aspects of information processing (Hellige, 1993). Hellige supposes that this would increase the range of efficient processing in a brain of limited size. In addition, the evolution of the corpus callosum, a large fiber tract that connects the two hemispheres, supports hemispheric specialization. Perhaps not only does the corpus callosum provide an informational link between the two hemispheres, but it may also have evolved as a barrier that inhibits or reduces certain maladaptive cross-talk between homologous regions of the two hemispheres. This could "add to the pressure for complementary or mutually inconsistent processes to migrate toward opposite hemispheres" (p. 306).

SUMMARY AND CONCLUSIONS

This chapter speculated on an evolutionary basis for the phenomenon of insight in learning and problem solving. We have seen that the characteristics of insight have selective advantages, that is, the reorganization or restructuring of prior knowledge or experience in the solution of a new problem. I have discussed that insight or insightful learning allows an organism to short-circuit the inefficient process of purely random or blind trial-and-error learning and that insight can allow first-trial learning. Insight may provide greater retention of problem solutions and facilitate the solution of problems that are structurally similar. I have discussed insight in non-human species with examples of insightful learning in animals. Insight in animals is complicated by their lack of language capability; one reason insight is readily ascribed to humans is that we freely talk about our insight experiences.

I finally examined the striking parallels that Fiore and Schooler have drawn between the characteristics of insight problem solving and cognitive processes in which the right hemisphere of the brain has a relative advantage. These parallels include the nonverbal nature of both the RH and insight problem solving, avoidance of fixation or perseveration, access to non-dominant interpretations, and global pattern recognition and restructuring. I claimed that these functions with a RH advantage are likely to have evolved for adaptive reasons, thereby suggesting that insight has also provided an adaptive role in our evolution.

In conclusion, I point out that this discussion has treated insight as strictly a cognitive phenomenon, individualistic in nature. But in the end, insight relates to more than just the individual problem solver. If we return to the four-stage process of creative problem solving proposed by Wallas (1926) (i.e., preparation, incubation, illumination, and verification), we can see that insight represents an individual's brief moment of revelation that is contained in a larger creative process. But this process is complex, time-consuming, and fundamentally social in nature, in that the effort preceding the insight and the effort that follows it are embedded in social, interactional factors (Csikszentmihalyi & Sawyer, 1995). Thus, insight may have evolved as an inseparable part of the process of creative thought.

NOTE

I would like to thank Ludy T. Benjamin, Jr., and Ryan D. Tweney for their helpful comments and suggestions on an earlier version of this chapter.

REFERENCES

Allen, C., & Hauser, M. (1996). Concept attribution in nonhuman animals: Theoretical and methodological problems in ascribing complex mental processes. In M. Bekoff & D. Jamieson (Eds.), *Readings in animal cognition* (pp. 47–62). Cambridge: MIT Press.

Beeman, M. (1993). Semantic priming in the right hemisphere may contribute to drawing inferences from discourse. *Brain and Language, 44,* 80–120.

Beeman, M., Friedman, R. B., Grafman, J., Perez, E., Diamond, S., & Lindsay, M. B. (1994). Summation priming and coarse semantic coding in the right hemisphere. *Journal of Cognitive Neuroscience, 6,* 26–45.

Benjamin, L. T. (1988). *A history of psychology: Original sources and contemporary research.* New York: McGraw-Hill.

Birch, H. G. (1967). The relation of previous experience to insightful problem solving. In A. J. Riopelle (Ed.), *Animal problem solving* (pp. 116–136). Baltimore: Penguin.

Bradshaw, J. L., & Nettleton, N. C. (1981). The nature of hemisphere specialization in man. *The Behavioral and Brain Sciences, 4,* 51–91.

Chater, N. & Heyes, C. (1994). Animal concepts: Content and discontent. *Mind and Language, 9,* 209–247.

Csányi, V. (1988). Contribution of the genetical and neural memory to animal intelligence. In H. J. Jerison & I. Jerison (Eds.), *Intelligence and evolutionary biology* (pp. 299–318). Berlin: Springer-Verlag.

Csikszentmihalyi, M., & Rathunde, K. (1990). The psychology of wisdom: An evolutionary interpretation. In R. Sternberg (Ed.), *Wisdom: Its nature, origins, and development* (pp. 25–51) New York: Cambridge University Press.

Csikszentmihalyi, M., & Sawyer, K. (1995). Creative insight: The social dimension of a solitary moment. In R. J. Sternberg & J. E. Davidson (Eds.), *The nature of insight* (pp. 329–363). Cambridge: MIT Press.

Dominowski, R. L., & Dallob, P. (1995). Insight and problem solving. In R. J. Sternberg & J. E. Davidson (Eds.), *The nature of insight* (pp. 33–62). Cambridge: MIT Press.

Duncker, K. (1945). On problem-solving. *Psychological Monographs, 58,* whole no. 270.

Ellen, P. (1982). Direction, past experience, and hints in creative problem solving: Reply to Weisberg and Alba. *Journal of Experimental Psychology: General, 111,* 316–325.

Epstein, R., Kirshnit, C. E., Lanza, R. P., & Rubin, L. C. (1984). ''Insight'' in the pigeon: Antecedents and determinants of an intelligent performance. *Nature, 308,* 61–62.

Fallshore, M., & Schooler, J. W. (1995). Verbal vulnerability of perceptual expertise. *Journal of Experimental Psychology: Learning, Memory, and Cognition, 21,* 1608–1623.

Fiore, S. M., & Schooler, J. W. (1998). Right hemisphere contributions to creative problem solving: Converging evidence for divergent thinking. In M. Beeman & C. Chiarello (Eds.), *Right hemisphere language comprehension: Perspectives from cognitive neuroscience.* (pp. 349–371) Mahwah, NJ: Lawrence Erlbaum.

Foldi, N. S., Cicone, M., & Gardner, H. (1983). Pragmatic aspects of communication in brain damaged patients. In S. J. Segalowitz (Ed.), *Language functions and brain organization* (pp. 51–86). New York: Academic Press.

Gazzaniga, M. S. (1983). Right hemisphere language following brain bisection: A 20 year perspective. *American Psychologist, 38,* 525–537.

Gick M. L., & Lockhart, R. S. (1995). Cognitive and affective components of insight. In R. J. Sternberg & J. E. Davidson (Eds.), *The nature of insight* (pp. 197–228). Cambridge: MIT Press.

Gould J. L., & Gould, C. G. (1986). Invertebrate intelligence. In R. Hoage and L. Goldman (Eds.), *Animal intelligence* (pp. 21–36). Washington, DC: Smithsonian Institution Press.

Griffin, D. R. (1984). *Animal thinking.* Cambridge: Harvard University Press.

Gruber, H. E. (1995). Insight and affect in the history of science. In R. J. Sternberg & J. E. Davidson (Eds.), *The nature of insight* (pp. 397–431). Cambridge: MIT Press.

Gur, R. C., Packer, I. K., Hungerbuhler, J. P., Reivich, M., Obrist, W. D., Amarnek, W. S., & Sackeim, H. A. (1980). Differences in the distribution of gray and white matter in human cerebral hemispheres. *Science, 207,* 1226–1228.

Hebb, D. O. (1966). *A textbook of psychology.* Philadelphia: W. B. Saunders.

Hellige, J. B. (1993). *Hemispheric asymmetry.* Cambridge: Harvard University Press.

Hillger, L. A., & Koenig, O. (1991). Separable mechanisms in face processing: Evidence from hemispheric specialization. *Journal of Cognitive Neuroscience, 3,* 42–58.

Ippolito, M. F., & Tweney, R. D. (1995). The inception of insight. In R. J. Sternberg & J. E. Davidson (Eds.), *The nature of insight* (pp. 433–462). Cambridge: MIT Press.

Koestler, A. (1964). *The act of creation.* New York: Macmillan.

Köhler, W. (1925). *The mentality of apes.* New York: Liveright.

Köhler, W. (1947). *Gestalt psychology.* New York: Liveright.

Maier, N. R. F., & Schneirla, T. C. (1964). *Principles of animal psychology.* New York: Dover.

Mayer, R. E. (1995). The search for insight: Grappling with gestalt psychology's unanswered questions. In R. J. Sternberg & J. E. Davidson (Eds.), *The nature of insight* (pp. 3–32). Cambridge: MIT Press.

Metcalfe, J. (1986). Premonitions of insight predict impending error. *Journal of Experimental Psychology: Learning, Memory, and Cognition, 12,* 623–634.

Metcalfe, J., & Wiebe, D. (1987). Intuition in insight and noninsight problem solving. *Memory and Cognition, 15,* 238–246.

Neufeldt, V., & Guralnik, D. B. (1991). *Webster's new world dictionary* (3rd college ed.). New York: Simon & Schuster.

Rausch, R. (1977). Cognitive strategies in patients with unilateral temporal lobe excisions. *Neuropsychologia, 15,* 385–396.

Scheerer, M. (1963). Problem solving. *Scientific American, 208,* 118–128.

Schooler, J. W., Ohlsson, S., & Brooks, K. (1993). Thoughts beyond words: When language overshadows insight. *Journal of Experimental Psychology: General, 122,* 166–183.

Schooler, J. W., Fallshore, M., & Fiore, S. M. (1995). Putting insight into perspective. In R. J. Sternberg & J. E. Davidson (Eds.), *The nature of insight* (pp. 559–587). Cambridge: MIT Press.

Schooler, J. W., & Melcher, J. (1995). The ineffability of insight. In S. M. Smith, T. B. Ward, & R. A. Finke (Eds.), *The creative cognitive approach* (pp. 97–133). Cambridge: MIT Press.

Semmes, J. (1968). Hemispheric specialization: A possible clue to mechanism. *Neuropsychologia, 6*, 11–26.

Sergent, J. (1988). Face perception and the right hemisphere. In L. Weiskrantz (Ed.), *Thought without language* (pp. 109–131). Oxford: Clarendon Press/Oxford University Press.

Simon, H. A. (1981). The sciences of the artificial. Cambridge, MA: MIT Press.

Simonton, D. K. (1995). Foresight in insight? A Darwinian answer. In R. J. Sternberg & J. E. Davidson (Eds.), *The nature of insight* (pp. 465–494). Cambridge: MIT Press.

Smith, S. M. (1995). Getting into and out of mental ruts: A theory of fixation, incubation, and insight. In R. J. Sternberg & J. E. Davidson (Eds.), *The nature of insight* (pp. 229–251). Cambridge: MIT Press.

Springer, S. P. & Deutsch, G. (1985). *Left brain, right brain*. New York: W. H. Freeman.

Sternberg, R. J. (1996). *Cognitive psychology*. Orlando, FL: Harcourt Brace College.

Taylor, M. M. (1988). The bilateral cooperative model of reading. In D. de Kerckhove & C J. Lumsden (Eds.), *The alphabet and the brain* (pp. 322–361). Berlin: Springer-Verlag.

Tolman, E. C. (1951). *Purposive behavior in animals and men*. Berkeley: University of California Press.

Wallas, G. (1926). *The art of thought*. New York: Harcourt Brace Jovanovich.

Wertheimer, M. (1959). *Productive thinking* (2nd ed.). New York: Harper & Row.

Zaidel, E. (1983). A response to Gazzaniga: Language in the right hemisphere, convergent perspectives. *American Psychologist, 38*, 342–346.

7

The Evolution of Humor: Do Those Who Laugh Last?

JYOTSNA VAID

"Tell me comrade, what is capitalism?"
"The exploitation of man by man."
"And what is communism?"
"The reverse." (Koestler, 1964, p. 90)

On the evolutionary level where laughter arises, an element of frivolity seems to creep into a humorless universe governed by the laws of thermodynamics and the survival of the fittest.
(Koestler, 1964, p. 31)

Much like the capacity to use language, the capacity to perceive and generate humor appears to be present in all known cultures (Apte, 1985). Like language, humor has both universal and culture-specific aspects. The different varieties (e.g., riddles, puns, jokes, anecdotes) and techniques of humor (e.g., mimicry, ambiguity, exaggeration, mockery, irony) are found in practically all cultures. What seems to vary across cultures are the extent of use of a particular form or technique and the extent to which humor is socially permitted. Even within a given culture the form and acceptability of humor depend, to a large extent, on linguistic, regional, diachronic, sociocultural, and personal boundaries (Chiaro, 1992), for humor presupposes shared knowledge and worldviews, shared interpretations, and shared emotional significances that provide its meanings and determine its appropriateness (Palmer, 1994).

In view of its pervasiveness one may well raise the question as to the functional significance of humor and whether or not humor has a survival value. As will be discussed shortly, at least four different hypotheses regarding the adaptive significance of humor may be identified from the vast literature on theories of humor. Before turning to these hypotheses, it would be instructive to consider first the nature of humor and its perceived functions.

THE NATURE AND SIGNIFICANCE OF HUMOR

A sense of humor has certain attributes in common with a sense of the erotic. Both, as Clinton (1982) notes, demand our being fully present and responsive in a situation. Like erotic pleasure, the pleasure of mirthful laughter is highly desired and sought after; as Chafe notes, people "deliberately seek out humor, they deliberately create occasions for it and they are willing to pay money to get it" (1987, p. 21). Humor's societal importance in modern times is reflected in its growing commoditization. Humor is presented to us for consumption in almost all forms of the mass media—newsprint, magazines, books, television, film, and (increasingly) cyberspace. It is communicated as well through a variety of artifacts including bumper stickers, T-shirts, and greeting cards. In North America, stand-up comedy has become an immensely popular (and lucrative) form of performance art for a growing segment of the population, achieving the status that poetry or theater has. An annual international comedy festival ("Just for Laughs") takes place in Montreal and is estimated to draw in several million dollars to the local economy.

A sense of humor is highly valued in a prospective mate, a leader, or a coworker. Having a sense of humor indicates a mental flexibility and openness to experience that are typically lacking in those who are overly serious and is thus seen as a sign of psychological health and maturity. Being able to treat oneself with a sense of humor, as A. Penjon notes, "frees us from vanity, on the one hand and from pessimism on the other by keeping us larger than what we do, and greater than what can happen to us" (cited in Morreall, 1983, p. 106). Indeed, the more we learn about humor, the harder it is to escape the conclusion that "humor . . . is not only valuable in human life, but valuable in a way nothing else is . . . [in that it] . . . is essential to maintaining a healthy outlook on things" (Morreall, 1983, p. 106).

Humor has, nevertheless, been somewhat of an enigma to those who have sought to understand it. The diversity of situations in which it occurs or can occur makes it practically impossible to characterize it in some convenient formula. Nevertheless, we all recognize humorous content even if we may not agree on its appropriateness in a particular context. Moreover, although what is humorous is often thought of as being "somehow off the mark, dodging the issue, masking and hiding from something more serious" (Clinton, 1982, p. 37), nevertheless, humor can be a very effective (and sometimes the most apt) way of expressing and confronting reality. These and other paradoxical aspects of humor have been duly examined by many philosophers, humanists, sociologists, and psychologists (e.g., Bergson, 1950; Freud, 1963; Martineau, 1972; Koestler, 1964; Morreall, 1983, 1989).

Empirical research on humor has been fairly recent—undertaken largely within the past two decades—for humor (like play, love, etc.) was not considered a legitimate (i.e., serious) topic for scientific study. Several hundred studies have now appeared, and there is a journal devoted to humor research. Most psychological studies (e.g., McGhee, 1979; Thorson & Powell, 1993) have explored humor by measuring who finds what funny and to what extent, using "canned" humor (i.e., jokes and cartoons) for the most part. This research has been criticized for having a male bias (Crawford, 1995) and for lacking ecological validity (Norrick, 1993). As a result, we still know very little about humor perception and production in women and men interacting in natural contexts; nor has there been much empirical investigation of actual or perceived uses of humor (e.g., Crawford & Gressley, 1991; Quiros & Vaid, 1998). There clearly remains a need for more contextualized approaches that analyze how different forms and uses of humor operate and interact with variables such as age, gender, and social status in a variety of naturalistic settings.

Humor is often expressed behaviorally in terms of laughter. Indeed, many theories of humor make reference to laughter. As such, one needs to address the relationship between humor and laughter before proceeding further. Laughter is an overt behavioral indication that the individual is in an amused state. Just as we find different things funny, we express our amusement in different ways, ranging from the hint of a smile with the teeth showing only slightly to convulsive, hysterical, screaming laughter. The Sanskrit rhetorician Bharata categorized laughter into six types, adding that the roaring and hysterical kinds of laughter (*apahasita* and *atihasita*) are typical of vulgar, ill-bred, or disreputable characters (Siegel, 1987).

Laughter is not, however, a reliable index of being in an amused state, for humor is only one among several possible causes of laughter. Aside from humor, for example, one may laugh out of ignorance, anxiety, derision, or embarrassment or in response to tickling. Moreover, one can appreciate a joke or funny story without actually laughing. Thus, it would be wrong to regard laughter as the acid test of humor. Nevertheless, many authors have used mirthful laughter as a marker of humor.

Any comprehensive theoretical account would need to make reference to two properties that, I believe, are critical to humor. The first of these is what Freud (1963) referred to as economy of expression. As a skilled use of creative cognition (see Smith & Ward, Chapter 5 of this volume; Ward, Smith & Vaid, 1997), humor exploits the ambiguity, polysemy, and intertextuality of language, and it does so by using an understated, concise form to convey rich, implicit content. The other critical aspect of humor is its collaborative nature. For humor to succeed, it is not enough to make a joke: the listener has to *get* the joke, that is, mentally re-create it (Koestler, 1964) and communicate that it was pleasurable (or not). There is a sense of collaboration in the construction of even "canned" humor and, in the case of spontaneous humor, the possibility of joint authorship (as in banter or witty repartee). Indeed, this latter aspect may well account for the affective solidarity and even intimacy experienced by those who share a joke.

A wide range of functions has been proposed in the literature on humor. These include (1) psychological functions, such as arousal, social control, establishment of superiority, providing relief and release, ego defense, coping and saving face, gaining status, and healing, (2) educational functions, such as teaching and learning, arguing and persuading, and (3) social functions, such as signaling in- and out-bonding, promoting social stability and control, and social change. Although these functions seem intuitively plausible, empirical research on their scope remains to be done.

Yet even if humor *were* shown to subserve some or all of the functions attributed to it, the question can still be raised as to whether these functions in themselves provide satisfactory explanations for humor or whether one needs to examine humor at a still deeper level of analysis. As Alexander (1986) points out, "to say that a particular behavior or tendency exists . . . to satisfy pleasure, relieve frustration, or even to help one deal with an immediate situation . . . begs the question of the reason for the existence of the effect (pleasure, relief, comfort)" (p. 257). That is, it is not enough to point to proximate causes of behavior in seeking ultimate explanations. Rather than saying that we laugh because it is a form of release from tension, the question that needs to be considered is *why* laughter should be healthy or have beneficial physiological effects. The reason cannot be purely physiological (e.g., Fry, 1993) but must also be sought in social situations that evoke laughter.

In what follows, I first review various proximate causes of humor proposed in the literature, then consider four different theoretical analyses of ultimate explanations for the evolution of humor.

THEORIES OF HUMOR

Theories of humor include psychoanalytic, social/anthropological, cognitive, and metaphysical approaches. A brief overview of existing theories is provided here (for a more thorough review, see Morreall, 1983).

Psychological Theories

Among psychological theories, that of Freud, as described in his *Jokes and Their Relation to the Unconscious* (1963, pp. 100–101), is one of the earliest; distinguishing between innocent and tendentious humor, Freud suggests that the latter makes possible "the satisfaction of an instinct (whether lustful or hostile) in the face of an obstacle that stands in its way." He further notes that the pleasure in a joke arises from the savings in psychic energy made possible by the respite from conscious monitoring. Thus, for Freud, humor allows for the temporary expression of socially undesirable impulses from the subconscious. The association of humor with aggressive or sexual impulses has characterized subsequent accounts as well and has led to some debate over whether hostility is an inherent element of humor (Fry, 1987).

Proponents of the so-called superiority theory (Aristotle, Plato, Hobbes, and Bergson) view humor as reflecting a moral stance on the part of the humorist. As described in Hobbes's *Leviathan*, "The passion of laughter is nothing else but sudden glory arising from a sudden conception of some eminency in ourselves by comparison with the infirmity of others, or with our own formerly" (cited in Koestler, 1964, p. 53). For Bergson (1950), laughter asserts the human values of spontaneity and freedom and therefore erupts whenever a person behaves rigidly, like an automaton: "Humor consists in perceiving something mechanical encrusted on something living" (p. 29). Superiority may be expressed not just by laughing at others' defects but also by showing that one can laugh at (and rise above) one's own imperfections.

Social/Anthropological Theories

The social significance of laughter and humor has been noted by several thinkers, including the ethologist Konrad Lorenz: "Laughter (as the overt expression of humor) produces simultaneously a strong fellow feeling among participants and joint aggressiveness against outsiders. . . . Laughter forms a bond and simultaneously draws a line. If you cannot laugh with the others, you feel an outsider, even if the laughter is in no way directed against yourself or indeed against anything at all" (1963, p. 284). Social theorists of humor (e.g., Martineau, 1972) have viewed it as a marker of group membership and solidarity (for those who share a joke) or exclusion (for those who are the "butt" of the joke) and as a means of maintaining social control and group cohesiveness. In addition, the "joking relationship" (noted by Radcliffe-Brown, 1965) is a form of humor that may serve to defuse potential conflict among kin related by marriage. As noted by Radcliffe-Brown (1965, p. 90), a joking relationship refers to "a relation between two persons in which one is by custom permitted, and in some instances required, to tease or make fun of the other, who in turn is required to take no offence." Such relationships have been observed in traditional societies in widely dispersed geographical regions, including Africa, Asia, and Oceania.

The anthropologist Mary Douglas suggested a core structure underlying jokes: "a joke is a play upon form. It brings into relation disparate elements in such a way that one accepted pattern is challenged by the appearance of another which in some way was hidden in the first" (1975, p. 98). She claimed that the telling of a joke is a potentially subversive act in the sense that the joke's form consists of "a victorious tilting of uncontrol against control" and represents the "leveling of hierarchy, the triumph of intimacy over formality, of unofficial values over official ones" (1975, p. 98). This "subversive" aspect of humor is particularly evident among members of marginalized groups who use humor strategically to articulate and, thereby, subvert their marginal or powerless status.

Subversive undertones are especially evident in East European humor, so-called gallows humor, and much of feminist humor (e.g., Barreca, 1991).

The feminist humorist or "fumerist" Kate Clinton argues that the forms and uses of humor may be gendered: masculine humor, according to Clinton (1982), is "deflective. It allows denial of responsibility, the oh-I-was-just-kidding disclaimer. It is escapist, something to gloss over and get through the hard times, without ever having to do any of the hard work of change. It is about the maintenance of the status quo" (p. 39). In contrast, feminist humor "is about exposure. It is about shedding light on our experience. It is an active ethos, not a passive acceptance of an imposed status quo" (Clinton, 1982, p. 39).

Cognitive Theories

While psychoanalytic and sociological theories have focused on the content, effects, or social uses of humor, cognitively oriented theories, including the incongruity theory associated with Kant, Schopenhauer, Koestler, and Morreall, and the configurational theory developed by the Gestalt psychologist Norman Maier (1932) have sought to describe the mechanisms or mental processes underlying humor.

In the incongruity view, humor is thought to arise from a sudden restructuring of a schema or narrative upon recognizing some "ambiguity, inconsistency, contradiction and interpretive diversity" (Mulkay, 1988, p. 26). In other words, we may experience humor when we become aware of a sudden disruption in the status quo, whether the latter refers to a state of knowledge, an emotional state, or a social relationship. Arthur Koestler (1964) argued that bisociative thinking underlies humor and creativity alike: "the creative act of the humorist consist[s] in bringing about a momentary fusion between two habitually incompatible matrices" (p. 94). Indeed, experimental studies of humor appreciation indicate that structural incongruity perception is an important component (Staley & Derks, 1995).

In formulating a Gestalt perspective on humor, Maier (1932) acknowledged that a key element in producing a mental experience of humorousness is a sudden and unexpected restructuring of the elements of a configuration, not unlike the experience of insight (see Pierce, Chapter 6 of this volume). That is, a humorous narrative manipulates our expectations by leading us down a garden path only to present us with an altogether different conclusion from the one we were led to expect. Given that the conclusion disrupts the way in which we have been thinking about the events in the narrative, we are totally unprepared for it. After a momentary confusion of thought, we experience the newly restructured configuration with clarity, and we are amused by how we were misled. However, Maier noted that whereas incongruity may be a necessary ingredient for humor, it may not be sufficient, for incongruity could just as easily arouse fear. He therefore proposed two additional requirements for humor: an attitude of objectivity toward the content of the humor ("we can laugh only so long as our feelings and sympathies are kept out of the situation") and a recognition of the ridiculousness in the scenario (Maier, 1932, p. 71). With respect to the latter, humor entails the realization that the humorous situation has a definite logic (but only within the bounds of the narrative) and that it is not to be taken as "true" pragmatically. Making this connection, Gregory Bateson (1969) suggested that humor involves the setting up of a play frame that indicates to the listener that what is inside the frame is not to be taken seriously. There is, in other words, an element of deliberate (if momentary) deception involved in humor that requires a tacit approval from the listener for the humor to be acknowledged.

Metaphysical Theories

While humor has been shunned by many Western philosophers as being unsuitable because of its frivolous, irrational, or irresponsible aspects and therefore as having no place in metaphysical inquiries (Morreall, 1989), a different view is embraced in Indian and Buddhist cosmologies. Buddha, for example, is thought to have asked his disciples the following question: "How can anyone who knows of old age, disease, and death laugh?" The answer, as Siegel suggests, lies in the revelation that "satire is laughter at the vices and follies to which humanity is driven by the agonies of old age, disease, and death; humor is laughter in spite of disease, in acceptance of old age, in surrender to death" (1987, p. 5). Indeed, in the Indian cosmology, all human actions and aspirations, when viewed from the distant, detached perspective of the gods, "are in essence comical. Wisdom is getting the joke. But . . . the very source of that wisdom . . . is sown with seeds of sorrow [for] we are as funny as we are sad" (Siegel, 1987, p. 372). The parallels with Western existentialist philosophy are interesting here. "Nothing is funnier than unhappiness," states the character Nell in Samuel Beckett's *Endgame*. Or, as Nietzche is supposed to have said, man suffers so deeply that he had to invent laughter.

FUNCTIONS OF HUMOR

Though differing in their characterizations of the phenomenon, an implicit belief underlying most accounts of humor is that it is somehow healthy or good. Humor is valued alternatively as a pickup or a put-down, a strategy for coping or for hoping. Humor makes us feel superior and prevents us from feeling inferior; it relaxes, distracts, or comforts us. Humor gets us out of a sticky situation, provides a means for the expression of otherwise taboo subjects, sharpens our wit, makes us more flexible in our thinking, fosters solidarity or intimacy, and provides an alternative to despair.

ADAPTIVE SIGNIFICANCE OF HUMOR?

As mentioned earlier, these various explanations of humor may, at best, be viewed as proximate causes. A fundamental understanding of humor requires an inquiry, however speculative, into its potential adaptive significance. At this juncture we may raise the question of whether humor can be said to have an "ultimate" function that was selected for in the process of evolution. Until fairly recently, this issue was either not raised or else was implicitly dismissed at the outset, for, if anything, laughter would appear to be antithetical to natural selection. Weisfeld (1993) notes that laughter consumes metabolic energy and attracts the attention of predators. Koestler (1964) refers to laughter as a "luxury reflex" with no apparent utilitarian value except perhaps in bringing about a temporary relief from utilitarian pressures. Fry notes, "Breathless, weakened, with lungs and muscles already spoken for; this is certainly not a state in which one would find greatest advantage when faced with life threatening hazards. Laughter thus seem[s] to be in direct conflict with the evolutionary tendency" (1987, p. 64).

Appearances notwithstanding, there are reasons to suspect that humor may, indeed, have evolved. Following research strategies pioneered by Darwin (1965), Weisfeld (1993) considers a number of possible criteria that led him to conclude that laughter and humor are plausible candidates for having evolved in humans. He points, for example, to laughter's pervasiveness across the human species and its behavioral stereotypy (i.e., the characteristic staccato expirations of laughter are found in all cultures as an expression of amusement). Weisfeld also notes humor's relatively early developmental onset (laughter in response to tickling and play emerges by around four months in human infants, and smiling occurs even earlier), its presence in related species (facial displays resembling smiling and vocalizations resembling human laughter have been observed in tickling and play contexts in chimpanzees, gorillas, and orangutans (see van Hoof, 1972), and its neurophysiological mediation (via structures in the hypothalamus, the limbic system, and the right cerebral cortex or hemisphere) (see Fry, 1993).

PRECONDITIONS FOR HUMOR

> Beneath the human level there is neither the possibility nor the need for laughter; it could arise only in a biologically secure species with redundant emotions and intellectual autonomy. (Koestler, 1964, p. 63)

In view of what we know about humor, it would appear that certain preconditions have to be met for humor to arise in a species. These would include (in no particular order) (1) sociality, that is, organisms living together in a network of social relations, (2) a system of communication, allowing for the members to express and communicate beliefs and feelings, (3) an ability to mentally represent and order the physical world in the form of schemas and to construct possible, imaginary worlds, (4) an exploratory drive, intellectual curiosity, and playfulness, (5) the capacity to deceive or misrepresent the truth, (6) the capacity to use logic and reasoning independently of affective or real-world constraints, (7) the capacity for collaboration, reciprocity, and compassion, and last, but certainly not least, (8) a theory of mind.

Even if these preconditions are met, it remains to be determined just what humor may have evolved for. The type of explanation proposed for humor's adaptive significance (and, in turn, the adequacy of the explanation) depends on how (and how well) one defines humor and on the kinds of phenomena that would be predicted based on the explanation proposed.

EVOLUTIONARY HYPOTHESES

Four distinct hypotheses regarding the adaptive significance of humor may be gleaned from the literature: (1) humor as disabling (Chafe, 1987), (2) humor as a form of social learning (Weisfeld, 1993), (3) humor as social status manipulation (Alexander, 1986, 1989), and (4) humor as vocal grooming in the service of social bonding (Dunbar, 1996). In the remainder of this chapter, each of these hypotheses is first described and subsequently evaluated. It is argued that while each suggests how humor *can* function, a more comprehensive understanding would require an explicit attempt at relating the preconditions and the properties of humor with its presumed functions. In this way one could begin to make a case that humor does or must operate in the manner proposed and not merely that it *can* operate in such a way.

Humor as a Disabling Mechanism

When we are truly amused by something, more often than not, it takes us by surprise and distracts us from whatever it was that we were in the middle of doing or thinking. Indeed, while heartily laughing in response to a humorous narrative, we, quite literally, cannot think of, let alone do, anything else. Wallace Chafe (1987) suggests that this disruptive effect of humor may be evolutionarily significant, that humor's basic, adaptive function is a disabling one. As Chafe puts it, "The humor state arises in us in the first instance in order to keep us from doing things that would be counterproductive. The things it keeps us from doing are things that our natural, schema-based human reasoning might lead us into but which, given the larger reality of a particular situation, would be undesirable, bad, or sometimes even disastrous" (Chafe, 1987, p. 18). Chafe further suggests that "the sound of laughter overtly communicates to other humans the fact that the sound producer is in the humor state—and thus . . . cannot be expected . . . to act or think seriously" (p. 21). The infectiousness of laughter may, in turn, render other persons infected by it similarly disabled.

Humor as Social Stimulation

Weisfeld (1993) traces the origins of humor in laughter in response to tickling and play of young primates (and children). Just as laughter in tickling and play (or mock attack) contexts provides opportunities for the practicing of skills that are needed for survival, laughter in response to striking counterexamples (incongruities), as in wordplay, or in response to narratives from social experiences may also be socially instructive. In other words, for Weisfeld (1993, p. 141), "the pleasure of humor motivates us to seek out poignant, fitness-enhancing input," that is, in sexual, aggressive, and social poise domains. Moreover, laughter is "a pleasant social signal that prompts the humorist to persist in providing this edifying stimulation" (p. 141). In Weisfeld's view, then, humor provides exposure to fitness-relevant scenarios in a nonserious context, motivating the practice of social skills useful in serious contexts; laughter, in turn, conveys appreciation and gratitude to the humorist for having provided such stimulation. Weisfeld further suggests that humor is therefore not as often used by the elderly, who would no longer have need for social instruction.

Humor as Status Manipulation

The notion that mirthful laughter serves to create and solidify group boundaries forms the centerpiece of the most well developed evolutionary theory of humor, proposed by Alexander (1986, 1989). According to Alexander, humor is a way of favorably manipulating one's status in a group to improve one's access to resources for reproductive success.

As Alexander puts it, "humor is a principle according to which the evolved abilities and tendencies of people to . . . use ostracism to their own advantage, are manipulated so as to induce status shifts—humor has developed as a form of ostracism" (1986, p. 107). He further notes that ostracism, in turn, has repercussions for reproductive success, tending to restrict access to significant resources (and thereby impede the reproductive success) of the ostracized individual or group while improving that of the ostracizers.

More specifically, Alexander (1986) proposes that humor develops as two related forms: (1) jokes that explicitly exclude or lower the status of a party and thereby bond together those who share it (e.g., ethnic, racist, or sexist jokes) or (2) jokes that implicitly exclude or lower the status of a party by explicitly reinforcing the cohesiveness in the group among the individuals sharing the joke. In this view, then, humor is a means of manipulating one's social status in a group (and thereby one's access to critical resources) by facilitating bonds with certain members and ostracizing others, through explicit or implicit exclusion.

Alexander sketches the evolutionary development of humor in five stages, beginning with a stage of physical grooming where the organism scratches or grooms itself to remove parasites, and so on. At stage 2, grooming acquires a social significance, that is, one grooms relatives or mates. At stage 3, grooming signals selectivity or preference, that is, a willingness to invest in a particular individual over others and the beginnings of ostracism. At stage 4, special responses to grooming emerge. These include appreciative stances, movements, or vocalizations and tendencies to elicit those responses. At this stage grooming (and its associates such as tickling, horseplay, necking, etc.) takes on a social significance of attracting the attention of observers who may be better partners in such investments. Finally, at stage 5, characterizing the emergence of humor in its modern form, laughter and expressions of pleasure become freed from the contexts of physical grooming, tickling, and courtship, and they begin to appear in other social situations as well. The possibility of a sixth, affiliative or "integrative" stage of humor, is also entertained; Alexander concludes that such a use is possible only if it can be argued that "affiliative actions (humor) have as their ultimate function the competitive success of the thereby unified cooperative group as compared to other groups" (1986, p. 116). In other words, whether ostracizing or integrative, humor works by privileging one individual or group over another individual or group.

Humor as Vocal Grooming

The most recent formulation of the origins of humor appears in a book by Robin Dunbar (1996) on the evolution of language. Like Alexander (1986), Dunbar situates the origins of humor (and language in general) in the physical grooming undertaken by social animals as a way of bonding and forming intimacies. He notes that such grooming puts the participants in a euphoric and mildly narcotic state, given that grooming is associated with the release of endogenous opiates in the brain. He further proposes that language evolved in humans as a vocal extension of physical grooming, to allow, as it were, the simultaneous grooming across space of more than one partner and thereby the facilitating of social bonds with larger groups of animals. Language allows for social bonding by permitting the exchange of socially relevant information (i.e., who is doing what with whom). Hence, Dunbar claims that language evolved initially as a means of gossiping about others as well as sharing one's own social experiences. The fact that much of conversation is punctuated by laughter (Provine, 1993, 1996) and that laughter, in turn, is known to release endogenous opiates as well suggests that humorous discourse may have arisen as a means for eliciting more laughter, in the service of social bonding.

Dunbar further maintains that the emergence of language required that humans had evolved a theory of mind, namely, the ability to understand what another individual is thinking, to ascribe beliefs, desires, fears, and hopes to someone else, and to believe that others experience these feelings as mental states (Dunbar, 1996). Having a theory of mind, in turn, makes it possible for humans to produce works of fiction, develop religious or scientific frameworks, and (one might add) develop a humorous stance. Indeed, all these capacities have in common an ability to detach oneself from the immediacy of one's experiences.

"Without language, we each live in our own separate mental worlds. *With* language, we can share the worlds inhabited by others. We can discover that other peoples' worlds are not quite the same as ours, that in turn will prompt us to realize that the world can be other than we suppose it to be" (Dunbar, 1996, p. 105).

COMMENTS ON EVOLUTIONARY HYPOTHESES

Humor as Disabling. The notion that humor is a safety valve that saves us from undesirable consequences of our natural reasoning is an intriguing one, for it suggests a wisdom and purpose beneath the frivolity and apparent purposelessness of much humor. Indeed, we can all probably think of instances where a humorous intervention, in fact, removed a block in our normal way of thinking. Pugh (1977) has highlighted an aspect of humor that may fit well with Chafe's view; he proposes that humor is a way of pointing out and sharing counterexamples. Given that human reasoning tends toward seeking out confirmatory, rather than disconfirmatory, evidence, this aspect of humor may turn out to be useful for problem solving.

Yet is there not a sense in which Chafe's claim requires humor to accomplish more than it perhaps actually does? For it is one thing to argue that in some cases humor *can*—by disabling us—prevent us from pursuing a counterproductive path (one may term this the weak version of the argument that humor is disabling). It is another to maintain (as Chafe seems to) that humor *always* or necessarily does (the strong version of the argument).

Both versions of the claim that humor's disabling effect is beneficial can be tested empirically: the role of humor could be examined in much the same way that the variable of incubation has been studied in problem-solving tasks. The question of interest would be whether individuals presented with a humorous interruption (as opposed to some neutral interruption) would be more efficient in solving a problem upon returning to it. Would the effect depend on the type of humor, the type of problem, the relevance of the humor content to the problem content, the presence of others, and so on? Moreover, one could examine the processes underlying the purported beneficial effect induced by this "disabling mechanism." One could investigate whether the benefit is a general one, as might arise from taking a break, or whether it is one specific to humor, that is, where the humor itself provides a fresh insight on the matter at hand.

Humor as Social Learning. In Weisfeld's view, humor is basically a form of social-intellectual play that allows for the seeking and practicing of social skills that are fitness-enhancing at some later point (1993). Whereas play typically occurs early in development, humor occurs throughout the life span, although it takes different forms reflecting the different stages of cognitive development (e.g., McGhee & Chapman, 1980). However, while suggesting that humorous scenarios typically involve some (usually poignant) fitness-relevant situation, Weisfeld does not explicitly propose why *humor* is particularly useful; that is, why gossip or fantasizing may not suffice for social learning purposes. Perhaps *humorous* discourse is more salient, memorable, or socially cohesive than other modes of social scenario building. This possibility, though not entertained by Weisfeld, could be examined by comparing the retention of gossip in the presence or absence of humor. If humor is, indeed, claimed to have evolved, it should show distinct effects beyond those that can be attributed to other forms of social learning, unless, of course, one contends (as Dunbar, 1996, e.g., does) that they, too, have an evolved basis.

Weisfeld's claim regarding the relative absence of humor among the elderly seems counterintuitive and is easily tested. Although it may be that the elderly do not employ humor for the same purposes that younger individuals may use it, humor may still serve a critical need even (or especially) for them. After all, the elderly in particular have to confront particularly poignant, fitness-relevant issues of illness, infirmity, and mortality (see Richman, 1995).

Humor as Status Manipulation. Alexander's (1986) scheme, while presenting humor primarily as a means of competing for critical resources, nevertheless, provides no rationale for why humor *per se* is necessary or useful in accomplishing the goal. That is, why are humorous put-downs necessary when direct criticism or insults could suffice? Is it because establishing dominance through vicarious or symbolic means (as humor allows) is a more cost-effective (since face-saving) way of manipulating status than more direct displays of hostility or strength? Alexander (1989) suggests that humor, as one form of social scenario building, provides a cost-effective edge in learning how to negotiate in fitness-relevant domains. In this latter portrayal, the role of humor is conceptualized more broadly than in Alexander's earlier (1986) framework, in which he appears to be referring only to jokes and to jokes that have someone as their butt. Many varieties of humor, for example, wordplay or self-deprecatory humor, lack a competitive element. Yet even if the competitive aspect of humor refers to how humor (whatever its content) is being used, the question remains as to whether competitiveness is a central or an incidental aspect of humor. As Weisfeld (1993) argues, for example, many behaviors such as running, cooking, and so on, can be performed competitively, but one would hardly want to argue that these incidental applications explain the evolutionary origins of these behaviors. In Alexander's (1986) view, humor appears to function primarily as a means of creating solidarity with some members of a group by excluding or demeaning others. Yet, while this may characterize one, albeit frequent, application of humor, it surely does not do justice to what Freud referred to as the finer side of humor. Humor may well have evolved as a particularly effective weapon of aggression, but it has also served well as a peaceful mechanism for disarming potential opponents. That is, humor may best be regarded as a device that wins people over rather than winning over them.

Humor as Vocal Grooming and Social Bonding. Although addressing humor only in passing, Dunbar's (1996) theory of language as a vehicle for social bonding through its origins in grooming and gossip has interesting implications for an understanding of humor. One might suggest, for example, that the pleasure that humor conveys parallels the pleasure we feel upon being physically touched. The importance of touch for primate and human emotional development has been well documented (Montagu, 1995). Humor has sometimes been characterized as a vicarious form of touching; sharing a joke has been likened to sharing a hug. Thus, if language evolved as a means of gossiping, humorous discourse may have evolved as a shorthand code for expressing attitudes toward others and toward life itself as a means of forming affectional ties with others who share those attitudes. As Lorenz noted, "Finding the same thing funny is not only a prerequisite to a real friendship, but very often the first step to its formation" (1963, p. 284). Thus, while language facilitates social bonding, humor in language may be a shortcut to making friends and, having made them, keeping them. With friends one can assume a tacit common ground that permits the sharing of humorous quips and anecdotes without having to spell things out or worrying about being misunderstood. In this view, both elements identified earlier as being critical—economy of expression and collaboration—are incorporated into the role proposed for humor.

CONCLUSION

Taken as a whole, the four perspectives on the evolutionary underpinnings of humor capture interesting and relevant aspects of the phenomenon: how it disrupts our routine (for the better), how it teaches and rewards us in our social interactions in fitness-relevant domains, how it can unify a group but also create group divisions, and finally, how it can create and strengthen bonds among intimates.

It is difficult to find ways to falsify evolutionary theories yet imperative to think along those lines. Some areas for future research were already discussed in the context of Chafe's theory and Weisfeld's theory of humor. Given that three of the four views discussed specifically highlight humor's social nature, one would want further data on the uses and perceptions of laughter and humor in same- and mixed-sex groups in a variety of contexts (e.g., Crawford & Gressley, 1991; Grammer, 1990; Quiros & Vaid, 1998). Studies of mate selection, for example, have shown that a sense of humor is an important element in self-presentation and is viewed as a highly desired trait in an ideal partner. Further research is needed to determine whether humor is used equally often or in the same way by men and women for self-presentation or sought after to the same degree in male and female partners alike. If, for example, humor's primary adaptive significance is as a form of male competition for female mates (as Alexander implies), one would expect to find certain forms of humor to predominate in men, with women taking only a passive role. However, if the affectional aspects of humor are what is critical (as Dunbar's view might suggest), one should find a more equal distribution of humor production and appreciation among men and women friends/partners. It remains for future research to test, clarify, and refine the existing hypotheses.

REFERENCES

Alexander, R. (1986). Ostracism and indirect reciprocity: The reproductive significance of humor. *Ethology and Sociobiology, 7,* 253–270.

Alexander, R. (1989). Evolution of the human psyche. In P. Mellars and C. Stringer (Eds.), *The human revolution: Behavioral and biological perspectives on the origins of modern humans* (pp. 455–513). Princeton, NJ: Princeton University Press.

Apte, M. (1985). *Humor and laughter: An anthropological approach.* Ithaca, NY: Cornell University Press.

Barreca, R. (1991). *They used to call me Snow White but I drifted.* New York: Penguin.

Bateson, G. (1969). The position of humor in human communication. In J. Levine (Ed.), *Motivation in humor* (pp. 159–166). New York: Atherton.

Bergson, H. (1950). *Le rire: Essaie sur la signification du comique.* Paris: Presses Universitaires.

Chafe, W. (1987). Humor as a disabling mechanism. *American Behavioral Scientist, 30(1),* 16–25.

Chiaro, D. (1992). *The language of jokes: Analysing verbal play.* London: Routledge.

Clinton, K. (1982). Making light: Another dimension—some notes on feminist humor. *Trivia, 39,* 37–42.

Crawford, M. (1995). *Talking difference: On gender and language.* London: Sage.

Crawford, M., & Gressley, D. (1991). Creativity, caring and context: Women's and men's accounts of humor preferences and practices. *Psychology of Women's Quarterly, 15,* 217–232.

Darwin, C. (1965). *The expression of emotions in man and animals.* Chicago: University of Chicago Press. (Original work published 1899)

Douglas, M. (1975). Jokes. In *Implicit meanings: Essays in anthropology* (pp. 90–114). London: Routledge.

Dunbar, R. (1996). *Grooming, gossip and the evolution of language.* Cambridge: Harvard University Press.

Freud, S. (1963). *Jokes and their relation to the unconscious.* New York: Norton.

Fry, W. (1987). Humor and paradox. *American Behavioral Scientist, 30,* 42–71.

Fry, W. (1993). The biology of humor. *Humor, 7(2),* 111–126.

Grammer, K. (1990). When strangers meet: Laughter and nonverbal signs of interest in opposite sex encounters. *Journal of Nonverbal Behavior, 14(4),* 209–236.

Koestler, A. (1964). *The act of creation.* New York: Macmillan.

Leacock, S. (1938). *Humor and humanity: An introduction to the study of humor.* New York: Henry Holt.

Lorenz, K. (1963). *On aggression.* New York: Bantam.

Maier, N. (1932). A Gestalt theory of humour. *British Journal of Psychology, 23,* 69–74.

Martineau, W. (1972). A model of the social function of humor. In J. Goldstein & P. McGhee (Eds.), *The psychology of humor: Theoretical perspectives and empirical issues.* New York: Academic Press.

McGhee, P. (1979). *Humor: Its origin and development.* San Francisco: W. H. Freeman.

McGhee, P., & Chapman, A. (Eds.). (1980). *Children's humor*. Chichester: John Wiley and Sons.

Montagu, A. (1995). Animadversions on the development of a theory of touch. In T. Field (Ed.), *Touch in early development* (pp. 1–10). Mahwah, NJ: Lawrence Erlbaum.

Morreall, J. (1983). *Taking laughter seriously*. Albany: State University of New York Press.

Morreall, J. (1989). The rejection of humor in Western thought. *Philosophy: East and West, 39*, 243–266.

Mulkay, M. (1988). *On humor: Its nature and its place in modern society*. Cambridge, U.K.: Polity.

Norrick, N. (1993). *Conversational joking: Humor in everyday talk*. Bloomington: Indiana University Press.

Palmer, J. (1994). *Taking humor seriously*. London: Routledge.

Provine, R. (1993). Laughter punctuates speech: Linguistic, social and gender contexts of laughter. *Ethology, 95*, 291–298.

Provine, R. (1996). The study of laughter provides a novel approach to the mechanisms and evolution of vocal production and perception and social behavior. *American Scientist, 84*, 38–45.

Pugh, G. (1977). *The biological basis of human values*. New York: Basic Books.

Quiros, A. & Vaid, J. (1998, February). *Gendered perceptions of humor uses and effectiveness*. Paper presented at the annual meeting of the Eastern Psychological Association, Boston.

Radcliffe-Brown, A. (1965). *Structure and function in primitive society*. New York: Free Press.

Richman, J. (1995). The lifesaving function of humor with the depressed and suicidal elderly. *The Gerontologist, 35*, 271–273.

Siegel, L. (1987). *Laughing matters: Comic tradition in India*. Chicago: University of Chicago Press.

Staley, R. & Derks, P. (1995). Structural incongruity and humor appreciation. *Humor, 8*, 97–134.

Thorson, J., & Powell, F. (1993). Development and validation of a multidimensional sense of humor scale. *Journal of Clinical Psychology, 49*, 13–23.

van Hoof, J. (1972). A comparative approach to the phylogeny of laughter and smiling. In R. Hinde (Ed.), *Nonverbal communication*. Cambridge: Cambridge University Press.

Ward, T., Smith, S., & Vaid, J. (Eds.). (1997). *Creative thought: An investigation of conceptual structures and processes*. Washington, DC: American Psychological Association.

Weisfeld, G. (1993). The adaptive value of humor and laughter. *Ethology and Sociobiology, 14*, 141–169.

8

Evolutionary Memory

HOLLY L. HUSTON, DAVID H. ROSEN, AND STEVEN M. SMITH

Researchers in the scientific fields of ethology, linguistics, visual perception, and anthropology have investigated and described the presence of innate collective predispositions to biological development and social behavior. To designate these predispositions as innate means that they are based in biology and transmitted genetically. To designate them as evolutionary means that they are universal and shared in common by all members of a species. In the behaviorally based study of ethology, researchers such as Lorenz (1969) and Tinbergen (1953) investigated instincts and hypothesized the existence of an "inborn basis of knowledge" and "innate releasing mechanisms," respectively. Both Lorenz and Tinbergen theorized that certain types of behavior and expressions of learning are programmed or hardwired within the central nervous system of a species. In linguistics, Chomsky (1968) posited that an inborn "language acquisition device" permitted children to acquire language. Some cognitive models of language acquisition (Marslen-Wilson, 1980) have postulated the existence of "primitives," or basic phonemic building blocks, from which language can be constructed. The existence of a small, finite set of linguistic primitives may be sufficient to construct any language currently spoken in the world. These primitives are assumed to be common to all members of the human species. Biederman (1987) proposed the concept of "geons," types of simple visual primitives from which more complex objects, such as symbols, can be visually constructed. Again, geons are considered to be based in biology and are structured in the brain's perceptual mechanisms. In anthropology, Levi-Strauss (1967) developed the concept of "infrastructures," which are commonly shared unconscious processes that give rise to, and direct, cultural universals. Furthermore, Schuster and Carpenter (1986) have carefully cataloged similarities in symbols and artistic patterns from all over the world.

In psychology, Jung (1964) postulated the existence of an innate structure of human recognition and recollection based on "archetypes" and the "collective unconscious," which can be thought of as an evolutionary form of memory. Theoretically, the contents of the collective unconscious are made up of the common, repeated experiences of all humankind, accumulated since the origin of the species. The contents of the collective unconscious are thought to owe their existence to heredity (Stevens, 1983, 1993) and, therefore, like "geons" and "innate releasing mechanisms," are considered to be biologically based. Within the collective unconscious, Jung (1964) posited the existence of archetypes: affectively charged predispositions to forms, instincts, and patterns of behavior. For example the mother–infant attachment bond, à la Bowlby (1969), can be thought of as based on the mother archetype, that is, a psychobiological template for organizing maternal behavior. Archetypes exist in two states: potential and actualized (Jacobi, 1973). Actualized archetypes often appear as an archetypal image or representation such as a symbol and are considered to be inherently meaningful. Symbols are images that convey a meaning greater than that of the pattern or picture itself. According to Jung, archetypal symbols transcend both time and culture, making them truly collective and universal phenomena (Jung, 1964). These symbols may result from human attempts to assign form to innate archetypal structures.

Despite the convergence of Jung's thought with the thinking of scholars in diverse disciplines, Jung's theories of archetypes and the collective unconscious have been virtually ignored by researchers due to their apparent experimental untestability. This chapter describes empirical research that seeks to answer several questions about Jung's theory of archetypes and their meaningful relationship to symbols. Jung analyzed and compared symbols and their meanings that were common to various cultures at different periods in history, including cultures that developed with no knowledge of each other. An example of one such collective archetypal symbol is the snake. In India, from the prehistoric to the present time, the snake has symbolized the rise of the kundalini energy in the body and is viewed as a powerful natural healing force (Jung, 1968). In the region of the Lower Pecos in Texas serpent motifs expressed in rock art appear to have been used in healing rituals that occurred about 5,000 years ago (Shafer, 1986). In ancient Greece, Asklepios, the divine physician, carried a staff with an entwined snake (Kerenyi, 1959). In various forms, the snake remains a symbol of today's health professions. Nevertheless, the advent of modern mass communication makes this type of comparative research more complicated to conduct, because few cultures now exist in isolation, making it increasingly difficult to sort out what has been learned (acquired) from what has been inherited (innate).

Researchers in the area of cognitive psychology (Kihlstrom, 1987; Schacter, 1987) have developed a renewed interest in the unconscious part of the mind that contains information and processes that influence our behavior without our awareness. Fodor (1983) has proposed that the mind contains innate, domain-specific cognitive modules orchestrating such activities such as language and visual perception, hardwired in the brain and operating outside conscious control. Methodologies, such as indirect memory tasks and priming (Thomson & Tulving, 1970; Tulving, Schacter, & Stark, 1982), have been developed to facilitate research into the unconscious, a concept whose theoretical validity had been questioned because it did not appear to be experimentally testable. The authors thought that some of the methodologies developed by cognitive psychologists might be useful in investigating Jung's theories of innate unconscious collective memory as manifested by archetypal symbols and their meanings.

EXPERIMENTAL EVIDENCE OF EVOLUTIONARY (ARCHETYPAL) COLLECTIVE MEMORY

We have investigated three basic questions about Jung's theory of archetypes. First, are archetypes associated with commonly accepted universal meanings? According to the theory, archetypal symbols have emotion (affect) and meaning (cognition) associated with them that can be expected to be somewhat stable across time and place. The Archetypal Symbol Inventory (ASI) was developed by Rosen, Smith, Huston, and Gonzalez (1991) to investigate this question. The ASI consists of 40 archetypal symbols and their associated meanings. Whereas some of the symbols are relatively obscure, such as the Egyptian symbol for birth, others are more commonly known, for example, the heart.

Second, if archetypal symbols are found to be related to their meanings, are such associations conscious or unconscious? Our investigations into this question utilizing the ASI provide evidence that the associations are unconscious, and these findings are discussed later.

Third, if knowledge of these symbols and their associated meanings is found to be unconscious, then is it learned or not? At this point, we can only infer that knowledge of archetypal symbols and their associated meanings is innate. A conclusive answer to this question is beyond the scope of the current chapter, but we suggest some ways that researchers could address this question.

Five experiments, as part of two separate studies, have been conducted by Rosen et al. (1991) and by Huston (1992) to specifically address the first two questions. Two studies (Rosen et al., 1991, Experiment III, & Huston, 1992, Experiment I) were conducted using a simple paired-associate learning task with appropriate controls. In this task, subjects were first shown the symbol-word pairs, then after a break, they were shown only the symbols and asked to recall the associated word.[1] Research in human memory and learning (Thomson & Tulving, 1970) has shown that words are remembered better if they are cued by associated and related words (like dog and bone), rather than by unassociated/ unrelated words (like dog and telephone). Our results using this method, with ASI symbol-word pairs, demonstrated that subjects do associate the archetypal symbols with their putative meanings.

Three additional studies (Rosen et al., 1991, Experiments I & II, and Huston,

1992, Experiment II) addressed the second question of whether this knowledge of the association between the symbol and its meaning is conscious or unconscious. Subjects in these experiments were found to be unable to generate the correct ASI meanings or even closely related meanings for the archetypal symbols (as determined by a *Roget's Thesaurus*, 1942); even using a lenient criterion, subjects could generate only 5% of the ASI meanings (Rosen et al., 1991, Experiment I). Subjects have also been unable to pair the symbols with their associated meanings in a matching task (only 6.5% success) (Rosen et al., 1991, Experiment II). Furthermore, subjects were unable to correctly name a symbol when given part of the word in an uncued word-fragment completion task (only 16% success) (Huston, 1992, Experiment II). This information indicates that people have little or no *conscious* knowledge of the relationship between the archetypal symbols and their meanings. Although this evidence does not conclusively demonstrate that the symbols are innate, rather than learned, it does suggest that the association between archetypal symbols and their meanings appears to be unconscious and merits further investigation.

In Rosen et al.'s (1991) paired-associate, cued-recall study, matched verbal meanings associated with their correctly assigned archetypal symbols were recalled at a significantly higher rate [$F(1, 234) = 67.91$, $p < .0001$] than mismatched meanings and symbols. In this study, 54% of the meanings for matched ASI symbol/word pairs were accurately recalled, compared to only 46% of the meanings for mismatched ASI symbol/word pairs ($N = 235$), indicating that the accurate associations are known to the subjects, but at the collective unconscious level of the human mind.

In a subsequent study conducted by Huston (1992), which included two extra symbols for methodological purposes, subjects studied paired-associates and were given either a typical cued-recall test (Huston, 1992, Experiment I) or a word-fragment completion task (Huston, 1992, Experiment II). For example, the fragment H__A__T__ (health) was given with ASI symbol of a serpent or snake, and the subject was asked to make a complete word from the fragment. The word fragments should serve as an additional aid to memory, even for mismatched pairs. Although the word fragments improved recall of all test items, it was still the case that matched paired archetypal symbols and meanings were again completed at a significantly greater rate [$F(1, 254) = 120.94$, $p < .0001$] than mismatched paired symbols and meanings.

It is noteworthy that the best items in the ASI were equally effective in both the Rosen et al. (1991) study and the Huston (1992) study. In an item analysis of the ASI, 100% (13/13) of the top third repeated as being associated with their meanings. In the middle third, 93% (13/14) were appropriately matched. Therefore, out of the top 27 archetypal symbol/word pairs, 96% (26/27) were matched to their meanings. Figure 8.1 presents the Archetypal Symbol Inventory-Revised or ASI-R, a 30-item revised ASI. This includes the addition of one new symbol (the yin/yang) that was effective in both conditions of the Huston (1992) study. These 30 archetypal symbol/word pairs have been empir-

Figure 8.1
Archetypal Symbol Inventory Revised (ASI-R)

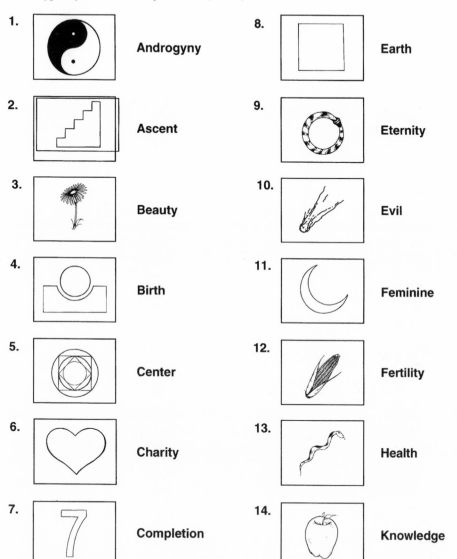

1.	Androgyny		8.	Earth
2.	Ascent		9.	Eternity
3.	Beauty		10.	Evil
4.	Birth		11.	Feminine
5.	Center		12.	Fertility
6.	Charity		13.	Health
7.	Completion		14.	Knowledge

Figure 8.1 (continued)

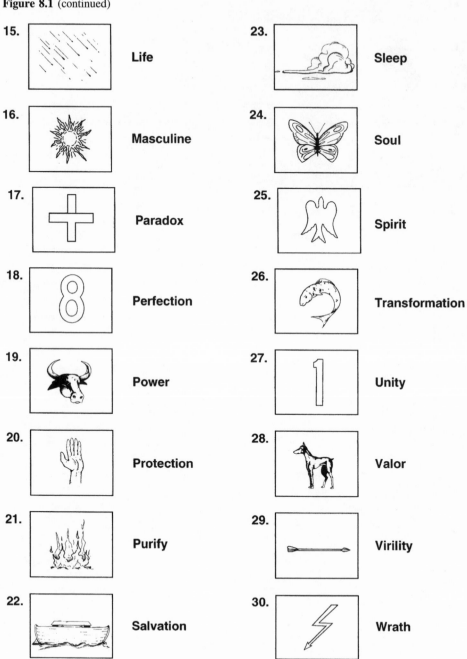

15.   **Life**

16.   **Masculine**

17.   **Paradox**

18.   **Perfection**

19.   **Power**

20.   **Protection**

21.   **Purify**

22.   **Salvation**

23.   **Sleep**

24.   **Soul**

25.   **Spirit**

26.   **Transformation**

27.   **Unity**

28.   **Valor**

29.   **Virility**

30.   **Wrath**

ically demonstrated to be strongly associated with each other, even though the knowledge of this association seems to be unconscious. The ASI-R, therefore, ought to be a useful instrument in future research exploring the existence of unconscious collective memory.

A POSSIBLE MECHANISM FOR EVOLUTIONARY MEMORY

Why are these archetypal associations operating beyond the subjects' awareness? A possible explanation for this is that the subjects are unable to consciously retrieve these associated meanings because they were never learned experientially (realm of the personal unconscious). We suggest that these associations are unconsciously available to the subjects because they are innate (realm of the collective unconscious). This would account for the subjects' ability to retrieve correctly paired associations (once primed) at a significant level without being able to consciously generate or match them.

We propose that, initially, archetypal symbols and their meanings (matched and mismatched pairs) are transmitted through conscious perceptual mechanisms and the personal unconscious. If the symbol and meaning are accurately matched, we postulate that an archetypal affective charge in the collective unconscious is triggered that then allows for later personal unconscious recognition. In other words, subjects remember better if there are existing knowledge structures (the archetypes[2] and their associated meanings). Therefore, later, when only the symbols are shown, the subjects know and report the accurate meanings at a significantly higher rate since they fit with something they already know unconsciously (evolutionary memory).

The phenomenon that has been demonstrated in these studies is a memory priming effect (see Figure 8.2). When symbols are paired with the accurate associated meaning word, subjects exhibit a higher frequency of recall for the words than when the symbols are paired with inaccurate or mismatched words. It is clear that when a symbol is presented along with its associated matched meaning, there is a priming effect for later accurate recall. Therefore, presentation of the symbol with the correct meaning actually primes and facilitates the memory for the word, while there is not such priming effect or facilitation when a symbol is paired with a word that is not its true meaning. This is the basis for the earlier supposition that the symbols and meanings are somehow cognitively and affectively connected or associated.

Previous research indicates that the right hemisphere of the brain appears to be the seat of archetypal patterns and symbols and their affectively charged visual images, whereas the left hemisphere seems to be the seat of verbal and cognitive knowledge (Gazzaniga, 1973; Galin, 1974, 1977; Rossi, 1977; Yates, 1994). The facilitation of memory when symbols are paired with matched meanings is theorized to be an interhemispherical connection, mediated by the corpus

Figure 8.2
Proposed Mechanism for Evolutionary Memory

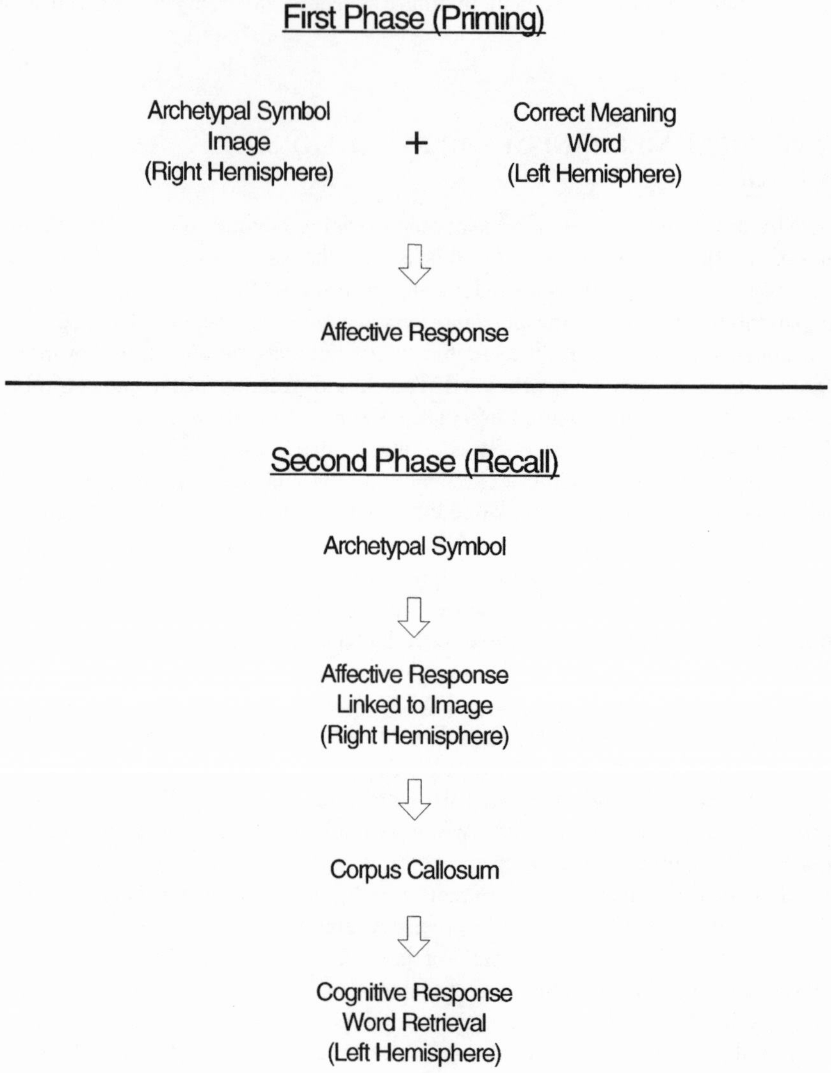

First Phase (Priming)

Archetypal Symbol		Correct Meaning
Image	**+**	Word
(Right Hemisphere)		(Left Hemisphere)

⇩

Affective Response

Second Phase (Recall)

Archetypal Symbol

⇩

Affective Response
Linked to Image
(Right Hemisphere)

⇩

Corpus Callosum

⇩

Cognitive Response
Word Retrieval
(Left Hemisphere)

callosum, which allows for the recall of the accurate meaning of the archetypal symbol triggered by the affective response.

Theoretically speaking, it would probably be feasible to say that the presentation of an archetypal symbol along with its associated accurate meaning activates the constellation of an archetypal image in the right cerebral hemisphere. This constellation of the archetypal symbol and its associated meaning in the left cerebral hemisphere apparently catalyzes a priming of memory for the association.

As noted before, it is theorized that archetypes are affectively charged. That is, there is always an affective response involved in the activation and constellation of an archetypal image. From this, there follows the possibility that the presentation of an archetypal symbol along with its putative meaning produces an affective response, while the presentation of the same symbol with an inaccurate meaning does not seem to produce such a response. This is consistent with the finding (Huston, 1992) that subjects were more likely to accurately recall an item when they gave the pair a rating of "well-matched" but were more likely to miss an item when they gave it a "neutral" rating. It may be the case that the mechanism underlying the priming effect is an affectively mediated reaction.

Subjects in both sets of studies seemed to know, based on intuition or evolutionary memory, that certain symbol-meaning pairs went together. This relates to several studies reported on by Pierce in Chapter 6 in this volume, specifically those of Fiore and Schooler (1998), Hellige (1993), and Semmes (1968), which stress the importance of the right cerebral hemisphere, the corpus collosum, and integration with the left cerebral hemisphere in this type of insightful knowledge.

QUESTIONS TO BE ADDRESSED BY ADDITIONAL RESEARCH

This work leads to several areas for future research. Research ought to focus on the affective response associated with symbol meaning presentations and whether or not this affective response seems to be the trigger for priming evolutionary (archetypal) memory. Visual-field effect studies using split-brain patients (Yates, 1994) might also be useful to study this memory priming effect when the symbol/word pairs are presented to only one cerebral hemisphere or the other. Additionally, innovative research with children would be useful in order to more conclusively demonstrate that this knowledge is innate rather than acquired. Studies using the ASI-R with amnesiacs à la Graf & Schacter (1985) might also shed light on the distinction between personal and collective memory due to the fact that amnesiacs experience varying degrees of impairment of personal memory. We expect that amnesiacs would be able to accurately associate archetypal symbols and their meanings, even though their memory for other types of information of a personal nature is impaired. Finally, our work needs to be replicated cross-culturally to lend further support to the theorized universality of the meanings of the archetypal symbols.

CONCLUDING COMMENT

Just as "geons" are theorized to function as the building blocks of visual perception in humans, we propose that "archetypes" serve as the "primitives" of evolutionary memory for symbolic meanings. Much as particular animal instincts stimulate biological unfolding and maturation, so human archetypes could be considered to stimulate psychological unfolding, maturation, and evolutionary adaptation. Additionally, with the resurgence of investigative activity concerning unconscious memory, this chapter expands this area of research to include unconscious collective or evolutionary memory.

NOTES

Portions of this chapter were presented at the Conference entitled "Evolution of the Psyche" held at Texas A&M University, September 13–14, 1996. The authors are grateful to presenters and participants for helpful comments and suggestions. Also the authors wish to acknowledge the assistance of Randolph C. Arnau and Laura Anderson. The input of Angela Lozano, Mary Lenn Dixon, Ernie Goetz, and Jyotsna Vaid was greatly appreciated.

1. To be specific, subjects were initially exposed to each symbol-word pair for eight seconds with a second between exposures. Following the exposure to all symbol-word pairs (half matched and half mismatched as well as randomly ordered) there was a two-minute break. Then each symbol was shown alone again for eight seconds, and the subjects were asked to recall the associated word they had seen before.

2. It is noteworthy that Plato used the term "archetypes" to represent archaic, primordial, and universal ideas and images that were inborn.

REFERENCES

Biederman, I. (1987). Recognition-by-components: A theory of human image understanding. *Psychological Review, 94*, 115–147.

Bowlby, J. (1969). *Attachment and loss*. New York: Basic Books.

Chomsky, N. (1968). *Language and the mind*. New York: Harcourt Brace Jovanovich.

Fiore, S. M., & Schooler, J. W. (1998). Right hemisphere contributions to creative problem solving: Converging evidence for divergent thinking. In M. Beeman & C. Chiarello (Eds.), *Right hemisphere language comprehension: Perspectives from cognitive neuroscience*. Mahwah, NJ: Lawrence Erlbaum.

Fodor, J. (1983). *The modularity of mind*. Cambridge: MIT/Bradford.

Galin, D. (1974). Implications for psychiatry of left and right cerebral specialization: A neurophysiological context for unconscious processes. *Archives of General Psychiatry, 31*, 572–583.

Galin, D. (1977). Lateral specialization and psychiatric issues: Speculation on the development and evolution of consciousness. *Annals of the New York Academy of Science, 299*, 397–411.

Gazzaniga, M. S. (1973). The split brain in man. In R. Ornstein (Ed.), *The nature of human consciousness* (pp. 87–100). New York: Freeman.

Graf, P., & Schacter, D. (1985). Implicit and explicit memory for associations in normal and amnesic subjects. *Journal of Experimental Psychology: Learning, Memory and Cognition, 11*, 501–518.

Hellige, J. B. (1993). *Hemisphere asymmetry*. Cambridge, MA: Harvard University Press.

Huston, H. (1992). Direct and indirect tests of archetypal memory. Master's thesis in psychology, Texas A&M University.

Jacobi, J. (1973). *The psychology of C. G. Jung.* New Haven, CT: Yale University Press.

Jung, C. G. (1964). *Man and his symbols.* New York: Doubleday.

Jung, C. G. (1968). In H. Read, M. Fordham, & G. Adler (Eds.), *The Collected Works of C. G. Jung* (Vol. 12). Princeton, NJ: Princeton University Press.

Kerenyi, C. (1959). *Asklepios: Archetypal image of the physician's existence.* New York: Pantheon.

Kihlstrom, J. F. (1987). The cognitive unconscious. *Science, 237,* 1445–1452.

Levi-Strauss, C. (1967). *Structural anthropology.* Garden City, NY: Anchor.

Lorenz, K. Z. (1969). Innate bases of learning. In K. H. Pribram (Ed.), *On the biology of learning* (pp. 13–93). New York: Harcourt, Brace, & World.

Marslen-Wilson, W. (1980). Optimal efficiency in human speech processing. Unpublished manuscript. Nijmegen, The Netherlands: Max-Planck Institut fur Psycholinguistik.

Roget's international thesaurus (1942). New York: Thomas Y. Crowell.

Rosen, D., Smith, S., Huston, H., & Gonzalez, G. (1991). Empirical study of associations between symbols and their meanings: Evidence of collective unconscious (archetypal) memory. *Journal of Analytical Psychology, 36,* 211–228.

Rossi, E. (1977). The cerebral hemispheres in analytical psychology. *Journal of Analytical Psychology, 22,* 32–51.

Schacter, D. (1987). Implicit memory: History and current status. *Journal of Experimental Psychology: Learning, Memory, and Cognition, 13(3),* 501–518.

Schuster, C., & Carpenter, E. (1986). *Social symbolism in ancient and tribal art: A record of traditional continuity: Vol. 1.* New York: Rock Foundation.

Semmes, J. (1968). Hemisphere specialization: A possible clue to mechanism. *Neuropsychologia, 6,* 11–26.

Shafer, H. (1986). *Ancient Texans: Rock art and lifeways along the lower Pecos.* San Antonio: Texas Monthly Press.

Stevens, A. (1983). *Archetypes: A natural history of the self.* New York: Quill.

Stevens, A. (1993). *The two million-year-old self.* College Station: Texas A&M University Press.

Thomson, D., & Tulving, E. (1970). Associative encoding and retrieval: Weak and strong cues. *Journal of Experimental Psychology, 86,* 255–262.

Tinbergen, N. (1953). *Social behavior in animals.* New York: Wiley.

Tulving, E., Schacter, D., & Stark, H. (1982). Priming effects in word-fragment completion are independent of recognition memory. *Journal of Experimental Psychology: Learning, Memory and Cognition, 8,* 336–342.

Yates, J. L. (1994). *Psyche and the split brain.* Lanham, MD: University Press of America.

9

On the Evolution of Interest: Cases in Serpent Art

BRETT COOKE

INTRODUCTION

Art is a medium that by definition should exemplify interest. As Kathryn Coe (1992) surmises, the aim of art is to draw attention. It does not have to provide us with beauty or pleasure, but it has to be noticed to be viable (Aiken, 1992). If it fails to catch our eye, it is not likely to be either influential or replicated. As a result of the nonlinear process of selection that is the immediate consequence of this self-organizing dialectic, works of art will tend to compete for our attention by focusing on topics that most effectively capture our interest. We are not disappointed, for artistic texts everywhere make it quite clear that certain themes elicit strong interest and do so in a manner that may persist or be repeated almost infinitely. Other issues that, by contrast, attract little attention are almost wholly ignored. Indeed, objective study shows that our attention is apportioned in a disproportionate manner.

Obviously, not everything is of equal interest, but rather, as art indicates, our attention span is quite skewed in favor of activities closely relevant to our biological advantage. Patterns of artistic imagery probably reflect our shaping by means of natural selection. Can we ever fail to be intrigued by representations of reproductive strategies, including both mate selection and the troublesome process of parenting, matters pertaining to justice and property, the possibility of genetic mutations, and various phobias? In other words, narrative plotlines the world over are replete with standard motifs dealing with romantic love, concern over the fate of children, a fascination with gold and precious objects, the maintenance of a viable society, and the mixture of curiosity and terror that characterizes our concern regarding things that might cause sudden death, such as the serpent. In the meantime, many of the activities that actually assure our livelihood—commerce, industry, education—are underrepresented compared to the actual time we devote to them.

Most, if not all, of the themes that readily attract our attention are rooted in real concerns that probably distinguished reproductive success from failure in the environment of the Pleistocene. It stands to reason that the manner in which we direct our attention was shaped in these ancient conditions. This consideration leads me to propose that we can use the tenets of natural selection to account for what I term differential interest, the uneven attention we render to diverse facets of our environment. Since we share virtually the same evolutionary heritage, these patterns of asymmetrically apportioned interest are largely common to all of us. This leads to a further prediction, namely, that we have learned to discern this asymmetry in each other, at least intuitively, the better to utilize it for our own selective advantage. We generally sense how to attract someone's attention, whether by pointing to real concerns, like the "epigenetic rules" mentioned in the previous paragraph, or merely to their images, separated from their reality (Lumsden & Wilson, 1983). As we shall see, we can augment our ability to attract attention by compounding our references to points of genetically prepared interest or, even more, by counterpoising them. The arts provide ample evidence of how we have exploited this asymmetry; works of art largely consist of intentionally created artifacts, not accidental or found objects. Indeed, by merely recognizing this asymmetry and how we have taken advantage of it, we are taking steps toward the articulation of a new "biopoetics," a theory of the arts that we can construct on evolutionary principles. Evolutionary psychology thus can help us address the difficult issue of artistic value, how it is that some works of art attract more interest than others and, in the case of some masterpieces, exert an inexhaustible hold on our attention. I propose to investigate this potential biopoetics by uniting art with something also of undeniable interest, snakes. Representations of snakes in art are widespread both in contemporary cultures and in archaeological and historical records; by their omnipresence they constitute a well-recognized artistic universal. For this reason snake depictions provide nearly ideal evidence in support of the evolution of interest.

SNAKE IMAGES IN ART: A CASE STUDY IN BIOPOETICS

Art is a hypertrophied expression of our partially innate inclination to devote incommensurate attention to certain phenomena. Inevitably, focusing on one object or event requires giving other objects and events in our proximate environment relatively little consideration. With limited mental capacity, time, energy, and, consequently, focus, how are we to cope with virtually infinite sensory and nonsensory data available to us if we do not preselect on some basis what we will give our attention to? As a case of such preselection, we have no problem accounting for the phobia regarding snakes that we share with some primates. Phobias amount to a heightened context-sensitivity that greatly accelerates our reaction time in actual encounters; for our forebears in the Pleistocene this quickened response certainly yielded an adaptive advantage, compensating for a loss in objectivity. Such a phobia is easily transmitted and absorbed, even in the medium of artistic images, where the number of ophidian forms is truly legion. Clearly, this greatly accelerated learning curve gives us evidence of a powerfully biased and undying interest in the serpent that can be elicited by images alone.

What is particularly significant about art is that it works to attract our attention usually without being anything other than an image of something. Rather, according to Ellen Dissanayake's (1992) notion of "making special," art is so fashioned as to attract our interest. It overcomes its lack of immediate utility often by elevating experience to a supranormal level. Dissanayake's observation seems to explain why snakes are universally depicted in art in an exaggerated and even sometimes anachronistic manner; they are given a presence that commonly exceeds realism. The immediate reason is quite simple: when it comes to grabbing your attention, the snake rarely fails to make a great impact. Also, we often want to be moved by art, a function that snake imagery is extraordinarily adept at performing. To introduce the snake into a text is playing with fire; certain emotional and, therefore, aesthetic consequences are all but inevitable, thanks to our highly primed phobia regarding ophidian images. Any phenomenon that evokes hysterical reactions with statistically anomalous frequency begs for study in terms of ultimate causes per natural selection. But what is most advantageous for evolutionary psychologists is that snake imagery sometimes confounds proximate explanations. Ophidian images are often found in environments that have no snakes. As a result, we are forced to attend to the genetic influences that possibly underlie this strange behavior if we are to find an adequate stimulus. For this reason we examine the art of three largely snakeless realms: ancient and medieval Ireland, the age of nineteenth-century European decadence, and the twentieth-century genre of science fiction. For what seem to be genetic reasons, all three are teeming with serpentine forms.

In his brief chapter on "The Serpent" in *Biophilia*, Edward O. Wilson (1984) set out what can be received as a basic evolutionary model for the selection of artistic themes, indeed, for interest itself. Working largely on the basis of Balaji Mundkur's monumental study *The Cult of the Serpent*, Wilson suggests a genetic dialectic. A species must first be exposed to a significant source of selection pressure. Mundkur says that we obtained our ophidiophobia (fear of snakes) from our primate predecessors; this possibly originated in the early Miocene period with the Proto-Simiae about 25 million years ago. Not only were venemous snakes present in the EEA (environment of evolutionary adaptation), but they included precursors of the much-feared cobra. As a result, we appear to share a genetically based regard for snakes with a number of species of monkeys, but not, for example, with our more distant relatives, the lemurs of Madagascar, which followed a different evolutionary path (Mundkur, 1983, p. 224). Second, there also must be a sufficient period of exposure to translate differential success in coping into genetic information that can be passed on to descendants. Our former habitats are still crawling with vipers, and snakes have been in close proximity to the genus *homo* virtually throughout our history. The phobia often leads to exaggeration; because our apprehension grows out of proportion to the actual danger, all the better that we should flee it. Drawing on Mundkur's extensive database of information, Wilson notes how in depictions of the mythical serpent, the snake gains powers never observed in nature (1984, pp. 99–100). Finally, ophidian imagery may reach environmental release, whereby the development of this theme can proceed free of its original stimulus, actual snakes. Although our race has been in intimate contact with snakes in virtually every native habitat, there are some exceptions, notably, Ireland, where snakes seem to have been totally absent since the Ice Age. Despite their apparent absence, their images persisted in Irish art. As Wilson noted in *On Human Nature*, such anachronistic phobias constitute wonderful evidence of the hold that our evolutionary history continues to maintain on us despite massive changes in our living conditions: "It seems significant that they are most often evoked by snakes, spiders, rats, heights, close spaces, and other elements that were potentially dangerous in our ancient environment, but only rarely by modern artifacts such as knives, guns, and electrical outlets" (1978, p. 70).

Wilson and Mundkur both note the great variety of associations conveyed by snakes, but they are unable to account for the apparently contradictory nature of ophidian imagery; for example, snakes are common symbols of both extreme evil and great good. An adequate explanation of the semiotic variation of serpent images may help settle a series of issues: (1) why the snake is treated so specially, (2) how it gains its strangely positive associations, (3) why so many features constitute extreme exaggerations of ophidian qualities, and (4) how these associations interact and amplify one another. In order to make sense of some of the semiotic ramifications of serpent images, we offer seven propositions on the evolution of interest, all illustrated by our artistic treatment of snakes.

Differential Interest Reflects Genetic Biases

Differential interest pertains to the snake, whose image is commonly associated with each of our semiotic issues. As Levy-Strauss said, snakes are "bons à penser," good to think about (cited in Mundkur, 1983, p. 39). They rarely are regarded with tedium. It is hard to tear one's eye away from this *fascinating* creature. In an instant they can make a life-or-death difference; therefore, they deserve our attention and continue to hold it, even from the pages of a book. As a result, they provide an artist with a ready supply of aesthetic power.

What is especially curious is that in art snakes are given a prominence much greater than the actual selection pressure they exert on us in almost any environment. Mundkur noted that both spiders and scorpions cause about nine times as many deaths as snakebite in Mexico, yet the Aztec pantheon was swarming with snakelike beings, leaving the arachnids quite unrepresented (Mundkur, 1983, pp. 51, 93).

A strikingly similar pattern of response in traditional literature may be discerned in the hundreds of entries devoted to snake, serpent, reptile, and dragon themes in Stith Thompson's *Motif-Index of Folk Literature* (1955–1958). All four can be regarded as the same animal, since their features are clearly derived from those of snakes. The volume of stories about these ophidian creatures simply dwarfs the oral representation of the far more dangerous arachnids and is rivaled only by the ever-present threat of disease. Thompson lists 72 themes involving dragons, 34 with unspecified large reptiles, 173 about serpents, and 232 pertaining to snakes, which sums to a total of 511. By contrast, there are only 12 motifs about scorpions and 56 concerning spiders; arachnid themes amount to less than a seventh of the ophidian subjects. If Mundkur's mortality rate for Mexico is at all representative, the greater mortality caused by scorpions and spiders, compared to that of snakelike creatures, is understated in narratives by a factor of more than 60 times. The effects of germs are more comparable to those of reptiles: there are 32 motifs involving disease; illness 30, sickness 60, and plague 28, but the total of 150 is still less than 30% of the total motifs dealing with serpents and similar beasts (Thompson, 1955–1958).[1] Keep in mind that these numbers involve only *themes*; the actual number of stories, which is difficult to determine, is much higher.

Elsewhere Thompson estimates claims that there are on the order of 1,100 folktales worldwide involving dragons alone (cited in Evans, 1987, p. 49). This interest in dragons also persists today in hundreds of children's books and other forms of juvenile literature (Evans, 1987, p. 50). A similar pattern may be found in science fiction literature. My survey of about 6,700 titles noted 41 references to ophidian creatures, with only 13 to disease and 8 to arachnids.[2] Whereas about 1 in 150 book titles makes a probable reference to snakes, spiders and scorpions are mentioned at only about one-sixth this frequency, a proportion matched by their representation in Thompson's *Motif-Index*. Once again, microscopic life, which is much more likely to harm us, registers at less than a third of the frequency of ophidians.

Indeed, a myriad of titles play exploitative and repetitive variations on our phobia of the snake. The fact that in English alone 116 science fiction and fantasy books were published with titles *beginning* with the word "dragon" between 1985 and 1991 supports our notion that the serpent elicits an untiring interest (Reginald, 1992, pp. 1165–1166). Such is the virtually involuntary attention evoked by serpents that some science fiction books mention them on the cover, almost as if only to catch a reader's eye. I was disappointed to find that Ivan Yefremov's famous story "The Heart of a Serpent" refers only to a constellation, much as Frank Herbert's *The Dragon in the Sea* describes not some sort of marine reptile but a submarine. Despite the apparent deception of such false covers, these ophidian allusions have served their writers well by merely attracting our attention; subsequently, the snakeless text has a chance to complete the task of art, that of holding our interest, something that would never have been possible if the work had been ignored in the first place.

Another illustration of the same principle may be found in advertising art, where images of snakes are utilized not to sell snakes but, instead, automobile alarm systems and tires. As Madison Avenue knows, pictures of something crucial to our reproductive fitness, such as a beautiful woman, can readily be exploited to direct interest to something else. We can quite understand the connection of snakes with deterrence, but they can also be attractive: surely, many people would wish to drive a Cobra and wear a boa.

Of course, these are not snakes but only their images. We need not agree with Andre Agassi that image is everything, but it will often suffice to evoke a phobic response. Anthony Stevens described to me a patient who would immediately and violently hurl away any magazine in which she saw a picture of a snake (personal communication, 1996). With snakes, rumor of fantasy is often every bit as alarming as the slithering intruder. The part, indeed, may well suffice for the whole in that the image may be treated as if it were the real phenomenon. When encountering an actual snake in the wild, a glimpse of its sinuous tail, its scaly back, or its squinty eyes should raise an alarm. Given the prospect of sudden death, it is far better to err by beating a quick retreat without the benefit of fulsome identification than to linger and risk snakebite (LeDoux, 1994, p. 56). Mundkur describes experiments with American coeds in which the mere mention of a snake often brought about a phobic response (Mundkur, 1983, pp. 239–240). On the other hand, repeated actual exposure may evoke contempt, as a number of informants in our snake-infested Brazos County tell me. Since mundane actuality seems to curb our fantasy, we may be more likely to fantasize about the snake in a relatively snake-free milieu. Nature accomplished adaptation not by striving for perfection but by achieving minor selective advantages. These gains may compensate for relatively harmless flaws in perception. One important consideration is that natural selection operates, to a large extent, on the basis of images, leaving plenty of room for slippage. We can be fooled. That perceptual slips are often permitted in nature bears enormous consequences for the arts, which are thereby empowered to exploit our phobic responses.

Differential Interest Correlates with Issues of Adaptive Significance

Given our limited resources of time, energy, and attention, it pays us to focus on those factors that are most likely to yield a significant selective advantage. There is little point to wasting much time on matters that are known to be trivial in terms of our fitness. It stands to reason that the closer a particular behavior lies to the issue of reproductive success, then the more likely it will conform to tenets of evolutionary psychology. We further suggest that as one approaches that necessary bottleneck of genetic influence from one generation to another, the more readily will behavior elicit our interest. The rationale is quite simple.

If the correct performance in a given sphere is somehow crucial to our fitness, then it behooves us to at least pay more careful attention. This line of thinking helps us understand why representational art is so rife with issues such as mate selection, reciprocal altruism, and our common phobias.

Mundkur (1983) outlined the likely genetic link between the initial danger posed by snakes and the special awe we hold for them. Natural selection does not dictate a necessary phobia of snakes and similar hazards but, rather, a greatly accelerated and facilitated tendency to acquire such a response. Snakes constituted humankind's earliest cult and certainly one of its strongest, a point that is reflected in the sheer volume of ophidian artifacts found all over the world. According to Wilson, this reflects a significant selection pressure, one exerted on each continent by venomous snakes. Over large portions of Asia and Africa, 5 persons per 100,000 die each year from snakebites (Wilson, 1984, p. 96). These figures must have been much higher prior to the advent of modern medicine, a consideration that suggests why the snake continues to earn our respect.

Apart from actual dangers, ideas, like sensory data, compete for our attention. Not only can they help catch our eye, as we saw with advertising art and science fiction titles, but they also work to energize a story. Thanks to their propensity to mingle with us silently, snakes keep us from resting easy, forcing us to stay on the alert. The same neural mechanisms that bring about an involuntary rise in our emotional state can, of course, be exploited for artistic reasons. Art that explicitly depicts snakes manipulates us by taking advantage of our innate biases, as does art that merely evokes serpentine forms, such as wavy or zigzag lines and, especially, spirals. Coss (1965) discovered that a coil elicited more eye dilation than other abstract serpentine images; this, after all, is the snake's posture when it is about to strike. Indeed, coils and spirals figure prominently in art, especially in amulets intended to ward off evil spirits. On the other hand, a number of book titles convey a positive attitude to a snake's trail; this may derive from our sense of relief at seeing a dreaded reptile slither away. It stands to reason that the level and character of interest roughly correlate with the degree of danger posed.

The snake is a readily available trump card in situations that call for strong rhetoric. If you wish to get someone's goat, call him a snake; it rarely is honorific. Consider, for example, the semantic weight of such terms as viper, reptile, venomous, or cold-blooded *when applied to someone*. Here again, single parts or attributes will suffice to get a rise. It is hard to imagine such words as slither, clammy, poisonous, fang, scaly, hiss, serpentine, or even sinuous and slick being used in a flattering context. They all give us the "creeps" and make our skin "crawl." The *Oxford English Dictionary*, for example, provides one definition of "reptilian" as "having the characteristics of reptiles, low, mean, malignant, underhand." Such is connoted when one "speaks with forked tongue" in an attempt to deceive others. We all know what it means to be "snakebit." Ever since Virgil's third *Eclogue* we have been on the lookout for "a snake in the grass," no doubt lying in silent ambush, and a dice player usually fears a roll of the double one, "snake eyes." Indeed, in the presence of anything ophidian it is difficult to remain indifferent.

Interest Is Constrained by Perceived Negotiability

Mundkur (1983) and Wilson (1984), however, are unable to account for snakes' privileged status. We can be fairly certain that diseases and senescence took a greater toll of victims in the EEA, yet these virtual constants did not bring about known phobias—other than our reluctance to try new foodstuffs. These threats are significantly underrepresented in our compendium of artistic themes. Their infrequent appearance may be explained, in part, by the seeming inevitability of their destructive impact. Whereas only religion or magic seemed to stem the danger of infection, there is no conceivable defense against old age. For this last consideration I added the qualifier *perceived* to my notion of negotiability. For example, in the most famous of the Greek tragedies, Oedipus saves Corinth from plague by solving the Sphinx's riddles. We pay much more attention to problems that are both significant to our reproductive fortunes and yet within the range of our capabilities. However, when pressures are either trivial or simply overwhelming, it probably does us little good to pay much attention to them.

Artistic plots tend to focus on issues that lie at the upper threshhold of our talents. Threats popular in narrative fiction typically demand every last ounce of our physical abilities, character and, often, some luck for us to survive. In terms of art, we generally like a good fight, including the common theme of being put to a severe test in a vicarious, therefore safe manner. In folklore, the actual struggle may be as brief as a heavyweight fight, but interest is created by the all-important buildup in tension, not in its resolution. For this reason, science fiction reptiles are often elevated to human scale, as with the alien Dracs that contend with our own kind on interstellar battlefields, often in a satisfyingly *mano a mano* struggle with anachronistic swords.[3] Their appellation is quite obviously derived from the Greek term for serpent, *drakon* (Cooke, 1987). All the better that we imaginatively endure a cliff-hanger and spine-tingler yet emerge unscathed. It thus makes sense that art puts us on the alert for snakes, for we usually can avert snakebite if we pay attention.

Interest May Reflect an Adaptive Drag

This proposition, of course, pertains to one of the essential observations of evolutionary psychology. We are not ideally adapted to the environment we inhabit. Indeed, in some respects, we are better suited to ancestral habitats. Clearly, there is a time lag in the response of our genome to conditions that are now changing quite rapidly. For example, although we should have nightmares about guns, knives, and speeding cars, we continue to be obsessed with animals that might bite, kill and, especially, eat us. These fantasies include unlikely magnified forms of the snake. There is little to worry from sharp teeth in our modern world, yet films like *Jaws* will terrify millions with fear of shark attack, while the far greater number of us who die from drowning will be almost wholly ignored in our arts. We hardly have to worry about dinosaurs, but recently *Jurassic Park* became one of the best-selling films of all time.

It is remarkable how serpentine themes persist in areas that suffer little or no danger from snakes. As Wilson and Mundkur both noted, the art of Ireland, which has known no snakes since the Ice Age, nevertheless swarms with ophidian forms all the way from the fourth millennium B.C. up to the present. In some cases, they are represented by coiled and spiral forms, such as those that appear to guard the entrances to ancient passage graves, like the one at Newgrange.[4] We also see so-called Celtic spirals on the borders of church vestments and in the margins of illuminated manuscripts such as the famous *Book of Kells*, pew cards, and modern art, posturing as if to defend figurative territory from evil spirits.[5] This reminds us both of the many myths in which a dragon guards a treasure, which would also include Fafner in Wagner's *Siegfried*, as well as of the auto security ads we noted earlier. The ophidian nature of "Celtic spirals" is made quite explicit in *The Book of Kells* as well as in other examples of medieval ornamentation bearing animal heads with gaping jaws and, often, forked tongues.

A problem comes up with Irish art and all other cultures that depict serpents. How are we to distinguish a chance or random ophidian referent from iterative behavior that evinces a genetic substructure? What level of frequency is significant? Mundkur, for example, notes that American city dwellers dream of serpents at about one-tenth the frequency of the urban themes that represent their immediate environment. Given the environmental displacement, he finds it "remarkable ... that [such American adults] dream of serpents at all" (1983, pp. 236–237). As previously noted, serpentine images appear in almost 1% of science fiction titles. We could regard this figure as insufficient support for a possible panhuman genetic propensity for giving special attention to snakes or as "remarkably" sufficient, if we consider the unlikelihood of encountering them in Ireland, a city, or outer space.

There is no problem assessing the serpentine images of old Irish art. First of all, they persist over eons of significant cultural change, ranging from pre-Celtic artifacts like the passage grave at Newgrange, to artworks by the pre-Christian Celts, and finally to their Christianized successors through the fifteenth century, a period of over four and a half thousand years in length. No one believes that the Irish dreamed up this imagery entirely on their own; obviously, representations had been conveyed to them by immigrants from the European continent. But we should not lose sight of the fact that snake references were conveyed and disseminated inevitably at the cost of other myths. These images successfully competed for Irish attention. Furthermore, any model of influence has to contend not just with sources but also with reception. We discard or entirely ignore the great majority of thoughts that occur to us. Only a few are "made special.'' What is remarkable about Irish art is that it literally is crawling with snakes. Indeed, the Irish gave surprising valuation to snakes. Serpentine imagery prominently bedecks all four of the most hallowed artifacts of the Irish Middle Ages: the Ardagh Silver Chalice, the *Book of Kells*, the Tara Brooch, and the High Cross of Drumcliffe. Undoubtedly, this intimate association with Ireland's major national treasures helps to account for the resurgence of serpentine imagery in later centuries. Serpent imagery, like ''Celtic spirals,'' was revived with Irish nationalism during the latter part of the nineteenth century; whereas the prevailing myth had been that St. Patrick, patron saint of the Emerald Isle, had rid Ireland of snakes, now serpents were being closely associated with the emerging national identity.[6]

Interest Is Nonlinear

Another factor that requires comment is how artistic images of the snake are magnified well beyond their natural size and capabilities into a serpent of gargantuan scale with supernatural powers. Serpentine myths depict reptiles that are able to stand on their tails, talk, suckle women and cows, fly, breathe fire or blow smoke, strike water from the earth, take revenge for human sins, conceive human children, and found tribal groups. Some become full-fledged dragons or nine-headed hydras. Snakes in myth can be bearded, feathered, or immortal, as in the case of the Worm Ouroborous. Furthermore, they are closely associated with such anthropomorphic attributes as evil, wisdom, the punishment of human sins, and divinity; snakes are often regarded as the carriers of prayers to the gods, as witnessed in Hermes' caduceus, now the symbol of medical doctors.

Given the danger that actual snakes pose, it is far better to overreact than to have a muted response to evidence of their presence. Whereas the consequences of neglect may well be dire, the cost of hysteria is relatively trivial. As a result, there is every reason to expect interest to wax by means of a positive feedback loop. Due to the particular neural structures involved, this magnification is somewhat beyond our conscious control. Snakes in myth and art are usually exaggerated in size and capacity. They are never minimized. Clearly, their aesthetic effect readily exceeds realism. They are never depicted as ordinary and inconsequential, which, of course, they often are.

With interest derived from adaptive considerations comes the potential for power. Mundkur claims that shamans developed their proclivity for handling snakes in order to gain influence over followers (1983, p. 41). Charisma requires attention. Behavior with a large adaptive potential attracts differential interest, which can be manipulated so as to derive a greater selective advantage. Building charisma for the beholden brings about a greater degree of gullibility in the beholder, often causing the latter to jump to wholly unwarranted conclusions. That we are not ideally objective in such situations elsewhere has been adduced to our inclusive fitness, given that our gullibility contributes to the formation of social organizations. Such trump cards like snake myths also make much representational art possible, if only because they impel us to "suspend" our sense of disbelief, allowing us to get emotionally involved with the otherwise unbelievable.

This nonlinear dialectic may well explain why a number of leaders are closely associated with snakes. The early Hebrews represented Jehovah in the shape of a serpent. Moses transformed his staff into a snake in order to free his people. Volkh Vseslavich, the greatest shaman in Russian folklore, was born of the union of a serpent with a peasant maid. A myth persists that a snake was seen lying beside Olympias, subsequently the mother of Alexander the Great (La Barre, 1969, p. 72). In *Agamemnon*, Clytemestra describes a dream in which a snake lay on her stomach. This is interpreted as a portent of how her future child Orestes, termed "the serpent's son," will take revenge on her for the murder of her husband, his father. The infant Hercules grasped two serpents that invaded his cradle, a sure sign of the future hero. Significantly, there are many heroes whose mythologies include dragon-slaying: Marduk, Indra, Horus, Thor, Jason, Cadmus, Perseus, Sigurd (later, Wagner's Siegmund), Beowulf, Apollo (who founds the Pythian games named after his victim), Baal, King Arthur, Srs. Lancelot, Gawain, Tristan, and Yvain, Alexander the Great, the Irish hero Finn, and, of course, Hercules, who as an adult kills Ladon, the dragon of the Hesperides. St. George is only 1 of about 40 saints in the Catholic canon to make the list; these include two Irish saints, Beicheart and Ciaran, who each drove a dragon into a lake (Simpson, 1980, p. 24). Last and probably least, the hero of the recent film *Escape from L.A.* is called Snake. Due to the awe evoked by serpents, people may prefer ophidian appellations; this is evident in the many dragon images that bedeck pennants, weapons, battleships, and athletic teams. My under-twelve soccer team recently voted to name themselves the Vipers; one does not have to go far in Texas to find rattlers, cobras, and sidewinders on a playing field. An additional reason is that these images work as amulets; for example, such images are also found on churches, as if to protect believers and their houses of worship against the elements and/or evil spirits. The pagan Celtic god Cernunnos, for example, is traditionally depicted with a ram-horned serpent encircling his waist for apotropaic reasons.

The Object of Interest Becomes Overdetermined

The negative qualities of snakes can become positive attributes for their bearers. Snakes or serpents also represent healing, that is, they are symbols of transformation, facilitating the passage from symbolic death to rebirth (Rosen, 1996, p. 91). Thanks to the charisma of interest, especially when it is conjoined with a perception of power, the focus of our attention may well accrue a number of unsifted, even contradictory associations. Mundkur admits his bewilderment at the sheer variety of meanings attributed to the serpent, concluding, "The only sentiment conspicuously shared in . . . myths is that of aversion to the animal"

(1983, p. 206). Whereas there is little reason to expect natural selection to assign fixed meanings to symbols, we note that most snake associations are striking—further evidence that snakes are highly marked in terms of semiotic value; they are positive or negative but rarely neutral. That is, snakes evoke strong interest; only very rarely would we ever ignore one. The reasons for this are quite obvious. Notably, most snake associations are themselves closely linked to issues of reproductive success.[7] As a result, they also manage to further stimulate our emotions. An excellent indication of markedness is the manner in which serpentine connotations can be readily organized into diametrical opposites (Willis, 1990, p. 250; La Barre, 1969, p. 94n.; Stevens, 1995, p. 187). Various myths depict the serpent as creator; others, as destroyer. It is linked with the sky and the coming of rain but also with the earth and the origin of water. The serpent is both an oppressor and a punisher. Most importantly, it is closely tied to good and evil. The snake is found at extremes, rarely in between, which is another way of saying that we are not likely to be indifferent to it.

A second consideration is that with snake imagery there is no necessary reason that the serpent's image should have one and only one imparted meaning. There is every reason to believe, thanks to our nonlinear model, that a highly charged phenomenon will gather connotations. This process of accruing meanings only adds to the positive feedback loop of gathering interest. As Mundkur observes, "the evidence from modern experimental psychobiology suggests that more than one simple, direct response may be stimulated by any phenomenon that evokes fear" (1983, p. 210). Interest behaves like a wild card, being simultaneously capable of a wide range of actions. The artistic world is characterized by overdetermination. It satisfies many questions or needs with a single answer. The chief property of artistic thought is its syncretism; it brings various forms of cognition together into precise accord on particular points, often creating something that is more than the sum of its parts. Syncretric cognition, however, produces a structure that may defy simplistic analysis, given that one allusion will be interdependent with the others. The more simple the original image, the stronger the resultant aesthetic effect. Such is true with the snake.

One of the most remarkable linkages of the serpent is with human sexual activity. There is simply too much cross-cultural evidence to ignore the likelihood of a significant underlying pattern. Freudians, as we see with Weston La Barre, simply speak of it as the human penis, noting similarities in appearance and function (1969, p. 106). There are many tales in which snakes inseminate women, much like the sire of Volkh Vseslavich. On the other hand, evidence abounds that links snakes with the vagina. Various metaphors evoke castration anxiety, such as the Medusa's head of snakes or the *vagina dentata*, whereby ophidian forms denote detached phalli. In the horridly misogynist art of late nineteenth-century Europe, women are represented cavorting with snakes in a salacious manner; examples include Lucien Levy-Dhurmer's *Eve*, Jean Deville's *The Idol of Perversity*, Gabriel Ferrier's *Salammbo*, and, most infamously, Gustav Flaubert's *Salammbo*, whose title heroine dances naked with a snake coiled around her arms.[8] Women were also depicted as if they *were* snakes.[9] Returning to semiotics, it requires only a single shift to get us from male to female associations, from phallic to vaginal, given that both are intimately linked to sexuality and that creation, in turn, is only a step away from destruction. The same goes for good and evil.

But this begs the question of how the sexual association originated in the first place. Daniel Rancour-Laferriere suggests that the essential link lies in the phallic display utilized by some apes as a form of territorial defense against other monkeys (1985, pp. 270–271). The ophiophobia that we share with them may have served as a preadaptation for this curious behavior. How could it deter alien monkeys if their highly colored phalli did not remind others of snakes? While there is plenty of clinical literature suggesting that snakes represent penises, can we not turn the equation around and see how the penis may get us to think of snakes? Rancour-Laferriere cites the Yiddish term for male genitalia, "Schlang," which primarily means "snake" (1985, p. 271). In my own experience I have heard American males speak of the penis as a "snake." The impudent hand gesture known as the "bird" is obviously a representation of a penis. Notably, it is used not to encourage lovemaking but, rather, to repel others, much as with phallic display. Meanwhile, Bedaux (1989, 1991) and Sutterlin (1987, 1989) have observed human beings defending their territory with both phallic *and* vaginal display, evidence that supports our point about semiotic shifts. As we noted earlier, similar territorial defense is often mounted by explicitly ophidian forms.

Interest Waxes with Counterpoised Associations

Aesthetic interest is only magnified when simplistic explanations are frustrated. A conundrum only gives us yet more to think about. The decadent linkage of women with snakes demonstrates another feature of interest, namely, that curiosity increases when biologically significant associations are directly counterpoised, especially when it is to the point that no resolution is possible. Such is the essential substructure of dramatic tragedy, wherein the protagonist is beset with a choice between two evils. This artistic form continues to generate enormous emotional energy. One need only note the continued power of *Oedipus Rex*, a story in which an exemplary man of talents and reproductive resources unwittingly commits incest with his mother. The same fascination is achieved when the snake is associated with irresistible forces such as sex.

Interest typically focuses on new phenomena or novel combinations of the familiar. This tendency reflects our evident need to be alert regarding changes in our environment. European decadent art of the latter part of the nineteenth century was born of the public's exhaustion with civic themes like the search for social justice. Often given the misnomer of "art for art's sake," artists in this school turned to their fantasy to create images that would gain a more extreme emotional response than anything ever created before. Notably, in their competition for public attention, they made recourse to ancient motifs of obvious adaptive significance. Time and again one can discern the essential recipe of counterpoising phenomena that are, on one hand, undeniably beneficial to fitness and, on the other, clearly threatening to the same. A common combination was that of lightly dressed beautiful women with snakes. Evolutionary sexologists would no doubt approve of the adaptive features of these women, noting their generous hip-to-waist ratios, skin complexions free of blemishes or parasites, and beautifully balanced facial and bodily symmetries, all signs of genetic health. On the other hand, these women are allowing a dangerous viper to come within very close proximity. But these images are problematic because, however negotiable these elements are if confronted singly, their juxtaposition frustrates easy resolution. As a result, the viewer cannot take a representation for granted and discard it but instead is seduced to peer still deeper.

Franz von Stuck's infamous *Sin* (1893) owes its immense aesthetic energy to the fact that it exemplifies all seven of our propositions inspired by serpent art (Figure 9.1). This painting includes images of clear adaptive significance to our genetic fortunes that lie within the grasp of our capabilities. We are presented with a comely woman near her reproductive peak potential; she seems to be receptive—indeed, her breasts are exposed to us—and we are tempted to approach. But she is wearing a real boa! Notably, the snake seems to have a relaxed body, the better to conform suspiciously with the contours of her torso. Its eyes confront us. It reflects an ancient threat, possibly reminding us of the similar association of a nude woman and an insidious serpent in the Garden of Eden: sexual desire and ophidiophobia both are truly venerable. Furthermore, however simple in appearance the picture may be, *Sin* conveys a myriad of carefully balanced contradictory associations. The sharp contrast between the light that gives prominence to the woman's naked flesh and the shadow that conceals an almost subliminal ophidian threat evokes our ambivalence. We are torn between attraction and the impulse to flee, a condition yielding a delicious sense of masochism that we are unable to resolve. We are left suspended in utter fascination, thanks the artist's exploitation of our evolved capacity for differential interest.

CONCLUSION

Paintings like von Stuck's *Sin* give us a glimpse of a plausible—and testable—semiotic structure for a biopoetics based on invariant principles of evolutionary psychology. Yet at the same time the context in which art strives to catch our eye is changing. This very fact probably requires new degrees of complication in the thematic structures of art. Over the past two millennia, especially in the elite circles of modern Western societies, art has gradually become at least potentially liberated from its ancient role as a complement to utilitarian objects and behaviors. As a result, it more and more has had to rely solely on its capacity to attract our attention. By the same token, matters of

Figure 9.1
Franz von Stuck, *Sin*, 1893, Oil on Canvas

Source: Gibson (1988), p. 85. Copyright © 1988 by Franz von Stuck Estate. Reprinted by permission of Museum Villa Stuck, Munich, Germany.

empirical necessity such as dominant ideologies have relaxed their control over the arts, which are increasingly free to explore a widening range of thematic and stylistic alternatives. We have more plastic materials with which we can fashion a greater range of objects. Nevertheless, despite all this rapidly expanding variety in artistic expression, our posited "epigenetic rules" and the artistic themes that derive from them remain unchanged. We have merely developed new semiotic structures to utilize them better in competing for attention. As we have seen in our examination of serpent images in art, these epigenetic themes continue to reveal themselves in our primitive fascinations and fears.

One may ask, How can we afford this anachronistic bias today? Admittedly, our genetic heritage may not be so evident in our everyday actions, given that we typically have to be acutely aware of our immediate environment. The arts, by contrast, allow us to escape our proximate concerns and to entertain ourselves with anything we wish—whereupon our evolutionary history, sometimes quite stripped of contemporary reference, may be seen to exert a greater hold on us. The themes of representational art have changed with the development of Western society, as we should expect, but it is just as remarkable that ancient motifs persist, that we still focus on the same phenomena that were associated with significant adaptive differentials in the Pleistocene.

Yet another consideration greatly helps to account for the waxing differential between empirical experience and aesthetic fantasy, as well as for the manner in which art ever more becomes a hypertrophied expression of genetically conditioned behavioral tendencies. Art, as we noted, has to compete for our attention with nonaesthetic phenomena. It overcomes its lack of utilitarian consequence by appearing to appeal to our selective benefit.[10] But aesthetic objects and performances also compete with each other. Whereas ancient societies typically were content with a limited range of aesthetic styles for long periods of time, modern societies are increasingly complex in the artistic media, themes, and styles they support. Thanks, in part, to our greater awareness of our history and of the cultural diversity provided by other societies, we have more to choose from, and the artist is locked in serious competition with other artists, who probably are also drawing on the same evolutionary sources for aesthetic response. Making greater recourse to anachronistic motifs that are energized by genetic conditioning is at least one of the major alternatives for artists to take in trying to gain a larger share of the artistic marketplace.

There are several likely corollaries to our biopoetics that we do not have the space to fully explore here: (1) an acceleration of aesthetic change, (2) an ever-growing diversity and individuality in artistic styles,[11] (3) the option of a greater and more outlandish irrealism in artistic themes, and (4) the possibility of a greater complexity in thematic structures, such as we find with the dramatic irony of von Stuck's *Sin*. All of these consequences have strongly characterized the rapidly expanding forms of Western art over the past four centuries. Yet, it seems likely that, despite all of this bewildering diversity, we will continue to discern the same relatively small set of genetically shaped interests and semiotic structures, thanks to our common evolutionary history.

NOTES

I would like to thank Nancy Aiken, Kathryn Coe, Hal Hall, and Daniel Rancour-Laferriere for their help in the preparation of this study.

1. Although stepparents have been much noted in critical literature about folktales, they figure in only 22 narrative motifs (Thompson, 1955–1958).

2. My survey covered Day (1975) and Bleiler (1978).

3. By contrast a cartoon was once advertised as the world's shortest: *Bambi Meets Godzilla*—hardly an even match and not at all the kind of parity required for extended narrative interest.

4. See Harbison, Potterton, and Sheehy (1978, pp. 14–15).

5. See *Treasures of Ireland* (1983, pp. 56, 39); Sheehy (1980, p. 175); Knowles (1982, p. 35).

6. See Sheehy (1980, p. 183); Knowles (1982, pp. 34, 47).

7. Anthony Stevens says as much by observing, "That one symbol can express so many different meanings must be because the sinuous, slithery schema is susceptible to contamination by other archetypal schemata—e.g. those concerned with sex, evil, healing, etc." (1995, p. 186). He suggests that, taken together, these diverse associations constitute a "semantic field" linked by the serpent (personal communication, 1996).

8. See Jullian (1973, p. 17); Dijkstra (1986, frontispiece, p. 308).

9. See Gibson (1988, pp. 129, 97); Delevoy (1982, p. 131).

10. We are subject, at the same time, to both proximate—contemporary, environmental—and ultimate—genetic—forces, and, given the imperfection of our evolutionary heritage, we may confuse one with the other. On the other hand, art can be said to provide a utilitarian benefit of another order by conditioning us as to what deserves our attention.

11. See Cooke (in press).

REFERENCES

Aiken, N.E.B. (1992). *A biological basis for the emotional impact of art.* Unpublished doctoral dissertation, Ohio University.

Bedaux, J. B. (1989). Laatmiddeleeuwse sexuele amuletten (Late medieval sexual insignia). In J. B. Bedaux & A. M. Koldeweij (Eds.), *Annus quadriga mundi* (pp. 16–30). N.p.: De Walburg Pers.

Bedaux, J. B. (1991). Marino Marini's Angelo dell cittadella: Beeldhouwkunst in biologisch perspectief. *Jong Holland, 3,* 26–31.

Bleiler, E. F. (1978). *The checklist of science-fiction and supernatural fiction.* Glen Rock, NJ: Firebell Books.

Coe, K. (1992). Art: The replicable unit—An inquiry into the possible origin of art as a social behavior. *Journal of Social and Evolutionary Systems, 15,* 217–234.

Cooke, B. (1987). The human alien: In-groups and out-breeding in *Enemy mine.* In G. E. Slusser & E. S. Rabkin (Eds.), *Aliens: The anthropology of science fiction* (pp. 179–198). Carbondale: Southern Illinois University Press.

Cooke, B. (in press). Pushkin and the memetics of reputation. In B. Cooke & J. B. Bedaux (Eds.), *Sociobiology and the arts*. Amsterdam: Editions Rodopi.

Coss, R. G. (1965). *Mood provoking visual stimuli: Their origins and applications*. Unpublished master's thesis, UCLA.

Day, B. M. (1975). *The checklist of fantastic literature in paperbound books*. New York: Arno Press.

Delevoy, R. L. (1982). *Symbolists and symbolism*. New York: Rizzoli.

Dijkstra, B. (1986). *Idols of perversity: Fantasies of feminine evil in fin-de-siecle culture*. New York: Oxford University Press.

Dissanayake, E. (1992). *Homo aestheticus: Where art comes from and why*. New York: Free Press.

Evans, J. D. (1987). The dragon. In M. South (Ed.), *Mythical and fabulous creatures: A source book and a research guide* (pp. 59–74). Westport, CT: Greenwood Press.

Gibson, M. (1988). *The symbolists*. (M. Gibson, Trans.). New York: Harry N. Abrams.

Harbison, P., Potterton, H., & Sheehy, J. (1978). *Irish art and architecture: From prehistory to the present*. London: Thames and Hudson.

Jullian, P. (1973). *The symbolists*. London: Phaidon.

Knowles, R. (Ed.). (1982). *Contemporary Irish art*. New York: St. Martin's Press.

La Barre, W. (1969). *They shall take up serpents: Psychology of the southern snake-handling cult*. New York: Schocken Books.

LeDoux, J. E. (1994). Emotion, memory and the brain. *Scientific American, 270*, 50–57.

Lumsden, C. J., & Wilson, E. O. (1983). *Promethean fire: Reflections on the origin of mind*. Cambridge: Harvard University Press.

Mundkur, B. (1983). *The cult of the serpent: An interdisciplinary survey of its manifestations and origins*. Albany: State University of New York Press.

Rancour-Laferriere, D. (1985). *Signs of the flesh: An essay on the evolution of hominid sexuality*. Berlin, New York, & Amsterdam: Mouton de Gruyter.

Reginald, R. (1992). *Science fiction and fantasy literature, 1975–1991: A bibliography of science fiction, fantasy, and horror fiction books and nonfiction monographs*. Detroit: Gale Research.

Rosen, D. H. (1996). *Transforming depression: Healing the soul through creativity*. New York: Arkana/Penguin.

Sheehy, J. (1980). *The rediscovery of Ireland's past: The Celtic revival, 1830–1930*. London: Thames and Hudson.

Simpson, J. (1980). *British dragons*. London: B. T. Batsford.

Stevens, A. (1995). *Private myths: Dreams and dreaming*. Cambridge: Harvard University Press.

Sutterlin, C. (1987). Mittelalterliche Kirchen-Skulptur als Beispiel universaler Abwehrsymbolik. In Johann Georg Prin von Hohenzollern & Max Liedtke (Eds.), *Vom Kritzeln zur Kunst* (pp. 82–100). Bad Heilbrunn: Verlag Julius Klinkhardt.

Sutterlin, C. (1989). Universals in apotropaic symbolism: A behavioral and comparative approach to some medieval sculptures. *Leonardo, 22*, 65–74.

Thompson, S. (1955–1958). *Motif-index of folk-literature*. Vols. 1–5. Bloomington: Indiana University Press.

Treasures of Ireland: Irish art 3000 B.C.–1500 A.D. (1983). Dublin: Royal Irish Academy.

Willis, R. G. (1990). The meaning of the snake. In R. G. Willis (Ed.), *Signifying animals: Human meaning in the natural world* (pp. 246–252). London: Unwin Hyman.

Wilson, E. O. (1978). *On human nature*. Cambridge: Harvard University Press.

Wilson, E. O. (1984). *Biophilia*. Cambridge: Harvard University Press.

10

The Survival
Value of Forgiveness

MICHAEL C. LUEBBERT

In the postmodern era, the act of forgiveness has often been treated with skepticism and even disdain by philosophers and social scientists espousing a secular weltanschauung. In prefiguring the arguments of social Darwinists, Nietzsche (1887) argued that forgiveness is frequently a strategy of weaklings incapable of asserting their will in competition with others. Nietzsche implied that forgiveness necessarily leads to a state of alienation because it separates a person from his or her true nature as an aggressive being. Viewed from this perspective, forgiveness seems to function as a power play, enabling the forgiver's continued sense of superiority and disguised hatred vis-à-vis the forgiven one. Mental health care professionals have also objected that forgiveness may operate dysfunctionally by making a person masochistically vulnerable to repeated attacks by the other. Misguided, premature calls for forgiveness issued to victims of sexual, physical, or emotional abuse may simply ensure that perpetrators escape punishment and that victims continue to suffer. Moreover, when viewed from a popular, evolutionary perspective, it appears that a willingness to forgive simply weakens one's fitness in the ongoing individualistic struggle for mates, economic resources, and power. From these perspectives, forgiveness has long appeared to possess no intrinsic survival value. To be sure, the common association of forgiveness with neurotic expressions of religiosity has also contributed to its neglect in the psychological and social sciences.

This chapter advances the thesis, however, that forgiveness is not merely the province of religious neurotics, masochists, unconscious power wielders, and moral weaklings unable to battle with the fittest. It is argued that forgiveness can be viewed as a fundamental human potentiality whose proper development and unfolding possess an intrinsic survival value both today and in the human species' original environment of evolutionary adaptedness. This argument starts with evidence for the survival value of forgiveness, demonstrating reconciliation behavior in non-human primates. Next delineated are factors that may have led to a natural selection for forgiveness behaviors in the human community's original environment of evolutionary adaptedness. Development of the human capacity to forgive is examined beyond this original environment of adaptedness as well. Specifically, the effects of the development of literacy on the evolution of the human person's capacity to forgive are discussed. This analysis attempts to explain how human forgiveness had its infancy in human attachment drives described by kinship selection, its adolescence in the reciprocal altruism promoted by strong in-group pressures limiting the exacting of revenge, and its maturation as a limited self-transcendence as new capacities for objective thought and selfless behavior developed through an internalization of literacy.

Contrary to a postmodern perspective that associates forgiveness solely with the unfortunate rise of a largely neurotic Judeo-Christian tradition, forgiveness served as an important theme in classical Greek society. To counter an anachronistic and unjust animus against the topic of forgiveness per se, this chapter briefly examines the profound treatment of forgiveness presented by Aeschylus, a Greek playwright, in his *Oresteian Trilogy* in the fifth century B.C. It is hoped that recognizing the topic of forgiveness as an important part of our pre-Christian intellectual patrimony will help postmodern Westerners to view forgiveness with renewed eyes, unjaundiced by the destructive uses that believers and nonbelievers alike have made of the human capacity to forgive. Moreover, subsequent analysis suggests that Aeschylus's dramatic treatment of forgiveness in the *Oresteian Trilogy* signaled the changes in human consciousness upon which many of the world religions have built their call for universal forgiveness.

TRANSFORMING THE FURIES: THE DYNAMICS OF FORGIVENESS IN AESCHYLUS'S *ORESTEIAN TRILOGY*

The Greeks, in laying the foundation for our Western philosophical and scientific worldview, struggled with the possibilities and limits of forgiveness. For the Greeks, forgiveness was a universal theme, worthy of treatment by one of its most celebrated playwrights, Aeschylus, in his *Oresteian Trilogy*. As Aeschylus presented the tragic story of the house of Atreus, he wielded a deep insight into the powerful attachment bonds uniting parent and child. For a modern, psychologically minded audience, Aeschylus's narrative serves as a powerful expression of the chaotic and destructive forces unleashed when primal attachment bonds between blood relatives are broken by betrayal and violence. In his trilogy, Aeschylus unfolded a multigenerational tragedy of betrayal, vengeance, and countervengeance that leads, surprisingly, to a process of forgiveness with deep human transformation in the protagonist, Orestes, and in his pursuers, the Furies. This hopeful denouement of transformation through forgiveness is doubly surprising, given the thoroughgoing determinism of the Greek worldview. Nevertheless, in spite of the classical Greek treatment of humans as playthings of destiny and of the gods, they did not commit the hubris of attempting to explain away human freedom.

In the first play of the trilogy, entitled *Agamemnon*, Aeschylus portrayed the return of the Greek general Agamemnon from the Trojan War and his subsequent murder by his wife, Clytemnestra. In the background of this action lay a multigenerational drama of betrayal and revenge. Agamemnon's father, Atreus, had been cuckolded by his friend Thyestes. To secure his revenge, Atreus invited Thyestes to a banquet whose main course was Thyestes's two small children. In the next generation, Aegisthus, a son of Thyestes, became Clytemnestra's lover and accomplice in murdering Agamemnon. The horror of betrayal extended beyond these bounds as well. Agamemnon himself had offered his daughter Iphigenia as a sacrifice to the gods to secure favorable winds as the Greek armies set sail for Troy, an offering that Clytemnestra abhorred and that precipitated her desire for murderous revenge.

In the second play, *The Libation Bearers*, Orestes, son of Agamemnon and Clytemnestra, committed matricide to avenge his father's death. In the third play, *The Eumenides*, the Furies, spirits of vengeance unleashed by his murderous act, pursued Orestes. In his flight from the Furies, Orestes sought refuge in the temple of Athena in Athens. The Furies pursued him there, intent on vengeance for his violation of the sacred bond of mother and offspring. Just at the climactic moment when the Furies have descended on Orestes, and their retribution seems imminent, the goddess Athena came to Orestes's aid.

Athena set up a jury of twelve citizens to decide Orestes's fate, but she reserved the right to cast the deciding vote in the event of tie. As fate or the gods would have it, the jury deadlocked at six apiece, and Athena cast her vote in Orestes's favor. At first, the Furies were loath to relent their intended vengeance. From their perspective, the violation of the blood bond between mother and son could not be satisfied by facile rationalizations or social exoneration. Four times Athena attempted to deflect the "immortal rage" of the Furies, promising them a new home in Athens, honor, and a new status as spirits of blessings whose favor alone could ensure individuals happiness and prosperity. Four times, the Furies refused to relent. On the fifth attempt, Athena succeeded in melting their anger. Having vented their murderous spleen without rejection or retaliation, the Furies finally relented of their insistence on vengeance and forgave Orestes for his matricide. They finally heard and accepted Athena's promise to protect and prosper all who revere the Furies. From henceforth, they would be honored not as spirits of vengeance and curse but literally as "kindly spirits" bearing the title Eumenides.

Like a good clinician, Athena did not insist that the Furies relent of their desire for vengeance as a price for continued dialogue. She listened to the compulsive, repetitive chorus of their strong strains of hurt, grief, and sorrow without judgment, rejection, or retaliation. Athena served here as a midwife to authentic forgiveness by not requiring of the Furies premature relinquishment of hurt or encouraging a compensatory power struggle characterized by forgiving but not forgetting. Her willingness to hear the Furies' outrage and pain enabled them to move beyond blood lust to gratitude, generosity, and a sense of usefulness. In the *Oresteian Trilogy*, Aeschylus had Athena facilitate a process of authentic forgiveness that resulted in the Furies being transformed into spirits of blessing, not vengeance. Despite the Greek worldview's strong sense of destiny and fate, Aeschylus dramatically expressed the fundamental human capacity for radical transformation through forgiveness.

In Aeschylus's dramatic economy, forgiveness required the intervention of Athena, a facilitator who could tolerate the expression of hurt and anger without defensive maneuvering or retaliation. In her expression of detached concern for the pain of the Furies, for Orestes's plight, and for the good of the state, Athena transcended the urge for vengeance flowing from a betrayal of the primal bond uniting mother and child, but not without honoring the spirits who protect this sacred bond. In short, Aeschylus portrayed forgiveness as a human potential whose roots lie in the unrelenting fidelity to this sacred bond but whose ultimate fulfillment lay in a wisdom capable of detached love as well.

EVIDENCE FOR RECONCILIATION BEHAVIOR IN NON-HUMAN PRIMATES

Viewed from the perspective of Darwin's notion of the survival of the fittest, forgiveness and evolutionary theory may seem like strange bedfellows. Nevertheless, an evolutionary account of forgiveness holds that the capacity to forgive developed and persisted because it facilitated reproduction and survival among individuals exhibiting such a capacity. Finding forgiveness behavior in animals close to humans on the evolutionary chain, notably, non-human primates, would provide support for the survival value of forgiveness claim. Indeed, for two decades, primatologists have undertaken intensive research on the reconciliation behavior of primates (Aureli van Schaik, & van Hooft, 1989; de Waal & van Roosmalen, 1979; de Waal & Yoshihara, 1983; de Waal & Ren, 1988; de Waal, 1989, 1993; York & Rowell, 1988). In his contribution to a recent book, *Good Natured: The Origins of Right and Wrong in Humans and Other Animals*, de Waal (1996) reported that reconciliations among non-human primates frequently occur after fights both in naturalistic settings and in captivity. De Waal defined reconciliation as a systematic increase in the number of friendly interactions "between former opponents shortly after an aggressive conflict between them" (p. 63). A number of these studies suggested that more friendly contacts involving former adversaries occurred during postconflict periods compared to control periods. Primatologists have argued that these reconciliation behaviors represent a "selective attraction" between individuals who have recently been engaged in open conflict. This selective attraction with its accompanying forgiveness or reconciliation behavior has been noted with patas monkeys, chimpanzees, bonobos, mountain gorillas, vervet monkeys, capuchin monkeys, red-fronted lemurs, baboons, and a variety of macaques (de Waal, 1996). De

Waal has also pointed out that with rhesus monkeys and patas monkeys, the reconciliations are instigated mostly by aggressors (de Waal, 1993).

De Waal and van Roosmalen (1979) reported in one study of chimpanzees in the Arnhem Zoo in the Netherlands that the process of reconciliation between former opponents involved special behavior patterns rarely seen outside this context: an invitational hand gesture, involving an outstretched hand and an open palm, then often followed by mouth-to-mouth kissing. De Waal (1987) reported that bonobo aggressors inspected the wound they had inflicted to lick and clean it. Bonobos also achieved reconciliation through genital stimulation and kissing. Chimpanzees enacted reconciliation through kissing, embracing, held-out hand invitations, gentle touching, and sometimes mounts (de Waal & van Roosmalen, 1979; Goodall, 1986). Rhesus monkeys utilized embracing, and stumptail monkeys used a bottom-hold ritual, involving one animal presenting its hindquarters while the other one grasped the presenter's haunches (de Waal & Ren, 1988). De Waal (1996) also reported evidence of reconciliation by proxy among macaques as relatives of a victim sought conciliatory contact with the aggressor on the victim's behalf.

Despite the impressive array of reconciliation behaviors displayed by diverse primates species, the authors cautioned that a large percentage of conflicts remain unreconciled among these animals. Nevertheless, they also pointed out that non-human primates do appear to exhibit a "selective attraction" to engage in reconciliation behavior with their partners in prior conflict. How can these reconciliation behaviors be understood from an evolutionary perspective? According to the theory of reciprocal altruism proposed by Trivers (1971), it is in an individual's long-term selfish interest to help others in need, because they will be more likely to help you in the future. De Waal (1996) himself readily applied this explanation to the reconciliation behavior of non-human primates. He argued that environmental pressures such as predation, food distribution, and the need for allies in the struggle for intragroup dominance impact the reconciliation behavior of each primate species. These pressures seem to interact, promoting an equilibrium between the centrifugal force of competition and the social cohesiveness required by the primate social life (de Waal, 1993). De Waal further argued that this apparent drive toward reconciliation among non-human primates may also be viewed as an expression of a kind of "community concern," tied to nature's intention to evolve primate social systems that would ensure survival and reproduction (de Waal, 1996, p. 206).

Some skeptics may object to the attribution of reconciliation behavior to non-human primates as an unjustifiable anthropomorphizing of these animals. An extreme skeptic might reject the attribution of all mental states and processes—both cognitive and emotional—as well as verbs of action and predicates of moral character and personality to animals (Fisher, 1996). In response to this critique, de Waal (1996) has argued that it is rationally parsimonious to assume that if species closely related in the evolutionary process act in similar ways, then the underlying process is probably the same also. Furthermore, he adds that to assume a priori that non-human primates cannot engage in reconciliation behaviors because such a claim wrongly likens them to humans merely begs the question (Fisher, 1996). The capacity of animals to engage in reconciliation behaviors is a question to be answered by empirical study, not by a priori definitions of how reality is structured. De Waal (1996) also noted that, whereas critics of such so-called anthropomorphizing object to attributions of reconciliation behavior to non-human primates, the attribution of aggression, violence, or competition—also so-called human activities—typically evokes no such objection. Such a double standard reflects, presumably, not judgments made on the basis of objective data but a fundamental bias toward viewing animal behavior—and perhaps even human behavior—as fundamentally selfish and aggressive.

THE EVOLUTION OF HUMAN FORGIVENESS WITHIN THE ORIGINAL ENVIRONMENT OF ADAPTEDNESS

Evidence of reconciliation behaviors among non-human primates provides some evidence for the evolutionary importance of forgiveness for species close to humans on the evolutionary chain. Nevertheless, the question of whether forgiveness has a survival value in terms of the phylogenesis of the human species can best be addressed by imagining the human person within the original environment of evolutionary adaptedness. This original environment of evolutionary adaptedness has been described as relatively small tribal communities of hunters or food gatherers, sharing a simple, common life without the aid of complex technologies for war or hunt, and without the technologies associated with written language. In his book, *The Two Million-Year-Old Self*, Stevens argued that such a cultural context existed between 15,000 and 40,000 years ago, during the late Paleolithic period. Stevens maintained that these early humans probably lived in organic, extended kinship groups, consisting of 40 to 50 individuals, living within social structures on which our species depended for 99.5% of its existence (Stevens, 1993, p. 67).

Perhaps a human capacity for forgiveness evolved in this context because these organic extended kinship groups required group cohesiveness and mutual cooperation to ensure the survival of the group against predators and to secure adequate amounts of food. From this perspective, the development of forgiveness behavior can be explained in terms of the theory of kinship selection. This theory suggests that individuals may sacrifice their needs or wants for the sake of others who also carry their genes. As society expanded beyond the boundary of the extended family, the community's need for protection against animal predators and marauding tribes and for cooperation in obtaining food may have also promoted forgiveness behaviors. As an expression of reciprocal altruism, forgiveness behavior may have been naturally selected for because it promoted the survival of one's own genes by solidifying mutual cooperation with non-kin whose help might help ensure the survival of one's progeny.

These two explanations for the selection of forgiveness behaviors in an en-

vironment of evolutionary adaptedness seem compelling in many respects. However, treating as normative for all times the human potential that may have been
actualized in the original environment of human adaptedness lacks a coherent
rationale. This original environment of human adaptedness is not necessarily the
type of society for which nature has equipped us. Nor does living under the
conditions of modern society result necessarily in a "frustration of archetypal
intent," as Stevens has suggested (1993, p. 67). The "archetypal intent" hypothesis suggests that evolution selected for the development of human brain
capacities that could not yet be actualized within this original environment of
evolutionary adaptedness. We know now that although evolution produced a
human mental apparatus capable of reaching high levels of analytic abstraction,
scientific reasoning, and penetrating self-analysis, this potential apparently lay
fallow in the illiterate human cultures of the late Paleolithic period.

Theories of kinship selection and reciprocal altruism serve well as complementary explanations of how forgiveness developed among illiterate humans
within their original environment of evolutionary adaptedness, but these evolutionary theories lose some—but certainly not all—of their explanatory value
when they are applied indiscriminately outside this original evolutionary context.
A new mode of analysis is required to treat the evolution of forgiveness in
cultures whose dynamic structures have been influenced by literacy. The analysis
to follow focuses solely on speculation about a single cultural phenomenon that
may have influenced the evolution of forgiveness in the West. Eastern cultures
and their religious traditions may have followed the same or different trajectories
in the evolution of the capacity to forgive. These cross-cultural comparisons are
beyond the scope of this chapter.

THE EVOLUTION OF HUMAN FORGIVENESS OUTSIDE
THE ORIGINAL ENVIRONMENT OF ADAPTEDNESS

Scholars concerned with the ways in which the development of written language has affected the evolution of human consciousness have pointed out that
preliterate humans do not possess the same sense of differentiated and internalized selfhood present in literate societies (Ong, 1982; Luria, 1976). Ong in his
book *Orality and Literacy* argued that persons in preliterate, or what he calls
primary oral, cultures tend to organize their knowing and knowledge around an
oral-aural synthesis. For the primary oral person, the word is experienced primarily as sound, as a dynamic event that exists only "when it is going out of
existence" (Ong, 1982, p. 32). Ong maintained that primary oral folk concep-
tualize and verbalize with close reference to the human life world, "assimilating
the alien, objective world to the more immediate, familiar interaction of human
beings" (Ong, 1982, p. 42). According to his analysis, preliterate folk achieve
knowledge through a close, empathic identification of the knower with the
known. Ong also noted that primary oral folk are notably "agonistic in their
verbal performance and their lifestyle," seeing life in the context of interper-

sonal struggle. In primary oral cultures, this agonism finds expression both in reciprocal name-calling and in a celebration of violent, physical behavior. Primary oral folk also use proverbs and riddles not only to communicate information and wisdom but also "to engage others in verbal and intellectual combat" (Ong, 1982, p. 44). Ong suggested that common and persistent physical hardships as well as the inability to understand natural causes for disease and disaster probably contributed to the development of this agonistic mental set. When such negative events could be explained only in interpersonal terms, the malevolence of another human being—a magician or a witch—must be assumed. Moreover, Ong argued that this agonistic structure of consciousness was connected with orality itself. As Ong put it, "when all verbal communication must be by direct word of mouth, involved in the give-and-take dynamics of sound, interpersonal relations are kept high—both attractions and, even more, antagonisms" (Ong, 1982, p. 45).

Ong further suggested that, in contrast to primary oral consciousness with its oral-aural focus, literate consciousness shifted the balance of the senses to the visual (Ong, 1967). This move toward "visualism" promoted a separation of the knower from the known, setting up conditions for objectivity. As Ong put it, "writing makes possible increasingly articulate introspectivity, opening the psyche as never before not only to the external objective world quite distinct from itself but also to the interior self against whom the objective world is set" (Ong, 1982, p. 105). According to Ong's account, the individual's sense of being a unique self with psychological depth may, indeed, be closely related to the increased capacity for introspection and analytic clarity facilitated, in part, by the development of written language. Although writing appears to have helped to heighten consciousness considerably, it has also undoubtedly led to an increased state of alienation from the natural milieu. Although he admitted the negative ramifications of this alienation, Ong noted that this alienation has also had a salubrious effect on human life. As Ong expressed it, "to live and to understand fully, we need not only proximity but also distance. This writing provides for consciousness as nothing else does" (Ong, 1982, p. 82). Nevertheless, as comprehensive as Ong's analysis of the effects of literacy on consciousness appears to be, Ong argued for a kind of relationism, not a thoroughgoing, causal reductionism throughout his analysis. Certainly, many factors other than the rise of literacy no doubt contributed to massive changes in consciousness as well.

In a more empirical approach to a study of the effects of literacy on consciousness, the Russian developmental psychologist A. R. Luria examined the psychological characteristics of illiterate peasants in the Soviet province of Uzbekistan at the time of the cultural revolution in the 1930s, just before they were exposed to literacy in order to indoctrinate them into communism. Luria found that illiterates exhibited a pronounced inability to disengage themselves from direct experience. When asked to think imaginatively about contrary-to-fact situations, illiterate persons typically refused, citing their lack of necessary knowledge, while remaining entirely within the realm of their practical experience. Luria concluded that for illiterate folks, imagination remains largely tied to the person's immediate situation in a rigidly bound manner. Luria noted, however, that the acquisition of literacy freed a person's imagination from the immediate context and made it available for problem solving (Luria, 1976).

In another task, Luria asked illiterates to analyze themselves in terms of their personal attributes. Respondents either did not grasp the task at all or simply described themselves in terms of their involvement in everyday situations. When one peasant was asked what sort of person he was, he responded: "What can I say about my own heart? . . . Ask others; they can tell you about me. I myself can't say anything" (Luria, 1976, p. 149). When asked to identify their positive or negative qualities, illiterate folk also sometimes pointed to having "bad neighbors" as one of their shortcomings. In other words, they attributed their bad characteristics to other people in their immediate life situation. Luria concluded, observing that, for illiterates "self-awareness is a secondary and socially-shaped phenomenon," one that is intimately related to one's appropriation of literacy (Luria, 1976, p. 145).

Luria also found that illiterates were unable to "immediately perceive the logical relation between the parts of the syllogism" (Luria, 1976, p. 103). Instead, the illiterate person treated the syllogism as a series of isolated, concrete, and logically unrelated judgments. When asked to pay attention to the logical relationships between the syllogistic statements, illiterate folk denied it was possible to draw conclusions from statements about things with which one had no personal experience (Luria, 1976). With the appropriation of literacy, Luria's peasants became able to understand syllogistic, logical relationships.

When Luria examined the illiterate subjects' capacity for generalization and abstraction, he found that illiterates typically exhibited concrete or situational thinking. Illiterate subjects did not sort objects into logical categories but incorporated them into "graphic-functional situations drawn from life and reproduced from memory" (Luria, 1976, p. 49). When one peasant was presented with a series of objects, that is, a hammer-saw-log-hatchet, he did not classify them categorically as tools. Rather, the peasant commented that these objects were alike because they interacted in a situational context: " 'A saw, a hammer, and a hatchet all have to work together. But the log has to be there too!' " (Luria, 1976, p. 56). Luria noted, as well, that the peasants, operating as they did in a situational mode, were decidedly rigid and unable to switch to other, alternative modes of classification. By contrast, Luria found that persons with even a year or two of schooling used categorical classification as their chief method of grouping objects.

While Luria explored empirically the characteristics of illiterate folk, Havelock in *Preface to Plato* approached the development of literacy in the West from a historical point of view. Havelock pointed out that the Greeks of Aeschylus's fifth-century B.C. culture were midway in the process of appropriating literacy (Havelock, 1963). Havelock noted that, although the Greeks had used the alphabet since the eighth century, most individuals in fifth-century B.C. Greece learned to read in late adolescence, if at all. He argued that it was not until the middle of the fourth century B.C. that Greek culture had been largely assimilated into literate habits of thought. In a fascinating analysis, Havelock contextualized Plato's railing against the poets in the tenth book of the *Republic* in the context of this shift from a superficial appropriation of literacy characterized by strong strains of residual orality to a literate mode of consciousness.

For Plato, the poets represented the Greek culture's commitment to a mimetic style of learning, closely tied to an earlier culture of primary orality. Havelock's analysis suggested that for Plato mimesis was a code word that described habits of thought that Luria would later come to associate with illiterate consciousness. Havelock argued that, according to Plato, mimesis was to be abhorred because it required "a state of total personal involvement and therefore of emotional identification with the substance of the poetized statement" (Havelock, 1963, p. 17). In its place, Plato argued for a dialectical rationality that broke down the participatory identification reminiscent of primary oral consciousness, by promoting awareness of the "I" as distinct from the object of knowledge.

Havelock argued that the Greeks' introduction of vowels into their written alphabet enabled them to objectify meaning to an extent never before realized in the West. In contrast to ancient Hebrew, which until very late in the pre-Christian era required readers to supply their own vowels as they performed the text in their reading of it, the Greek vocalic alphabet enabled them to reduce meaning almost entirely to textuality. In a development previously unthinkable for primary oral folk, ideas could now be treated as universal essences, somehow real, out there, and fully representable in a text. With this new capacity to objectify reality as a "not me" came a new capacity for abstract, objective analysis. The new technology of writing enabled the Greeks to separate the knower from the known to an extent never before possible in human history. Consequently, the anthropomorphic cast of primary oral thought with its agonistically toned focus on the collectivist, human life world of family and tribe began to lose its hold on consciousness. A new capacity for rational reflection, applied both to the self and the human life world, promoted, in turn, the development of philosophy, a protoscience, and genres of art with a new psychological depth.

Scholars building on Ong's work have pointed out that the shift to literacy that grounded the development of the capacity for rational reflection also helped the West to shift from a shame-based to a guilt-based social structure. Tradition-directed shame cultures use myth, lore, ritual, and religion to inform individuals of codes of honor and dishonor in social interactions. In short, the shame culture provides the individual with "unified images of character that a person emulates and against which one compares himself or herself in conducting life and action" (Payne, 1991, p. 225). Such cultures typically exert tremendous pressure on individuals to conform to tribal modes of behavior and provide strong negative sanctions for breaking with tradition. With the shift to literacy "the individual finds it possible to think through a situation more from within his own mind out of his own personal resources and in terms of an objectively analyzed situation which confronts him" (Ong, 1967, p. 135). In literacy-based "guilt cultures," the "individual is socialized to experience a psychological, inner sense of deviation and loss with behavior or thoughts that do not conform to the social code" (Payne, 1991, p. 225). The literate individual depends on the guidance of an interiorized moral sense that functions as a gyroscope that guides one's movements on a moral landscape. In the literate mode of consciousness, guilt has replaced shame as the highest expression of moral "dis-ease."

Nevertheless, guilt has not entirely replaced shame as the normative moral emotion in literate cultures. In fact, Lewis (1971) has argued that in our culture "shame is probably a universal reaction to unrequited or thwarted love" (p. 16). Lewis pointed out that experiencing shame brings both the self and the other into focal awareness, as one painfully experiences the other's rejection of the self. The experience of shame, therefore, "helps to maintain the sense of separate identity by making the self the focus of experience" (Lewis, 1971, p. 25). Although shame extends beyond the confines of shame-based cultures, differences exist between literacy-based expressions of shame and earlier, preliterate expressions. Whereas in primary oral, shame-based cultures shame involves the individual's almost complete identification with the community whose rejection he or she feels, shame in literate cultures reflects a heightened self-consciousness that directly judges the ultimate inadequacy of the self. In dramatic contrast to the largely unconscious, empathic identification of the self with the community in primary oral, shame-based cultures, in literate cultures shame involves even more self-consciousness about the self than guilt (Lewis, 1971).

Perhaps only with the development of self-reflection and detached objectivity associated with the rise of literacy can an experience of shame-free guilt be possible. Indeed, recent research by Tangney (1990) has shown that the two constructs can be measured independently and that shame-proneness, not guilt-proneness, is associated with pathological narcissism (Gramzow & Tangney, 1992), psychological maladjustment (Tangney, Wagner, and Gramzow, 1992), and anger and self-reported aggression (Tangney, Wagner, Fletcher, & Gramzow, 1992). This line of research suggests as well that shame-proneness will also predict problems with forgiveness because shame involves a judgment about the entire self, "stemming from internal, global, uncontrollable, and presumably stable attributions about the self" (Tangney, 1990). Given such a pervasive negative judgment of the self, failures in justice or empathy by others may result in shame-based rage and unconsciously motivated retaliatory reactions. Thus, the shame-based individual will likely exhibit greater difficulty in processing the motives and actions of the so-called perpetrator objectively, resulting in blockages in the forgiveness process. Caught in a swirling vortex of shame, the shame-based individual will experience difficulties in seeing the other or self compassionately, making the practice of authentic forgiveness unlikely. Indeed, Trainer (1981) differentiated authentic (intrinsic) and inauthentic (role-expected and expedient) forgiveness styles, laying the groundwork for specific predictions, relating shame-proneness and the capacity to forgive.

Aeschylus's *Oresteian Trilogy* represents a shift in the cultural significance of shame, as previously unconscious, shame-based collective forces such as the drives toward vengeance and countervengeance, symbolized by the Furies, were increasingly subjected to rational analysis and control. Athena's handling of the Furies in Aeschylus's play portrays the emergence of this new, objectifying viewpoint, as well as a shift from a shame-based to a guilt-directed mode of consciousness. In the old, primary oral cultural synthesis with its close identification of the knower with the known, forgiveness as a human potential found expression only when collective pressures put limitations on human vengeance. In this context, only refraining from retaliation would promote the ultimate survival of the group.

In the new synthesis emerging in Aeschylus's Greece, the motives for forgiveness were now subjected to a more rational consideration. According to the new contours of Athenian society, violations of community norms would hereafter lead to guilt for specific actions that, in turn, permitted rationally based expiation and exoneration. This shift from a shame-based to a guilt-focused culture called into question the efficacy of shame-based acts of vengeance. Indeed, Athena's rational appeal to the Furies to forgive Orestes in the final play of the *Oresteian Trilogy* represented the unfolding of this new, guilt-based synthesis. Newly forged intellectual capacities and relational dynamics, related in part to the rise of literacy, promoted a new capacity for forgiveness that was rooted, in part, in an individual's disinterested appreciation of the realities of the objective world. Indeed, Aeschylus implicitly portrayed the Furies as personification of the old agonistic, collectivistic, shame-based dynamics of primary oral consciousness. The encounter between Athena and the Furies represents the unfolding of a major cultural paradigm shift in which shame-based, residually oral modes of collective interaction are replaced by literacy-based guilt modes of moral self-consciousness. When, in Aeschylus's drama, they ultimately relinquished their right for shame-based vengeance, Athena awarded them a new place of honor in Greek society as "spirits of blessing," literally, Eumenides.

In the new intellectual climate of fifth-century Greece, fostered, in part, by a growing assimilation of consciousness to the effects of literacy, new potentialities for forgiveness evolved. The development of a more interiorized selfhood and the capacity for objective analysis lay a foundation on which the world religions' subsequent call for universal forgiveness could make sense. The new Greek synthesis grounded a guilt-based cultural milieu quite distinct from the original environment of human evolutionary adaptedness in which shame-based community norms were the standard. As we have seen, the capacity to forgive that evolved within the cultural matrix of primary oral cultures could be explained as the direct result of the forces of kinship selection and reciprocal altruism. Humans living in these preliterate tribal cultures possessed a sense of self substantially less differentiated than that of modern individuals in the West.

Their forgiveness behaviors probably evolved in response to collective needs for cooperation to ensure group survival in the face of predation, the threat of warring tribes, and a scarcity of food. Individuals who failed to restrain their desires for revenge threatened the stability and safety of the tribe. Collective sanctions and laws, heavily buttressed by the threat of shame-based punishment of recalcitrant individuals, probably reinforced compliance. Because this mode of forgiveness emerged out of what Havelock (1963) terms a mimetic tendency toward emotional identification with what is known, uncomplicated by a fully differentiated sense of self, a label of "mimetic forgiveness" seems appropriate. In essence, mimetic forgiveness represents the expression of a "natural" reconciliatory tendency in shame-based, oral cultures. For them, forgiveness stems from largely unconscious, collectivist pressures operating on the basis of kinship selection and reciprocal altruism.

In contrast, the differentiation of self promoted by the widespread internalization of literacy in fifth-century Greece promoted the evolution of a new mode of forgiveness best termed "dialectical forgiveness." In contrast to its predecessor, "dialectical forgiveness" involves the use of noetic capacities not fully developed by illiterates. As we have seen, Luria's illiterate peasants possessed a limited awareness of distinct self-identities. Although the mimetic forgiveness of illiterates may be motivated by group pressures to refrain from vengeful activity, such forgiveness does not require a fully differentiated or interiorized sense of self. As we have also seen, such forgiveness likely flows from shame-based, collective motives and not from an internalized and personalized sense of guilt. In contrast, dialectical forgiveness, built as it is on the differentiation of literate consciousness, is characterized by a heightened sense of self and by an appreciation of abstract and universal moral principles. As such, dialectical forgiveness stems more from guilt than from shame after a person has developed an attitude of fundamental self-respect and self-acceptance.

As we have seen, Luria noted that his illiterate peasants were unable to disengage themselves from direct experience, rendering them incapable of thinking imaginatively about contrary-to-fact situations. Forgiveness in the dialectical mode presupposes the person's ability to disengage the self from direct experience by placing oneself in the position of looking at a situation as the other person sees it. This ability to pivot back and forth between one's own viewpoint and that of the other differentiates it strongly from mimetic forgiveness. In this mode, the individual tied to direct experience apparently cannot easily enter into the other person's experience. Only strong, collective, shame-based pressures dissuade an individual from seeking revenge, because, according to Luria, illiterate individuals possess limited capacity for reaching beyond their immediate experience.

Luria also noted that illiterate peasants tended to exhibit concrete or situational thinking and do not classify objects categorically. Literates, by contrast, have a greater capacity for abstracting. The greater degree of abstraction associated with dialectical forgiveness means one can conceive of universal motives for forgiveness. By referring to God as a cosmic parent and all human beings as brothers and sisters, some world religions have symbolically extended the kinship ties on which mutual cooperation and forgiveness seem to have their natural basis. Indeed, traditional religious commentators have not grasped that seeing God as a Divine Parent, calling for universal love toward all members of the human family, requires a highly developed capacity for abstraction.

The limited self-awareness of Luria's illiterate peasants and their inability to disengage from immediate experience both make dialectical forgiveness problematic. Dialectical forgiveness implies a sense of personal integrity based on abstract principles that do not figure in mimetic forgiveness. Remaining tied to the concrete situation, one simply takes revenge unless shame-based group pressures for survival intervene. In dialectical forgiveness, however, a heightened sense of selfhood, a heightened capacity for categorical classification, and an ability to disengage from direct experience all allow the self to reflect analytically on the various modes of its own activity. The individual can identify specific acts that have evoked feelings of guilt and take personal responsibility for his or her moral failures. The dialectical forgiver can likewise examine whether his or her intentions, behavior, feelings, and thoughts surrounding the act of forgiveness are consistent with universal principles of justice or agapaic love.

A CONTEMPORARY, DIALECTICAL TREATMENT OF FORGIVENESS

One contemporary researcher in the area of forgiveness has developed three empirically based scales, implicitly in the dialectical mode, that purport to assess whether the person has achieved internal consistency or integrity in the act of forgiveness (Trainer, 1981). Trainer's nuanced, dialectical approach expresses both the defensive inconsistencies that interfere with an integral forgiveness of self or others as well as an integrated form of forgiveness that she labels as intrinsic. Trainer does not view intrinsic forgiveness primarily as a product of social pressures, such as those captured by the theories of kinship selection and reciprocal altruism. Rather, she depicts intrinsic forgiveness as "an inner change in attitudes and feelings toward the one who has done the injury, as well as by benevolent behavior" (Trainer, 1981, p. ix). She explains that intrinsic forgiveness involves a "free decision to disengage from hostile attitudes, feelings, and behaviors" and to step into a healing process that will result in a renewed capacity to experience positive attitudes and feelings toward the other who has wounded one (Trainer, 1981, p. 68). As such, intrinsic forgiveness requires both autonomous initiative on the part of the forgiving individual as well as a relaxed receptivity to the initiatives of the offender.

Intrinsic forgiveness requires that the person consistently act according to values integral to one's identity. Such consistency requires that the forgiver engage in nondefensive reappraisal and letting-go coping processes that lead to the cessation of hostile internal dialogue (Trainer, 1981, p. 36). Intrinsic forgiveness involves a decision based not on calculations of what is deserved but, Trainer argued, on the ethical belief that "one has the responsibility to refrain from treating offenders in ways that are less than human" (Trainer, 1981, p. 43). When viewed in the metaphorical language of Aeschylus's drama, intrinsic forgivers are those who, because they have experienced a capable advocate who loved and accepted them as they expressed their anguish and anger over rejection, are now habitually able to forgive and forget, more or less unconditionally. Through the help of attachment figures, wise and secure as the goddess Athena in Aeschylus's drama, these individuals master the difficult discipline required to transform Furies into Eumenides. With their own hard-won inner peace, they become spirits of blessing for the families and communities with which they share their love and work.

As a healthy, integrated expression of dialectical forgiveness, intrinsic forgiveness epitomizes the highest forgiveness potential possible in literacy-based and guilt-based cultures. Nevertheless, despite the shift from a shame-based to guilt-based cultural milieu, shame continues to operate in powerful and disruptive ways within the new cultural synthesis. The main difference between guilt- and shame-based cultures is that dialectical forgiveness, more so than mimetic forgiveness, depends on a much more distinct differentiation of the self from the community or persons whose sanctions have engendered in him or her feelings of shame. Moreover, in dialectical forgiveness, one can distinguish between the distinct realms of guilt and shame. As shame about the self detoxifies and separates from issues requiring forgiveness, the self increasingly assumes an other-centered stance. Of course, Trainer's work suggests that only with intrinsic forgiveness is the specter of interiorized shame adequately analyzed to allow an integrated forgiving and forgetting.

In describing two nonintrinsic, but dialectical, forms of forgiveness that lack an integral consistency between affect, cognition, and behavior, Trainer (1981) contrasts role-expected with expedient forgiveness. She defines role-expected forgiveness as "an overt manifestation of forgiving behavior accompanied by fear, anxiety, and resentment" (Trainer, 1981, p. xi). In role-expected forgiveness, the forgiveness behavior is a compulsive, automatic response to the perceived expectations of others or of oneself. In living up to these expectations, spontaneous feelings of anger, revulsion, or sadness are disregarded, denied, or repressed. In this relatively dysfunctional form of forgiveness, the forgiver may sometimes take the other off the hook for destructive behavior, but this, nevertheless, leaves oneself dangling, skewered by one's natural psychic distress. In role-expected forgiveness, the individual attempts to direct against oneself the Furies of rage, guilt, and shame that constitute the natural response to being wronged. The other person, defined by social role as justified in his or her behavior, seems exonerated of blame and spared the difficult work of holding the victim's psychic pain and anger as they are transformed into spirits of blessing, that is, Eumenides. Nevertheless, as members of the helping professions will attest, individuals who exhibit role-expected forgiveness often exhibit indirect hostility toward the persons they purport to forgive.

Trainer's second forgiveness type, expedient forgiveness, "consists in an overt manifestation of forgiving behavior performed as a means to an end" (Trainer, 1981, p. ix). The individual who exhibits expedient forgiveness knows that it is in his or her best interests to forgive. Therefore, forgiveness serves these individuals as a power strategy whereby one can reassert one's strength against the victimizer. Forgiveness functions as a way to get even for the injuries inflicted. Expedient forgiveness enables the forgiver to devalue both the injurer and the injury in condescending toward the other. The forgiver thus survives the injury while restoring the integrity of the self (Trainer, 1981, pp. 72–73). One might say that the expedient forgiver tricks the Furies into following the scent of the so-called guilty other. While superficially domesticated, the Furies of one's own rage, guilt, and shame hound one's enemies through the subtle stratagems of passive aggression, projection, and haughty superiority expressed as forgiveness for crimes temporarily pardoned but not forgotten.

Despite substantial differences from each other, all three forms of dialectical forgiveness express a literacy-based mode of consciousness very different than their earlier, orally based, mimetic predecessors. In the dialectical mode—in contrast with the mimetic mode—the self is sufficiently interiorized and differentiated from the group to make mutuality possible. Moreover, future research may demonstrate that intrinsic forgiveness, unlike nonintrinsic modes of forgiveness, promotes an active processing of shame that integrates personal experience on affective, cognitive, and behavioral levels. Such integrated processing likely promotes both objectivity and compassion as the victim grasps his or her solidarity with the perpetrator in the shared experience of shame and guilt. Furthermore, for intrinsic forgivers, the experience of solidarity should not promote a proliferation of abuse from rigid, unyielding demands for universal benevolence toward all. Indeed, when forgiveness is viewed as an active processing of traumatic events on cognitive, affective, and behavioral levels that involves an acknowledgment of hurt, a lowering of resentment, and a relinquishing of hatred, forgiveness need not lead to further abuse (Freedman & Enright, 1996). This distinguishes between an intrinsic, integrated act of forgiveness and potentially destructive, nonintrinsically based alternatives: pardoning that releases a perpetrator from blame, condoning that denies actual injury, and reconciling that riskily renews a relationship with a perpetrator (Freedman & Enright, 1996).

CONCLUSIONS

The present chapter has explored the development of forgiveness from an evolutionary point of view. Viewed through the dramatic artistry of Aeschylus, forgiveness was conceptualized as a theme of universal import for the ancient Greeks. Aeschylus's portrayal of Orestes's reconciliation with the Furies provided a template for understanding the process through which vengeance can give way to forgiveness, and individual and collective Furies can be transformed into Eumenides, spirits of blessing.

Evidence for the selective attraction between non-human primates previously engaged in conflict continues to accumulate. De Waal (1996) argued that, expressed as reciprocal altruism, reconciliation behaviors promote individual survival within the context of an interdependent community, helping the individual to deal with predation, food distribution, and the establishment of alliances to aid in the struggle for intragroup dominance. When viewed as a product of natural selection occurring within humankind's original context of evolutionary adaptedness, the twin theories of kinship selection and reciprocal altruism explain forgiveness behavior. A human capacity to forgive developed originally to cope with environmental pressures associated with food acquisition, mating, predation, and marauding bands. Cooperation among kin and non-kin alike ensured that one's genes passed on to succeeding generations. Strong, shame-based social pressures connected with promoting group survival presumably led to forgiveness behaviors that helped protect the fragile web of human solidarity, promoting survival in a hostile environment.

As humankind moved beyond the original environment of evolutionary adaptedness, the internalization of literacy led to a more highly differentiated and interiorized personal identity and a lessening of the agonistic character of primary oral consciousness. An increased capacity for separating the knower from the known encouraged by literacy led, in part, to a guilt-based morality and, consequently, to new possibilities for forgiveness. So-called dialectical forgiveness could now be imagined and, sometimes, even practiced. Athena's handling of the Furies in the final play of the *Orestian Trilogy* exemplified this new mode of dialectical forgiveness. The enhanced ability to disengage from direct experience related to the appropriation of literacy led to an attenuation of the old oral-agonistic consciousness, thus making an assumption of the other person's point of view more feasible. Likewise, an increasing capacity for abstraction laid the groundwork for the articulation of universal, moral, and religious appeals for forgiveness. Finally, a heightened sense of selfhood, an increased facility for abstraction, and a heightened ability to disengage from immediate experience all contributed to the development of a view of forgiveness as an integrated expression of one's identity.

As an exemplar of a dialectical approach to forgiveness, Trainer's (1981) three empirically derived forgiveness types both validate and qualify postmodern objections to the practice of forgiveness. Forgiveness in the expedient mode appears to be, sometimes, a sordid moral power play, and forgiveness in the role-expected mode appears to resemble masochistic self-hatred. Nevertheless, Trainer's research also provides evidence for the occurrence of forgiveness in an intrinsic mode. Both expedient and role-expected forgiveness, based as they probably are on personal shame as well as guilt, might be explained as defensively structured, dysfunctional versions of reciprocal altruism. In contrast, intrinsic forgiveness has the potential to be, sometimes, a relatively selfless act. Literacy-promoted self-reflection, the capacity to overcome determinisms through self-knowledge, and the capacity to coordinate the affective, cognitive, and behavioral dimensions of forgiveness all make unified integrity in forgiving possible. If intrinsic forgiveness, indeed, expresses this personal integrity, the person may replace selfish motives with universal religious or moral ones comprehensible only to literate folk.

For those who are no longer limited to the level of human actualization possible in the original environment of evolutionary adaptedness, forgiveness still has a survival value. Forgiveness remains of central importance for those committed to the cooperative development of a more human world, reflecting ever more completely the tender altruistic stirrings with which nature has equipped the human community. In practicing forgiveness, individuals can, like good organic gardeners, learn how to work as much with nature as against it. In the end, the answer to the question of whether to forgive may affect the ultimate destiny of our planet's evolutionary process. Indeed, the evolutionary evidence suggests that individuals skilled in forgiveness may possess a selective advantage, enabling them to act in ways best suited to promote the survival of the species and the planet (de Waal, 1996).

REFERENCES

Aeschylus (1956). *The Oresteian trilogy* (Philip Vellacott, Trans.). Middlesex, England: Penguin Books.

Aureli, F, van Schaik, C. P., & van Hooff, J. A. (1989). Functional aspects of reconciliation among captive longtailed macaques (Macaca fascicularis). *American Journal of Primatology, 19*, 39–52.

de Waal, F. B. M. (1987). Tension regulation and nonreproductive functions of sex among captive bonobos (Pan paniscus). *National Geographic Research, 3*, 318–335.

de Waal, F. B. M. (1989). *Peacemaking among primates*. Cambridge: Harvard University Press.

de Waal, F. B. M. (1993). Reconciliation among primates: A review of empirical evidence and unresolved issues. In W. A. Mason & S. P. Mendoza (Eds.), *Primate social conflict* (pp. 111–144). Albany: State University of New York Press.

de Waal, F. B. M. (1996). *Good natured: The origins of right and wrong in humans and other animals*. Cambridge: Harvard University Press.

de Waal, F. B. M., & Ren, R. M. (1988). Comparison of the reconciliation behaviour of stumptail and rhesus macaques. *Ethology, 78*, 129–142.

de Waal, F. B. M., & van Roosmalen, A. (1979). Reconciliation and consolation among chimpanzees. *Behavioral Ecological and Sociobiology, 5*, 55–66.

de Waal, F. B. M., & Yoshihara, D. (1983). Reconciliation and redirected affection in rhesus monkeys. *Behaviour, 85*, 224–241.

Fisher, J. A. (1996). The myth of anthropomorphism. In M. Bekoff & D. Jamieson (Eds.), *Readings in animal cognition* (pp. 3–16). Cambridge: MIT Press.

Freedman, S. R., & Enright, R. D. (1996). A manualized forgiveness therapy for incest survivors. *Journal of Consulting and Clinical Psychology, 64*, 983–992.

Goodall, J. (1986). *The chimpanzees of Gombe: Patterns of behavior*. Cambridge, MA: Belknap Press.

Gramzow, R., & Tangney, J. P. (1992). Proneness to shame and narcissistic personality. *Personality and Social Psychology Bulletin, 18*, 369–376.

Havelock, E. A. (1963). *Preface to Plato*. Cambridge, MA: Belknap Press.

Lewis, H. B. (1971). *Shame and guilt in neurosis*. New York: International Universities Press.

Luria, A. R. (1976). *Cognitive development: Its cultural and social foundations*. Cambridge: Harvard University Press.

Nietzsche, F. W. (1887). *On the geneology of morals*. (by W. Kaufman, Trans.). New York: Vintage Books.

Ong, W. (1967). *The presence of the word: Some prolegomena for cultural and religious history*. New Haven, CT, and London: Yale University Press.

Ong, W. (1982). *Orality and literacy: The technologizing of the word*. New York: Methuen.

Payne, D. (1991). Characterology, media, and rhetoric. In B. E. Gronbeck, T. J. Farrell, & P. Soukup (Eds.), *Media, consciousness, and culture: Explorations of Walter Ong's thought* (pp. 223–252). Newbury Park, CA: Sage.

Stevens, A. (1993). The two million-year-old self. College Station: Texas A & M University Press.

Tangney, J. P. (1990). Assessing individual differences in proneness to shame and guilt: Development of the self-conscious affect and attribution inventory. *Journal of Personality and Social Psychology, 59*, 102–111.

Tangney, J. P., Wagner, P., Fletcher, C., & Gramzow, R. (1992). Shamed into anger? The relation of shame and guilt to anger and self-reported aggression. *Journal of Personality and Social Psychology, 62*, 669–675.

Tangney, J. P., Wagner, P., & Gramzow, R. (1992). Proneness to shame, proneness to guilt, and psychopathology. *Journal of Abnormal Psychology, 101*, 469–478.

Tangney, J. P., Wagner, P., Hill-Barlow, D., Marschall, D. E., & Gramzow, R. (1996). Relation of shame and guilt to constructive versus destructive responses to anger across the lifespan. *Journal of Personality and Social Psychology, 70*, 797–809.

Trainer, M. F. (1981). *Forgiveness: Intrinsic, role-expected, expedient in the context of divorce*. Unpublished doctoral dissertation, Boston University.

Trivers, R. (1971). The evolution of reciprocal altruism. *Quarterly Review of Biology, 46*, 35–56.

York, A. D., & Rowell, T. E. (1988). Reconciliation following aggression in patas monkeys (Erythocebus patas). *Animal Behaviour, 36*, 502–509.

11

The Evolutionary Significance of Archetypal Dreams

HOLLY L. HUSTON

For those who are unfamiliar with the concept of archetypes, I begin by providing a brief introduction. Like Freud, Jung postulated the existence of a personal unconscious. However, Jung also postulated the existence of a collective unconscious, an inherited, instinctual substrate that underlies, and is separate from, the personal unconscious. Jung generally defined the collective unconscious as an inherited biological template for psychological and social development that has been derived from the evolutionary experience of our species over millions of years (Jung, 1966, 1968b).

Much as patterns of physical development are coded in our genes, Jung believed that the same was true for patterns of psychological and psychosocial development (Stevens, 1982, 1993). These patterns are called the archetypes and make up the "building blocks" of collective unconscious. These archetypal patterns can be expressed symbolically and are most identifiably expressed in dream imagery, art, myth, and ritual, although the archetypes themselves, like subatomic particles, are not visible and are observable only by their effects.

Jung first developed and then expanded his theory of archetypes by three different methods. The first method he used was examination of research data collected from administrations of the Word Association Test (Jung, 1972). The second method was comparison of common symbols found across cultures (Jung, 1989). The third method used by Jung to explore the existence of archetypes was his analysis of the unconscious mental activity (dreams, delusions, and hallucinations) of patients who produced certain symbols or obscure mythological material, even though it was clear these patients could not have been exposed to this material either by education or by travel (Jung, 1968a).

Through his observations and investigations, Jung documented a readily identifiable class of dreams different from everyday dreams in both content and impact. He identified these dreams as "archetypal dreams" and maintained that they were organized around particular archetypes and originated from the collective unconscious rather than from personal experience. This third aspect of Jung's investigations, the explorations of dreams, is the basis of this chapter.

What makes archetypal dreams so different from other kinds of dreams? Archetypal dreams are vivid, emotionally charged, impactful dreams that are often experienced as being intensely meaningful. Archetypal dreams are often nonrational and remote from everyday personal experience (Jung, 1968d). Archetypal images seem to be curiously resistant to interpretation. Jung noted that he had remembered dreams that were full of symbolic material that "Freud was unable to interpret . . . only incompletely or not at all" (1989, p. 158).

Typically, archetypal dreams and images are experienced as ego-alien or as qualitatively different from "normal," "everyday," or "personal" images produced in the dream state. On a related note, Hunt (1989) has found that clients' free associations to archetypal symbols, instead of becoming progressively more relevant to the dreamers' daily life, "tend[ed] to become more impersonal and to circle around the more striking details of the dream" (p. 129).

By comparison, Hunt described clients' free associations to typical (nonarchetypal) dream images as "usually branching out into background personal memories" (p. 129). Archetypal dreams contain unusual and often nonrational events and situations (such as primitive rituals), characters (such as mythical figures or talking animals), objects (such as a stone that turns into a deity), or behaviors (such as flying on one's own) that are not simply improbable but impossible in everyday experience.

Archetypal dreams can possess a mysterious, compelling, and gripping quality, related to spirituality and meaning, that Jung characterized as being "numinous" or holy. Archetypal images are often experienced by the dreamer as "strange, uncanny, and at the same time, fascinating" (Jung, 1968c, p. 311). The contents of archetypal dreams are not readily comprehensible to the conscious mind. Persons experiencing an archetypal dream often feel that the dream is highly significant and that they have encountered something profound, yet they often find it difficult to put the meaning into words.

Archetypal dreams tend to be impactful. They are more likely than other types of dreams to induce or accompany profound change in the dreamer. Also, archetypal dreaming is not an all-or-nothing proposition. Dreams can contain varying degrees of archetypal content.

Although I have long been interested in Jung's work, as a result of my personal experiences I became intensely interested in his theory of archetypes and its application to dreaming. I relate my own experience because it provides a graphic example of archetypal dreams and raises questions about some of the functions that archetypal dreaming may serve.

About six years ago, I became very ill. I saw many of the finest doctors in one of the world's best medical centers, but no one seemed to be able to fully identify or successfully treat my problem. In the eighteen months that followed the onset of my illness, I experienced a slew of nasty symptoms and received, at various times and from various experts, a myriad of scary diagnoses, which included systemic lupus erythematosus, myasthenia gravis, and polymyositis (a wasting disease of the muscles of the shoulder and hip muscles). I had to undergo a series of diverse and frightening medical tests and spent enough money on the drugs, the tests, and the doctor visits to purchase a small luxury automobile. However, at the end of this ordeal, I was still ill and was driving the same old car.

Ultimately and in despair, I gave up on Western medicine. The fact that something was amiss physically could be demonstrated on a number of laboratory tests, but no one seemed to be able to put the pieces together in a meaningful way. Doctors seemed to want to treat the pieces, saying that the eye problems that I was having were completely unrelated to the gastrointestinal distress that I was experiencing. Since all these parts were housed in the same body, I had difficulty following this line of reasoning.

By chance, I learned about a doctor of Eastern medicine, a Chinese doctor from a long line of doctors who had done amazing things for people, or so I had heard. I decided that I had nothing to lose by going to see him and at that point was ready to try anything.

My visit to his clinic was an experience quite unlike anything that I had ever encountered. In a small, storefront office, a row of red plastic chairs had been placed along the window. The floor was worn linoleum. A few simple drawings done on straw and bamboo scrolls adorned the walls. The bulk of the room was taken up by a glass and wood counter, and behind the counter were rows and rows and rows from floor to ceiling of tiny drawers. These drawers were the source of the most dense and amazing smells. I felt as though I had fallen into a jar of "Chinese 5-spice." I checked in with the doctor's wife and signed a form stating that I understood that this man did not have a doctor of medicine degree awarded by any recognizable American institution. Nervously, I sat with a friend awaiting my turn to see him.

When the doctor was ready to see me, he called me back to a small room. He placed my hand on a small, maroon satin pillow and gently began to feel along my wrist for the pulse. He was very quiet, sitting with his head cocked to one side, looking at a corner of the ceiling. He seemed to be listening with his fingers. After a time, in a very thick accent, he began to describe some of the symptoms I was currently experiencing. He asked me a few questions and then told me more about my symptoms. I was amazed by some of the things that he was able to tell me. My friend was equally amazed.

He told me that he could help me and prescribed herbs for my condition. I was to take the herbs for 30 days exactly as he had prescribed them. He wrote out the prescription in Chinese, and I carried the tiny white paper, covered with strange, lacy, black script, to his wife.

She filled the prescription from the rows of drawers. Thirty sheets of butcher-block paper were laid out on the glass counter. Using a very old, handheld scale, she measured out herbs from the drawers. Onto the papers, I saw spill from the scales a profusion of bark, dried fruits, leaves, mushrooms, dried flowers, resin, mosses, roots, twigs, and a dark powder that looked like very rich potting soil. Each packet was wrapped and taped. The packets weighed approximately one pound, with one packet to be taken per day. I left with two heavy shopping bags full of herbs. On the way home, we had to roll the windows down in the car because the intense smell became overwhelming.

Cooking the herbs was truly an ordeal. They could be prepared only in a glass pot, since cooking herbs in metal reputedly interferes with their medicinal properties. They had to be boiled and strained several times over the course of three hours. The tea that was then rendered from the herbs had to be taken warm but not too hot. Over the days that followed, the house became saturated with the pungent smell of the herbs. For weeks afterwards the sofa and rugs smelled faintly of astralagus and licorice.

Drinking the herbs was as much of an ordeal as preparing them. I can honestly say that those herbs were the worst-tasting stuff that I ever drank. However, my experience was that they made me well. Most interestingly, this treatment seemed to have a very powerful effect on my dream life. I began sleeping better almost immediately. Then, approximately two weeks into the treatment, cup after noxious cup, I felt an increased sense of calm, and my symptoms were rapidly diminishing.

During the second week of drinking the tea, I had a very powerful dream in which I was receiving communion from an Oriental priest. He wore red and white robes, with an elaborate, gold-embroidered design. I was alone with him in a room that was hung with rich tapestries. The floor was soft and covered with beautiful rugs. The room was a little bit smoky and smelled of incense. Before me stood the priest. He was balding and aristocratic with a white Fu Manchu mustache (very unlike the dark-haired, bespectacled Chinese doctor I had seen two weeks earlier). He had an air of perfect serenity and peace. Before him, on an elaborately carved rosewood table as tall as a lectern, stood a cup and a plate, both Oriental in design. He took a pinch of a loamy substance from the plate between his fingers and held this to my mouth. He said, "This is my body." It smelled like the forest, and I ate it. He held the cup to my lips. I saw that it was full of a dark and muddy liquid, like the tea. He said, "This is my blood," and I drank it. I woke from this incredibly vivid dream feeling better than I had felt in many months. I felt my strength returning and knew that I was going to get well.

Two days later, I dreamed of an Oriental woman coming toward me in a forest. She wore a flowing white gown. On her head, she wore a crown of twigs, berries, leaves, and all of the things of the earth that go into the tea. The woman approached me and smiled. Again, I woke with an intensified feeling of well-being and a sense that things were going to be OK.

I understood that the illness had forced me to reconnect with my body and, through the illness, with the earth around me in a new way. I had a powerful sense of the earth as savior and mother and the things of the earth as healing. In the dreams, I literally ingested the unadulterated earth and found that it made me well. For several weeks following these dreams, anytime I lifted food to my mouth, I was intensely aware of being sustained by the massive web of life.

I loved these dreams because they were such powerful integrations of the mystical and the mundane, the conscious and the unconscious, East and West, modern and primitive, body and soul. To this day, I am taken by the power of the images. If I close my eyes, I can call these images forth, and they are still evocative. They elicit feelings of deep peace, profound nurturance, and the sense of a connection that cannot be broken. I have wondered often about these dreams. My experience with them has fostered my subsequent interest in dream impact and has raised many questions.

Did the tea trigger the dreams? If so, how? Were the dreams a response to the process of preparing or drinking the tea or to the herbal chemistry? Were they an affirmation that I was finally engaged in the correct treatment for my condition? Was the external and somewhat exotic trigger of the Chinese doctor sufficient to trigger an internal, but foreign, healer that then manifested as a dream image? Perhaps all of these.

Jung conceived of the influence of the collective unconscious and archetypes as ranging on a continuum from the most basic level of human physiological development and survival to the more transcendent and spiritual aspects of human development. Jung also thought of archetypes in evolutionary and developmental terms as mechanisms of human psychological maturation. Common aspects of human psychological, social, and biological development were theorized by Jung to be governed by an archetypal program.

Jung's psychology focuses, in part, on the split between conscious and unconscious (and this includes his idea of the collective unconscious) and between the civilized and primitive aspects of ourselves. Integration of these and other potentially opposing aspects of ourselves is a major goal of Jungian analysis.

Jung has described our more primitive aspects as being closest to animal instincts and stressed that these primitive instincts inhabit the ancient corners of the collective unconscious, much as our primitive forebears lived in caves that had previously been inhabited by animals. The primitive aspects of ourselves are not dense in the sense of being "dumb"; rather, they underpin a type of intelligence or functioning that differs from that of our daily, "rational" functioning and is based on complex biology and instinct. According to Stevens (1993), "At the heart of Jungian psychology is the idea that beneath our conscious intelligence a deeper intelligence is at work—the evolved intelligence of humankind. . . . To Jung, the two million-year-old self was a vivid metaphor for an age-old dynamic at the core of personal existence, thereby the virtue of the evolutionary heritage of our species" (p. 2).

Accordingly, in dreams, we could certainly expect the 2 million-year-old within us to comment upon our bodies and what we need to maintain the general state of our physical as well as our psychological health. My own dreams seemed to reveal that I had taken a major step to be in harmony with my body's natural healing abilities.

In the past 25 years both the medical and behavioral sciences have witnessed an explosion of interest in, and research into, the issue of the mind/body "problem" (Rossi, 1993; Achterberg & Lawlis, 1980; Simonton, Simonton, & Creighton, 1978). Archetypes, as defined by Jung, function as a bridge between psyche and soma. Rooted in the neurobiological basis of the instincts, the archetype expresses itself in the form of imagery and affective energy within the individual psyche. Archetypes may serve as an internal psychobiological feedback mechanism. When fully operational, archetypes can serve as a medium of healing, helping to preserve psychological and biological homeostasis. They are powerful visual communications from the nonverbal 2 million-year-old self within us, to the abstract, thinking self of the neocortex (Stevens, 1993; Bohm, 1988).

Archetypal dreams may be the "2 million-year-old's" way of communicating with our more "modern" selves. Rossi (1993) acknowledges the importance of Jung's archetypal hypothesis and recognizes its similarities to more recent theories in the area of psychoneuroimmunology. He also notes that Jung is a largely unrecognized pioneer in the area of imagery and active imagination and its archetypal links to the body.

Over time, I have come to the conclusion that archetypal dreams are *strongly* related to physical states such as illness, healing, pregnancy, menopause, puberty, aging, and dying, as well as to personality growth. Some initial research has been conducted on archetypal dreams that explores the links between archetypal imagery and physiology.

For example, Schroer (1984) conducted a study investigating the frequency of archetypal dreams during first pregnancy. He assumed that archetypal dreams occur more frequently during critical life phases and reasoned that, therefore, archetypal dreams are likely to occur during a woman's first pregnancy. Schroer writes that "like other critical life phases, a first pregnancy has both a psychological and a biological component. The pregnant woman is taking on the identity of a mother for the first time, as well as experiencing massive hormonal and metabolic changes in her body." Schroer found that eight of the pregnant women reported archetypal dreams during the reporting period, compared to none of the nonpregnant women.

For those interested in possibly increasing the frequency of their archetypal dreaming, Hunt, Ogilvie, Belicki, Belicki, and Atalick (1982) found that the physical-motor characteristics of good balance were related to increased frequency of archetypal and lucid dream reporting. Consequently, one would expect that meditation, ballet, tai chi, yoga, and other disciplines that promote physical balance ought to increase archetypal dream recall.

Jung wrote, "Together, the patient and I address ourselves to the two million-year-old [self] that is in all of us. In the last analysis, most of our difficulties come from losing contact with our instincts, with the age-old forgotten wisdom stored up in us. And where do we make contact with this old man in us? In our dreams'' (Jung, 1971, p. 76).

To this day, the personal dream images that I described earlier defy a complete verbal analysis and remain ineffable in many respects. They are like shells washed up from some primordial inner sea—nothing that I made, just gifts that I stumbled across.

I never expected that my 2 million-year-old man, and woman, could wear a Chinese face. To me they represent the importance of balance and connectedness to the things of the earth. I cannot help but wonder today, when I think of these images, if they do not somehow have a physiological effect. Perhaps they stimulate production of endogenous opiates and a constellation of other beneficial neurotransmitters, such as serotonin.

The dream images, in conjunction with life experience, have led me to think in depth about the relationship among archetypes, imagery, psychneuroimmunology, and evolution. Rather than presenting answers about the significance of evolution in archetypal dreaming, I have shared with you my preliminary observations. I also hope that I have encouraged you to reflect upon the importance and the meaning of archetypal dreams, especially your own.

REFERENCES

Achterberg, J., & Lawlis, G. (1980). *Bridges of the mind/body*. Champaign, IL: Institute for Personality and Ability Testing.

Bohm, D. (1988). Beyond relativity and quantum theory. *Psychological Perspectives, 19*, 24–43.

Hunt, H. T. (1989). *The multiplicity of dreams: Memory imagination, and consciousness*. New Haven, CT: Yale University Press.

Hunt, H. T., Ogilvie, R., Belicki, K., Belicki, D., & Atalick, E. (1982). Forms of dreaming II: Findings with a phenomenologically based classification of "altered state" or "hallucinatory" experiences in dreams. *Perceptual and Motor Skills, 54*, 58–609.

Hunt, H. T., Ruzycki-Hunt, K., Pariak, D., & Belicki, K. (1993). The relationship between dream bizarreness and imagination: Artifact or essence? *Dreaming: Journal of the Association for the Study of Dreams, 3*, 179–199.

Jung, C. G. (1966). The personal and the collective (or transpersonal) unconscious. In H. Read, M. Fordham, & G. Adler (Eds)., *The collected works of C. G. Jung* (Vol. 7) (pp. 64–79). Princeton, NJ: Princeton University Press.

Jung, C. G. (1968a). The concept of the collective unconscious. In H. Read, M. Fordham, & G. Adler (Eds.), *The collected works of C. G. Jung* (Vol. 9I) (pp. 42–53). Princeton, NJ: Princeton University Press. (Original work published 1936)

Jung, C. G. (1968b). Instinct and the unconscious. In H. Read, M. Fordham, & G. Adler (Eds.), *The collected works of C. G. Jung* (Vol. 8) (pp. 129–138). Princeton, NJ: Princeton University Press. (Original work published 1919)

Jung, C. G. (1968c). On the nature of dreams. In H. Read, M. Fordham, & G. Adler (Eds.), *The collected works of C. G. Jung* (Vol. 8). (pp. 281–300) Princeton, NJ: Princeton University Press. (Original work published 1948)

Jung, C. G. (1968d). Synchronicity: An acausal connecting principle. In H. Read, M. Fordham, & G. Adler (Eds.), *The collected works of C. G. Jung* (Vol. 8) (pp. 417–531). Princeton, NJ: Princeton University Press. (Original work published 1952)

Jung, C. G. (1971). *Psychological reflections: A new anthology of his writings.* London: Routledge & Kegan Paul.

Jung, C. G. (1972). *Experimental researches. The collected works of C. G. Jung* (Vol. 2). Princeton, NJ: Princeton University Press. (Original work published 1904–1907)

Jung, C. G. (1989). *Memories, dreams, and reflections.* New York: Pantheon. (Original work published 1961)

Rossi, E. (1993). *The psychobiology of mind-body healing* (revised ed.). New York: Norton.

Schroer, T. (1984). Archetypal dreams during first pregnancy. *Psychological Perspectives, 15,* 71–80.

Simonton, O., Simonton, S., & Creighton, J. (1978). *Getting well again.* Los Angeles: Tarcher.

Stevens, A. (1982). *Archetypes: A natural history of the self.* New York: William Morrow.

Stevens, A. (1993). *The two million-year-old self.* College Station: Texas A&M University Press.

12

An Evolutionary Approach to Psychiatric Disorders: Group-Splitting and Schizophrenia

JOHN PRICE AND ANTHONY STEVENS

INTRODUCTION

> The search for hidden function in what seemed to be grossly maladaptive traits has been among the most fruitful procedures of evolutionary science ever since Darwin. (Alexander, 1979)

The evolutionary approach to psychiatric disorders seeks to identify the adaptive (functional) behavior patterns that are seen in disordered form in the various clinical states (Nesse & Williams, 1994; Gardner, 1995; McGuire & Troisi, 1998). For example, in the case of simple phobias such as snake phobia and fear of heights, the clinical state is likely to be an exaggeration of an inherited avoidance response that was adaptive in our ancestral environment. More complicated anxiety disorders can be conceptualized in terms of the avoidance of danger; the disadvantages of too much anxiety at one extreme of a normal distribution may be balanced by another type of disadvantage in those who suffer too little anxiety (e.g., mortality from accidents). However, in the case of the major psychoses there is no obvious normal behavior that has become exaggerated or distorted, and there is no general agreement as to what adaptive advantage, if any, the genetic tendency to either schizophrenia or affective disorders conferred during the course of our evolution.

Since the time of Kraepelin there has been a strong clinical impression that schizophrenia and affective psychosis are fundamentally different, even though no discriminant function has been found to separate psychotic patients into two discrete groups (Kendell & Gourlay, 1970; Kendell, 1991). Our own evolutionary analysis of psychiatric disorders (Stevens & Price, 1996) supports the clinical impression that schizophrenia and affective disorders are fundamentally different, for we suggest that the genetic tendency underlying them performs different and even opposite functions. We see both disorders as being the by-products of vital group processes, concerned with the integrity and the multiplication of human groups during evolution. Individual behavior has become adapted to subserve the emergent properties and processes of groups, and because of the evolutionary recency of group life, these behaviors have not yet been fine-tuned by the evolutionary process to the same extent as behavior subserving individual goals. Therefore, it is likely to be to behaviors serving group goals that we should attribute the incapacities that we see caused by the major psychoses.

GROUP COHESION AND GROUP SPLITTING

In the natural history of groups, two stages require very different behavior from group members. There is a stage of growth and competition with other groups that requires that the group should subordinate the goals of individual members to those of the group; in human groups over the past few million years this has been achieved by the development of a unified social reality (dogma and customs) for each group and the creation of cultural mechanisms for promoting group solidarity (McNeill, 1995). The social reality of each group is different and may well appear arbitrary to outsiders. The cohesive adoption of one social reality by a group required the evolution of the capacity for "indoctrinability" in group members (Eibl-Eibesfeldt, 1982).

During this cohesive stage of group development there is a premium on homeostasis, and deviations in group behavior that threaten group cohesion are counteracted. The sanctions exercised by the group include loss of status and prestige and even expulsion from the group. It has appeared to us and to others (Price, Sloman, Gardner, Gilbert, & Rohde, 1994; Stevens & Price, 1996; Leary & Downs, 1995) that the capacity for mood change might be a primitive mechanism for enabling the individual to accept the first of these sanctions (loss of status and prestige) and so to subordinate his or her individual goals to the goals of other group members. In this way the individual would avoid the sanction of expulsion from the group, and thus group homeostasis would be achieved at the expense of mood change in one or more individuals (Price, 1991).

When a group reaches a certain size, there is a need for the group to split into two or more daughter groups. This is a time of change, and the homeostatic mechanisms are put on hold, while other behaviors facilitating splitting are favored. Some splitting occurs when a group gets polarized between opposing attitudes such as left-wing and right-wing, young and old, mods and rockers, and so on. Then we can imagine that a sizable subgroup splits off, sharing common aspirations but with fundamental beliefs not very different from those of the remaining group members. Fissioning may also occur along kinship lines (Chagnon, 1980).

A related process is the dispatch of colonists from an established group to settle in a new area that has previously been identified as suitable for colonization. The colonists take with them the beliefs and aspirations of the mother group, but, to the extent that they are separated from the mother group, they have an opportunity for developing a new and different identity.

Another type of splitting occurs when a single individual develops an entirely new and arbitrary belief system and persuades a few other members of the group to share his or her beliefs. This "prophet" then becomes the leader of the new group, taking the new group to a new territory. Such a leader needs the sort of charisma traditionally granted by divine will and maintained through direct communication with the gods. This is a uniquely human phenomenon, quite unlike the forms of group fissioning that occur in other primates (Pusey, 1992; Ron, 1996). It is this type of splitting that we believe derives from the schizophrenic genotype. If the prophet is able to attract followers and persuade them to his or her unique beliefs, he or she takes them to the "promised land" and creates a new community; if the prophet fails to recruit followers, he or she is perceived as "mad" and, in some cases, becomes a psychiatric patient.

THE ROLE OF CULT LEADER

Contemporary studies of disaffected groups that separate from their host community and set off in quest of some promised land (Galanter, 1989) indicate that having a charismatic leader is indispensable to group survival. Especially relevant to our argument is the finding that many such leaders seem to be borderline or schizotypal personalities. In a brilliant investigation of charismatic leadership, Charles Lindholm (1990) describes how figures such as Adolf Hitler, Jim Jones, and Charles Manson inspire incredible loyalty in the followers who gather around them. Yet to others unaffected by their personalities, they appear half mad, "driven by violent rages and fears that would seem to make them repellant rather than attractive, while their messages look, from the perspective of the outsider, to be absurd melanges of half-digested ideas, personal fantasies and paranoid delusions" (p. 4).

The relationship between charismatic leaders and the followers who gather around them has long been a subject for systematic scrutiny, and many have contributed valuable insights and terminologies to describe them: Weber's "epileptic prophets," Durkheim's "collective effervescence," Mesmer's "animal magnetism" invested in the person of the hypnotist, Nietzsche's "superman," Eliade's shamanic "technicians of the sacred," the millennial cults of medieval Europe so vividly described by Normal Cohn, and Le Bon's "inspired leader" recruited from "the ranks of those morbidly nervous, excitable, half-deranged persons who are bordering on madness" (Le Bon, 1952).

Nearly all charismatic leaders are men (therefore, the male pronoun is mainly used in this chapter), though history records some outstanding female examples, such as Joan of Arc. Of those for whom personal details exist, most would probably satisfy the DSM-IV criteria for borderline, schizotypal, or paranoid personality disorder. The most striking thing about them is their *shamanic* quality. The Tungus noun *saman* means "one who is excited, moved, raised." As a verb, it means "to know in an ecstatic manner." Ethnological studies of shamans in Siberia, Africa, and North America suggest that shamans approach the borderline of insanity but do not actually cross it: in other words, they could be classified as schizotypal but not as schizophrenic. As with all charismatic leaders, their influence arises from the uncanny, hypnotic power of their personalities, the force of their rapidly shifting emotions, the bizarre manner of their speech, their capacity to enter into a state of dissociation and to leave it at will, and their apparent ability to put themselves in close touch with the unconscious and to articulate its archetypal contents in a way that convinces their followers that they are divinely inspired.

THE ROLE OF CULT FOLLOWER

If it is adaptive to have potential cult leaders proclaiming salvation through deviant and often bizarre systems of belief, there must be people ready to listen to them and to be converted by them. At least a proportion of the population must be susceptible to their message.

Indeed, we find in our society an enormous interest in fringe beliefs that is otherwise inexplicable. Not only do many young people actually join cults, but there is a large market for reading matter devoted to witchcraft and other paranormal phenomena. In spite of a large, even excess provision of religious capacity in the mainstream religions, the churches remain empty, and the services unattended; senior churchpeople describe an unsatisfied need for further spiritual experience—"a widespread spiritual hunger in the land"—that can be satisfied only by charismatic figures proclaiming some variation on the standard faith or practice.

The gullibility of people over reports of flying saucers, the Bermuda Triangle, cures by faith healing, astrology, the bending of forks, and miracles of various kinds is difficult to reconcile with standard models of human behavior; indeed, only in the context of the coevolution of charismatic qualities in leaders with complementary dispositions of gullibility in followers do all these phenomena make any sense at all.

This disposition in the follower to embrace the bizarre teachings of a prophet does not imply any mental abnormality. The cult followers described by Galanter (1989) were normal, and many of them had been relieved of mild depression by joining the cult; they tended to come from close and secure families. The same was true of the cult followers described by Ribeiro (1970), who made the point that millennial movements are a normal phenomenon in many cultures. They depend on a central myth that is reinterpreted anew by successive prophets, as we have seen in our own culture in the form of a series of millennial cults based on the Book of Revelation. Human aspiration for "salvation" and abhorrence of "evil" make such cults attractive. Normal citizens who are not preoccupied with fighting a neighboring group tend to see evil not in the enemy but closer to home; then they are liable to be dissatisfied with the society they live in and to be interested in the promise of personal salvation in a perfect age or in a "land without evil" (Ribeiro, 1970).

There is a strong and unique two-way interaction between the leader and his followers. The leader makes the follower feel special, uniquely loved, and valued. Even when the leader addresses an audience of thousands of people, this personal message is retained. A member of the audience at one of Hitler's large rallies reported: "I felt as though he were addressing me personally. My heart grew light, something in my breast arose. I felt as if bit by bit something within me were being rebuilt (Lindholm, 1990, p. 102). There is also an intense adulation of the leader by the followers, which no doubt confirms the aberrant beliefs and may well contribute to the leader's ability to maintain his difficult and lonely role. Indeed, as Lindholm put it: "if the postulate of the charismatic's volatile, borderline-like personality is correct, then such a man is particularly susceptible to psychotic collapse when not given needed social support (Lindholm, 1990, p. 171).

This leads us into our central concern, which is the transformation of the features of psychosis into the attributes needed to create a worldview so attractive and yet so deviant as to persuade normal people to leave their social group, their homes, and often their families to endure the rigors of cult life.

WHY SCHIZOPHRENIC SYMPTOMS PROMOTE GROUP SPLITTING

Delusions are a cardinal feature of schizophrenia, and the capacity for delusional thinking is essentially the capacity to create new belief. A new belief is a delusion only if it remains unshared; when a new belief is transmitted to followers, it becomes not a delusion but a dogma.

Group solidarity is maintained by a communality of belief, and, in order to split off, the new group has to establish a worldview that is at odds with that of the old group. The new worldview arises from the delusional belief system of the group leader. It must be impervious to attempts to persuade the believer that it is wrong, hence, the fixity of delusions and the certainty of the deluded patient that he is right, and all the world is wrong. Delusions are often of mission and are consistent with the process of leaving the old group and establishing a new group.

Because of the arbitrary nature of the belief systems on which group differences are based, only one member of the new group (the prophet) can generate new beliefs, and others must accept them. There may be one or more temporal leaders who interpret the beliefs of the prophet to the followers. In addition, paranoid delusions of persecution are experienced in relation to members of the old group and encourage the prophet to take the new group somewhere else.

The sudden, overwhelming force of "autochthonous" delusions is necessary to combat the strong forces that maintain conformity of belief within a group.

We know from Asch's experiments that people are willing to falsify their perceptions in order to express opinions that do not conflict with a majority view (Asch, 1956; Cialdini, 1984). Tolerance of deviant belief such as "heresy" is not a feature of groups. The Congregation of the Universal Inquisition, now the Congregation for the Doctrine of Faith, is a testament to the motivation of an organization to maintain conformity of belief. The common belief in many ways defines a group, and the extreme fear that most people have of losing the privileges of group membership is a source of motivation for conformity of belief. Against this background of ideological conformity the aberrant beliefs of the prophet need to be seen.

Auditory hallucinations provide a reference group for the prophet, composed of elements of his unconscious mind. Without at least one other person, it is difficult to maintain a belief system in opposition to the majority view (Asch, 1956). Evidence for this was found in U.S. troops being brainwashed in Korea; provided that they had one other prisoner with them, they could hold out. The hallucinations can also provide material to substantiate and elaborate the delusional beliefs.

Thought disorder cuts down communication between the prophet and the old group, facilitating splitting. Neologisms have the same effect. A common language is a unifying social force, while differences in language promote splitting. The meaning of neologisms is communicated to supporters and helps to establish a new language for the new group.

Some unusual motor features of schizophrenia may also be explained in the light of cult formation. For instance, schizophrenic patients have an unexplained capacity and tendency to walk for long distances. We have observed that on admission to hospital their feet are sometimes severely blistered. No other psychiatric patient group shares this tendency. Long walks are a feature of the early stages of cult formation (Webster, 1980) and may also be useful in the prophet for the purpose of reconnaissance. Another example is the reduced tendency to shrug the shoulders. Human ethologists have noticed that schizophrenic patients have a reduced frequency of "shoulder-shrug" compared to normal populations (E. C. Grant, personal communication). This gesture expresses doubt, resignation, and compromise, which are alien to the task of the prophet.

Hospitalized schizophrenic patients have been reported to prefer geographically isolated places and to avoid social contact (Singh, Kay, & Pitman, 1981). This would fit with our theory, assuming that the schizophrenic individual is behaving like a prophet lacking followers. The prophet is alienated from normal social intercourse because of his deviant beliefs, and in the absence of followers, his preaching of his mission having failed, he might be expected to withdraw from society and to refrain from social intercourse.

The schizophrenic patient and the prophet both manifest a certain inattention to problems of daily living. Schizophrenic patients tend to neglect themselves and require "chivying" by relatives or psychiatric nurses in order to maintain normal hygiene. Left to themselves, they do not wash themselves or change their clothes, and their living quarters become increasingly untidy. The same tendency may be seen in the prophet. Since the prophet has to convince his followers of the truth of his delusional beliefs, he must be seen as special, out of the ordinary, holy, and concerned with spiritual matters. Therefore, neglect of everyday routines such as comfort and hygiene will increase his credibility in the eyes of followers. These followers perform many of the functions of psychiatric nurses, with the difference that they operate within the delusional system rather than outside it. The defects that the followers ascribe to holiness the nurses ascribe to madness.

Since the beliefs propounded by the prophet are likely to be incompatible with reality, there must be some means of reconciling the followers to these disparities when they occur. An example of this is the way in which the Jehovah's Witnesses periodically proclaim the date of Armageddon, revising it when the day arrives and passes with no sign of the predicted cataclysm. The increased cognitive dissonance found in schizotypy would not only permit the prophet to ignore this embarrassment but to demonstrate to his flock that his faith is in no way affected by it. In one graphic instance of this dynamic, a Maori prophet, Rua, who prophesied that King Edward V11 would arrive in New Zealand in June 1906 with a gift of £3 million to enable Rua to buy back the Maori lands from the whites, gathered a group of approximately 1,000 people around him (Webster, 1980). When both king and money failed to materialize, more than half his followers loyally accompanied him on a long march into the Urawera Mountains, where they established a farming community. Rua had nine wives and many children and remained the respected leader of the commune, preaching a religion based on the Old Testament. The settlement flourished until it was attacked and overwhelmed by police in 1916. Indeed, Festinger (1957), who himself infiltrated a millennial cult, found that the nonoccurrence of the leader's prediction of the world's end actually intensified the loyalty of the group, thus confirming his predictions based on cognitive dissonance theory.

The "positive" features of schizophrenia are useful in group splitting. The negative features are not seen in the successful prophet, whose ego is inflated by his followers like a taut balloon. The prophet without followers, who lacks any form of social boosting or validation, succumbs to the negative features. Thus, the schizophrenic patient, like a punctured or uninflated balloon, has the balloon lining of his delusional system but none of the inflation that gives it "shape" and makes him an attractive and charismatic figure.

The Schizotypical Individual as Shaman

The similarity between schizophrenic illness and the experiences of prophets and shamans has not gone unremarked. We have already reviewed the anthropological literature (Price & Stevens, 1998). Taking a genetic perspective, Erlenmeyer-Kimling and Paradowski (1969) looked for some advantage in the schizotype that might balance the reduced reproduction seen in schizophrenia.

They examined the idea that, historically, schizophrenics were esteemed for mystical experiences and enjoyed privileged social status as shamans, prophets, or saints.

Schizophrenic behaviour may have conferred high social status upon affected individuals in earlier periods. The hallucinatory and delusional features of the disease might previously have earned the affected individual esteem and protection by presenting him to his community as visionary, mystic, shaman or saint. (Jarvik & Chadwick, 1973)

However, they considered this hypothesis to be untestable and also inherently unlikely, for the following reason: "Saints and prophets not being renowned for high fecundity, the benefits ordinarily garnered by them or their isomorphs would scarcely have bestowed a reproductive advantage of the needed magnitude" (Jarvik & Chadwick, 1973).

Erlenmeyer-Kimling and Paradowski (1969) considered the shaman only in the context of existing society and not in the role of founder of a new cult; they did not have our present knowledge of the widespread occurrence of world-rejecting cults (Wallis, 1984) or of the fact that male cult leaders often control the sexuality of their members so that they themselves have sexual access to all the female members, whereas the male followers live under strict sexual prohibitions (Lindholm, 1990). Thus, the founder of a successful cult may enjoy marked reproductive success.

Theories of Proximal Causation

Our theory concerns the ultimate or evolutionary origin of the schizotypal diathesis and therefore does not conflict with theories of proximal causation, whether these be sociological, psychological, or neurochemical. If the sudden conviction of an autochthonous delusion is an adaptive advantage, it does not matter whether it comes about due to a daytime breakthrough of REM sleep in a phenotype adapted to nocturnalism (Feierman, 1994), an abnormality of memory retrieval (Sengel & Lovallo, 1980), a lack of cognitive inhibition (Peters, Pickering, & Hemsley, 1994), or a surge of dopaminergic transmission in the nucleus accumbens. Nor does it matter if schizophrenia is shown to be associated with brain damage (Elkis, Friedman, Wise & Meltzer, 1995) due to either trauma or infection. Stranger forms of symbiosis have been shown to occur (Williams & Nesse, 1991).

IMPLICATIONS FOR RESEARCH

Evolutionary explanations concern what has happened in the past and so are difficult to refute directly; likewise, it is difficult to derive from them specific, testable propositions. Nevertheless, we feel that our theory has certain heuristic implications. Those who study the psychosocial origins of schizophrenia should direct their attention also to the psychological and social conditions that give rise to the formation of cults and to the psychological characteristics of cult leaders.

Malinowski reported that a significant proportion of the communication in primitive tribes concerned the social construction of a shared reality, consisting of ceremonies designed to appease the gods, ward off sickness, and so on (Cronen, Pearce, & Harris, 1982). We would predict that the capacity for this type of social participation would be impaired in the schizotypal individual, more than other categories of communication such as gossip and task-oriented talk. If it is the destiny of the schizotypal individual to create a new reality for a new group, he should not share in the communal reality of the parent group.

Among the relatives of schizophrenic patients we expect the schizotypal genotype to manifest itself not only in actual cult leaders but also in various forms of independent thinking and a tendency to strike out in new directions. Thus, the artistic person would not just flourish in an existing school but would create his own school. The rejection of orthodoxy and the search for a "promised land" might express themselves through the symbolic forms of the artist or the "new intellectual territory" of the scholar; thus, the satisfaction of achievement and even of recognition might give the boost to self-esteem and to mental stability that in the cult leader is provided by the adulation of followers. In a more contemporary context, we might expect to find creative people like Sigmund Freud, who turned his back on orthodoxy and carved out for himself and his followers a large territory of the mind.

IMPLICATIONS FOR TREATMENT

A major factor that distinguishes a successful cult leader from a schizophrenic patient is that the leader is surrounded by a group of devoted followers who hang on his words and adopt his beliefs, however crazy they might appear to outsiders. Thus, the group grants the leader enthusiastic validation of his ideas and powerful boosting to his self-esteem. Therefore, we predict a therapeutic effect from the provision of a group of adulatory believers for each schizophrenic patient.

Such provision would be impossible, even in the most generously funded research project. However, advances in computer technology, artificial intelligence, and the explorations of "virtual reality" offer the possibility that each schizophrenic patient might be allowed to generate his own group of followers within a computer system. He could indoctrinate his robotic followers with his beliefs, imparting to them his visions, his mission, the hierophantic dictates of his voices, his neologisms, and his syntactical eccentricities, forming a network of inspired communication with part personalities, projected from the recesses of his own psychic complexity through the miracle of silicon into a virtually existent world of his own devising. The consequent gratification of his otherwise frustrated social, religious, and political ambitions may well prove to be of therapeutic help, especially in the relief of negative symptoms. It is not possible to predict how the treatment would affect the patient's general behavior and his relation to society as a whole. Even the relative social withdrawal necessary for the computer work might be balanced by a rise in sociability due to increased self-confidence.

There is some evidence to suggest that a computerized cult follower might have reality for the patient. McGuire and Troisi (1998) describe a study in which undergraduates were told that they were "communicating through a teletype." They were, in fact, communicating with a simple computer program based on 100 rules to generate replies, but they experienced the replies as if they were communicating with another person. When asked afterward whether they were communicating with a computer or a person, 90% of the subjects answered, "a person." Moreover, 80% stated that they thought it impossible that they could have been communicating with a computer. This experiment was conducted in the 1960s, when computer software was in its early days. At the present time it seems not unreasonable to think that a program could be devised so that "computer-generated followers" would not only seem real and human but could elevate the schizophrenic patient into a leadership role.

Another study described by McGuire and Troisi (1998) provides evidence that to be placed in a leadership role has beneficial effects in chronic schizophrenia. In this study schizophrenic patients were allocated to work groups facilitated by nurses, but the nurses then withdrew from the groups, leaving the leadership position vacant. In each group one patient came to adopt the leadership role, and this patient showed clinical improvement, whereas the remaining patients showed no change. It is, of course, possible that, just by chance, one patient in each group showed spontaneous recovery and that this improvement enabled the patient to become a leader; but this seems unlikely, and it is more probable that some systemic process between the group members resulted both in one member's becoming leader and also in that particular member's showing improvement in symptoms. This promising study deserves to be repeated, but it also gives hope that by creating a leadership role in relation to computer-generated followers it might be possible to benefit all patients rather than limit the benefit to the leader at the expense of the human followers.

REFERENCES

Alexander, R. D. (1979). *Darwinism and human affairs.* Seattle: University of Washington Press.

Asch, S. E. (1956). Studies of independence and conformity: 1. A minority of one against a unanimous majority. *Psychological Monographs, 70* (Whole No. 416).

Chagnon, N. A. (1980). Mate competition favouring close kin, and village fissioning among the Yanomama Indians. In N. A. Chagnon & W. Irons (Eds.), *Evolutionary biology and human social behavior* (pp. 86–131). North Scituate, MA: Duxbury.

Cialdini, R. B. (1984). *Influence: How and why people agree to things.* New York: William Morrow.

Cronen V. E., Pearce, W. B., & Harris, L. M. (1982). The coordinated management of meaning: A theory of communication. In F.E.X. Dance (Ed.), *Human communication theory: Comparative essays* (pp. 61–89). New York: Harper & Row.

Eibl-Eibesfeldt, I. (1982). Warfare, man's indoctrinability and group selection. *Zeitschrift fur Tierpsychologie, 60,* 177–198.

Elkis, H., Friedman, L., Wise, A., Meltzer, H. Y. (1995). Meta-analyses of studies of ventricular enlargement and cortical sulcal prominence in mood disorders: Comparisons with controls or patients with schizophrenia. *Archives of General Psychiatry, 52,* 735–746.

Erlenmeyer-Kimling, L., & Paradowski, W. (1969). Selection and schizophrenia. *American Naturalist, 100,* 651–665.

Feierman, J. R. (1994). A testable hypothesis about schizophrenia generated by evolutionary theory. *Ethology and Sociobiology, 15,* 263–282.

Festinger, L. (1957). *A theory of cognitive dissonance.* Stanford CA: Stanford University Press.

Galanter, M. (1989). Cults and new religious movements. In M. Galanter (Ed.), *Cults and new religious movements* (pp. 25–40). Washington, DC: American Psychiatric Association.

Gardner, R. J., Jr. (1995). Sociobiology and its applications to psychiatry. In H. I. Kaplan & B. J. Sadock (Eds.), *Comprehensive textbook of psychiatry* (6th ed., vol. 1, pp. 365–375). Philadelphia: Williams & Wilkins.

Jarvik, L. F., & Chadwick, S. B. (1973). Schizophrenia and survival. In M. Hammer, K. Salzinger, & S. Sutton (Eds.), *Psychopathology: Contributions from the social, behavioral and biological sciences* (pp. 57–73). New York: Wiley.

Kendell, R. E. (1991). The major functional psychoses: Are they independent entities or part of a continuum? Philosophical and conceptual issues underlying the debate. In A. Kerr & H. McLelland (Eds.), *Concepts of mental disorder* (pp. 1–16). London: Gaskell.

Kendell, R. E., & Gourlay, J. (1970). The clinical distinction between the affective psychoses and schizophrenia. *British Journal of Psychiatry, 117,* 261–266.

Leary, M. R. & Downs, D. I. (1995). Interpersonal functions of the self-esteem motive: The self-esteem system as a sociometer. In M. H. Kernis (Ed.), *Efficacy, agency and self-esteem* (pp. 123–144). New York: Plenum.

Le Bon, G. (1952). *The crowd: A study of the popular mind.* London: Ernest Benn.

Lindholm, C. (1990). *Charisma.* Oxford: Blackwell.

McGuire, M. T., & Troisi, A. (1998). *Darwinian psychiatry.* New York: Oxford University Press.

McNeill, W. H. (1995). *Keeping together in time: Dance and drill in human history.* Cambridge: Harvard University Press.

Nesse, R. M., & Williams, G. C. (1994). *Evolution and healing: The new science of Darwinian medicine.* London: Weidenfeld & Nicolson.

Peters, E. R., Pickering, A. D., & Hemsley, D. R. (1994). "Cognitive inhibition" and positive symptomatology in schizotypy. *British Journal of Clinical Psychology, 33,* 33–48.

Price, J. S. (1991). Homeostasis or change? A systems theory approach to depression. *British Journal of Medical Psychology, 64,* 331–344.

Price, J. S., Sloman, L., Gardner, R., Gilbert, P., & Rohde, P. (1994). The social competition hypothesis of depression. *British Journal of Psychiatry, 164,* 309–135.

Price, J., & Stevens, A. (1998). The human male socialisation strategy set: Co-operation, defection, individualism and schizotypy. *Evolution and Human Behavior, 19,* 57–60.

Pusey, A. E. (1992). The primate perspective on dispersal. In N. C. Stenseth & W. Z. Lidicker (Eds.), *Animal dispersal: Small mammals as a model* (pp. 243–259). London: Chapman & Hall.

Ribeiro, R. (1970). Brazilian messianic movements. In S. L. Thrupp (Ed.), *Millennial dreams in action* (pp. 55–69). New York: Shocken Books.

Ron, T. (1996). Who is responsible for fission in a free-ranging troop of baboons? *Ethology, 102,* 128–133.

Sengel, R. A., & Lovallo, W. R. (1980). A random process model of cognitive deficit in schizophrenia. *Schizophrenia Bulletin, 6,* 526–535.

Singh, M. M., Kay, S. R., & Pitman, R. K. (1981). Territorial behavior of schizophrenics: A phylogenetic approach. *The Journal of Nervous and Mental Disease, 169,* 503–512.

Stevens, A., & Price, J. (1996). *Evolutionary psychiatry: A new beginning.* London: Routledge.

Wallis, R. (1984). *The elementary forms of the new religious life.* London: Routledge.

Webster, P. (1980). *Rua and the Maori millennium.* Wellington: Price Milburn for Victoria University Press.

Williams, G. C., & Nesse, R (1991). The dawn of Darwinian medicine. *Quarterly Review of Biology, 66,* 1–22.

13

An Evolutionary
Perspective on Treatment

ANTHONY STEVENS AND JOHN PRICE

What the evolutionary perspective brings to the treatment of psychiatric disorders is a new orientation, in that it adopts a transpersonal view of the patient's situation. Instead of seeing the illness purely as the product of familial and social circumstances, it examines it in the context of the evolved goals, needs, and strategies that have determined human behavior since our species came into existence on the African savanna. From the evolutionary standpoint, a psychiatric disorder is not a medical disaster like cancer or a stroke but an ancient adaptive response that for some contemporary reason has become maladaptive to the detriment of the patient's emotional and social life.

The first step in treatment, therefore, is to take the patient's history beyond the purely personal predicament and relate it to the story of humankind, for what psychiatry has traditionally classified as "illness" is often a consequence of a potentially healthy organism struggling to meet the demands of life: symptom formation is essentially an *adaptive* process. To consider symptoms as the products of a hypothetical disease entity does not necessarily make their meaning clear or their treatment easier. Viewed in an evolutionary context, they are more likely to be comprehensible. This permits a therapeutic approach that is both better informed and, we believe, more likely to lead to a lasting solution of the problem. A case history may serve to illustrate what we mean.

Albert Squires, a hospital porter, had been off sick for three months before his family doctor referred him to the psychiatric outpatient clinic of the hospital where he worked. He presented with the signs and symptoms of major depression—depressed mood, weeping, anhedonia, loss of interest and sexual libido, impaired sleep and appetite.

A decent, reliable, and conscientious man, with no previous psychiatric history, he had come to work at the hospital nine months earlier, having served for a number of years before that as a merchant seaman. All had gone well with this new job until, at the end of his first six months, the head porter sent for him and rebuked him for not taking any sick leave! Squires explained that he would certainly take sick leave if he became ill, but since he was in good health, this would not be necessary. "You're missing the point," said the head porter. "I don't care whether you're ill or not. When a man is off sick, the rest of us get paid overtime. So if you don't take your sick leave, you're letting the side down. You're cheating us out of money we're entitled to."

To Squires this was an important moral issue. Being an honest man, he didn't see how he could possibly stay off work and send in a sick note when he was feeling perfectly well. So he declined to go along with the head porter's scheme. Gradually, the atmosphere at work changed: his previously happy relationship with his fellow workers turned sour as they avoided him and showed their disapproval of his "uncooperative" attitude. He felt shunned and increasingly isolated, with the result that his slide into depression began. Eventually, unable to face going to work any longer, he was forced to go off sick. He brooded on the injustice of his position, but the irony did not escape him that his colleagues were drawing their overtime pay despite the moral stand he had taken on the issue.

What light does evolutionary theory throw on this case? How are we to understand the social situation in which Squires's depression had occurred? What evolved strategies were being used at different levels of the triune brain? What helpful advice could we give to the patient?

According to the "rank theory" of depression, the condition is an adaptive response to losing rank and conceiving of oneself as a loser (Price, 1967; Price & Sloman, 1987; Price, Sloman, Gardner, Gilbert, & Rohde, 1994). The adaptive function of depression, according to rank theory, is to facilitate losing and to promote accommodation to the fact that one has lost. In circumstances of defeat and enforced subordination, an internal inhibitory process comes into operation that causes individuals to cease competing and to reduce their level of aspiration (Gilbert, 1992). This inhibitory process is *involuntary* and results in the loss of energy, depressed mood, sleep disturbance, poor appetite, retarded movements, and loss of confidence, which are the typical characteristics of depression.

Viewed from an evolutionary perspective, the depressive state seems to have evolved to promote the acceptance of the subordinate role and the loss of resources that can be secured only by holding higher rank in the dominance hierarchy. The function of this depressive adaptation is to prevent the loser in a status conflict from suffering further injury and to preserve the stability and competitive efficiency of the group by maintaining social homeostasis.

How does rank theory help us to understand Squires's situation? Porters in a large hospital constitute a small tribal group with its own hierarchy, values, rituals, and modes of functioning. As with all such groups, membership depends on acceptance by other members of the group and the allocation of status within the group. Acceptance and status depend, in turn, on conformity to the group's ethos. Once membership has been granted on these terms, an individual's self-esteem, sense of personal health, and well-being become dependent on the continued good opinion of the group. The realization that one has offended the group, lost status, and been threatened with ostracism can result in a depressive disorder. A depression is particularly likely to result if the individual is forced into an *involuntary* use of the yielding subroutine, as was the case with Squires.

One important contribution of rank theory is that it has proposed a hypothesis of how depression actually evolved: it emerged as the *yielding* component of ritual agonistic conflict. This has been called the *yielding subroutine* (Price & Sloman, 1987). The adaptive function of the yielding subroutine is twofold. First, it ensures that the yielder truly yields and does not attempt to make a comeback, and, second, the yielder reassures the winner that yielding has truly taken place, so that the conflict ends, with no further damage to the yielder. Relative social harmony is then restored. Mania, on the other hand, evolved as the *winning* component of ritual agonistic behavior and may be called the *winning subroutine*.

These subroutines relate, then, to two fundamental vertebrate strategies for dealing with adversity. One is to attack, to escalate the action, to "go for it" with the determination to "win at all costs" (the *winning strategy*); the other is to yield, to back off or submit, to de-escalate, to "cut one's losses" (the *losing strategy*). The phylogeny of social competition has decreed that the decision to escalate or de-escalate should be taken quickly and synchronously *at all three levels of the triune brain.*

Paul MacLean conceived of the brain not as a unity but *three brains in one*, each with a different phylogenetic history, each with "its own special intelligence, its own special memory, its own sense of time and space, and its own motor functions" (MacLean, 1976).

In line with these suggestions, it is likely that the brain evolved in three stages. *The Reptilian Brain.* This, our most primitive component, evolved in our reptilian ancestors about 300 million years ago. We share it with all other terrestrial vertebrates, and it has remained remarkably unchanged by the march of evolution. It contains nuclei that are vital to the maintenance of life, such as those controlling the cardiovascular and respiratory systems. The main structural components of the reptilian brain are the basal ganglia, including the olfactostriatum (the olfactory tubercle and nucleus accumbens) and part of the corpus striatum (the caudate nucleus, putamen, globus pallidus, and satellite collections of gray matter).

At the early evolutionary stage represented by the reptilian brain emotions had not yet emerged, nor had cognitive appreciation of future or past events. Behavioral responses at this level are largely governed by instinct and appear to be relatively automatic. The typically reptilian behaviors of territorial acquisition and defense, as well as dominance striving, agonistic threat displays, and mating, are manifested at this stage of development.

The Paleo-mammalian Brain. This is made up of those subcortical structures that constitute the limbic system. This includes not only the hippocampus, the hypothalamus, and the thalamus but also the pituitary gland, which has been aptly described as ''the conductor of the endocrine orchestra.'' The limbic system is a homeostatic mechanism par excellence: it not only maintains a sensitive control of hormone levels but also balances hunger against satiation, sexual desire against gratification, thirst against fluid retention, sleep against wakefulness. It also plays an indispensable role in memory storage.

By this evolutionary stage the major emotions of fear and anger have emerged as well as those of love and attachment, together with their associated behavioral response patterns, bonding and mating. The thalamocingulate division of the limbic system performs the essential role in these mother–offspring and peer group behaviors, and there is no counterpart of this limbic subdivision in the reptilian brain. The other subdivisions of the limbic system—the amygdalar and septal subdivisions—are involved, respectively, in behavior promoting self-preservation and the procreation of the species. In all mammals, including man, this part of the brain is a structure of the utmost complexity, controlling basic psychophysical responses and attitudes to the environment.

Conscious awareness is more in evidence at this stage, and behavior is less rigidly determined by instincts, though these are still very apparent. The limbic system includes the oldest and most primitive part of the evolving cerebral cortex—the so-called *paleocortex*.

The Neo-mammalian Brain. This is the *neocortex*. It is responsible for cognition and sophisticated perceptual processes as opposed to instinctive and affective behavior.

Each of the ''three central processing assemblies'' of the triune brain (MacLean, 1985) has the autonomous power to select either a winning or a losing strategy. At the highest (neocortical) level a conscious assessment of the threat is made, and the decision whether to fight or yield is taken in full awareness of the circumstances. Meanwhile, at the middle (limbic, paleo-mammalian) level a semiconscious, emotionally loaded assessment of the threat is made, and the strategic selection proceeds with much less awareness of the circumstances. Simultaneously, at the lowest (reptilian) level an unconscious, instinctive assessment of the threat is made, and the winning or losing strategy is selected at a level beyond all awareness of the social circumstances involved.

How does the existence of these three strategic levels of operation help us to understand Squires's depression? Careful examination of his thoughts and feelings about his predicament made it apparent that his highest (neocortical) and middle (limbic) levels had selected the winning strategy, while his lowest (reptilian) level had selected the losing strategy. At the highest level, he was sticking to his moral principles and refusing to collaborate with the head porter's dishonest scheme. At the middle level he was sustained by powerful feelings of self-righteousness, disapproval of the head porter's chicanery, resentment at his colleagues' unfriendliness, and fury at the injustice of it all. But the lowest level had, without any voluntary participation on the part of consciousness, gone for the losing strategy and dragged him down into depression, effectively sabotaging all attempts by the higher centers to stand by correct moral principles and "fight the good fight" to the point of victory.

If these are the neuropsychic facts of the situation, how do they enable us to help him? First of all, they can give him some insight into what has been happening to him. That, in turn, might provide him with the data necessary to take action to resolve the conflict holding him in its grip. In view of his background, it was felt that a nautical analogy would advance his understanding.

He was asked to imagine a cargo ship sailing through icy waters. The captain is an extremely conscientious man, with a tight schedule to keep. He could make a wide detour south so as to avoid the ice, but since he hates being late and could not think of letting his company down, he decides to risk plowing on through the ice floes and keep on course. The helmsman, who knows nothing of the captain's schedule, though he can see the ice floes ahead, decides the captain must know best and holds his course as ordered.

The chief engineer down in the engine room knows nothing of all this, however, and busies himself maintaining the engine revolutions in accordance with the commands from the bridge. Soon the ship begins to take a battering from the ice. The captain, though anxious, refuses to alter course, while the helmsman, who is partially deaf, is aware of little apart from the captain's instructions. However, the chief engineer not only hears the ice clanging against the plates of the hull but sees water spurting through the joints between them and judges the situation too dangerous to proceed. On his own initiative, therefore, he throws the engines into reverse.

When this parable was put to him, Squires at once saw that his conscious mind was like the captain who had decided that virtue must prevail and that he must stick to his course at all costs. Squires also conceded that his emotions had been like the helmsman, who could see only part of the picture but carried on regardless, loyally convinced he was doing the right thing. It was the deepest level that Squires had most difficulty in understanding—the profound alteration of mood that had completely paralyzed his capacity for effective action. Nevertheless, he came to appreciate that, at this unconscious level, his mind had, indeed, behaved like the chief engineer. It was as if it had decided that the psychological damage and the emotional pain he suffered each day at work were too great to be endured, so that the engine room in his brain had refused to provide the energy to keep him on the course he had taken and had "gone into reverse" so as to pull him out of the intolerable situation.

Having understood this much, what—as Squires himself was quick to ask—should he do about it? From the "ultimate" standpoint of evolutionary processes, it does not matter whether a protagonist in a conflict wins or loses but that the conflict should be settled one way or the other. Then damage to both parties is minimized: both go their own way and live to fight another day. In selecting the winning or losing strategy, what matters from the individual combatant's point of view is that all three levels of the brain should agree in adopting the same strategy. If there is a fundamental disagreement between them (e.g., one level selecting one strategy while the others select the opposite strategy), then the likelihood of an affective disorder is greatly increased. Therefore, as far as the individual's mental health is concerned, it is unimportant which strategy is adopted provided that all three "central processing assemblies" are *pulling together toward the same objective*.

It follows that Squires can adopt one of two courses to deal with his predicament. If he decides to adopt a winning strategy and go on to the attack, he can, with the full backing of the psychiatric department, report his predicament to the District Health Authority and request suspension on full pay while his allegations are investigated. His objective will be to expose the irregularities of the portering department, have the head porter fired, and perhaps take over the post himself. This tactic, backed up with the threat of a civil suit against the Health Authority for negligence in failing to deal with a flagrant misuse of the sick leave system and for allowing the patient's health to suffer through bullying by the head porter, should be sufficient to galvanize the Authority into immediate action.

If he decides to adopt a losing strategy, however, he could come around to the head porter's point of view. He could bring himself to appreciate that the sick leave racket was a quasi-legitimate way of getting the porters more money. In fact, the Health Authority wished to pay the porters more but was prevented from doing so by the national guidelines. It consequently turned a blind eye to the routine abuse of the sick pay system, accepting that each porter would benefit by an extra two weeks' holiday a year and receive overtime pay as a bonus when his colleagues were on leave. Having come to see the essential fairness of this irregular arrangement, Squires could then write a letter of apology to the head porter, acknowledging the error of his ways and promising to be more cooperative in the future. The probability is that his anger against his colleagues will then subside and that in the future he will share their disapproval of any new porter who tries to buck the system.

Though Squires gave his enthusiastic consent for us to describe his case, in the hope that it might be of some help to others, he was not willing to permit us to divulge which of these alternative courses of action he chose to adopt. But, as far as the therapeutic outcome is concerned, the choice is immaterial. Winning and losing are both healthy activities: evolution has seen to that. It is in helping the patient to integrate the decision-making activities of all three levels of his brain that the therapeutic challenge lies.

The alternative strategies and their levels of operation are summarized in Table 13.1. Normally, all three levels escalate or de-escalate together. For example, D facilitates F, which facilitates B. This normally leads to yielding and reconciliation, which remove the circumstances responsible for D and F. On the other hand, F combined with A or C prevents resolution: F plus C produce the hostile depressive; F plus A produce the depressive who clings to unrealizable goals.

Table 13.1
Alternative Strategies for Social Competition at Three Brain Levels

	ALTERNATIVE STRATEGIES	
BRAIN LEVEL	WINNING (escalating)	LOSING (de-escalating)
CORTEX (reason)	(A) Fight to win	(B) Actively submit
LIMBIC (emotion)	(C) Get angry	(D) Feel chastened
REPTILIAN (mood)	(E) Mood elevation	(F) Depression

People develop a depressive illness when the losing strategy of the lowest (reptilian) level is activated in conjunction with an inappropriate adoption of the winning strategy at the highest (cortical) level and/or the middle (limbic) level. What keeps the patient depressed is the failure to resolve the situation by yielding at the higher levels. Since the reptilian depressive strategy is beyond the reach of conscious intervention, it cannot be changed by an act of will. Yet it continues to sabotage the patient's capacity to win. If the depression prevails, and the patient is eventually forced, despite himself, to give up at the higher levels and adopt a unifying losing strategy at all three levels of the brain, then the depression remits, its object achieved.

As the case of Albert Squires demonstrates, the winning strategy of the middle (limbic) level is characterized by the emotion of anger. The phylogenetic point of this is that *it is extremely difficult to give way if one is angry*. Anger is the emotion of *attack*. It facilitates winning by providing an uprush of energy. The outcome leads to mood change. If the circumstances are propitious, and the anger results in victory, then there is an elevation of mood. If the circumstances are unpropitious, and the anger has to be inhibited or leads to defeat, there is a depression of mood. Sometimes, however, the winning strategy is selected at the middle level, while the losing strategy is selected at the highest and lowest levels. This happened to a man who was falsely accused of sexually abusing his ten-year-old daughter. The accusation was made in public and permanently destroyed his reputation. At the cortical level he chose a losing strategy in that he refrained from taking legal action against the local authority on the grounds that further publicity would cause more harm to his daughter. At the lowest level the losing strategy was also selected, with the result that he became severely depressed. However, at the limbic level, he continued to nurture a murderous rage against the social workers responsible for the initial, grossly unjust accusation. His depression was consequently long-lasting and difficult to treat.

Intractable depressive disorders tend to occur when something appalling has been done to or by a patient, and the normal processes of yielding, atonement, forgiveness, and reconciliation have been unable to function. A man who, while drunk, caused a car crash in which his wife and children were killed developed a depression of this kind. Depression associated with posttraumatic stress disorder can follow a similar course.

While there is little doubt that evolutionary theory can improve our understanding of the nature and function of the common psychiatric disorders, it is still early to say how much it is going to help us to devise effective methods for their treatment. What is needed now is a corpus of informed knowledge about the relationships between individual experience, social influences, and the phylogenetic propensities that guide and inform all human development. This is the program that Freud and Jung embarked upon at the beginning of the century. We are now perhaps in a better position to bring it to fruition.

REFERENCES

Gilbert, P. (1992). *Depression: The evolution of powerlessness*. Hillsdale, NJ: Lawrence Erlbaum.

Maclean, P. D. (1976). Sensory and perceptive factors in emotional function of the triune brain. In R. G. Grennell & S. Gabay (Eds.), *Biological Foundations of Psychiatry* (vol. 1) (pp. 177–198). New York: Raven Press.

MacLean, P. D. (1985). Evolutionary psychiatry and the triune brain. *Psychological Medicine, 15*, 219–221.

Price, J. S. (1967). Hypothesis: The dominance hierarchy and the evolution of mental illness. *Lancet, 2*, 243–246.

Price, J. S. & Sloman, L. (1987). Depression as yielding behaviour: An animal model based upon Schelderup-Ebbe's pecking order. *Ethology and Sociobiology, 8*, 85s–98s.

Price, J. S., Sloman, L., Gardner, R., Gilbert, P., & Rohde, P. (1994). The social competition hypothesis of depression. *British Journal of Psychiatry, 164*, 309–335.

For Further Reading

Alexander, R. D. (1987). *The biology of moral systems*. New York: Aldine de Gruyter.

Axelrod, R. (1984). *The evolution of cooperation*. New York: Basic.

Barkow, J., Tooby, J., & Cosmides, L. (1992). *The adapted mind: Evolutionary psychology and the generation of culture*. New York: Oxford University Press.

Bowlby, J. (1969). *Attachment and loss*, Vol. 1. New York: Basic.

Bowlby, J. (1973). *Attachment & separation*, Vol. 2. New York: Basic.

Boyd, R., & Richardson, P. J. (1985). *Culture and the evolutionary process*. Chicago: University of Chicago Press.

Brown, D. E. (1991). *Human universals*. Philadelphia: Temple University Press.

Buss, D. M. (1998). *Evolutionary psychology: The new science of the mind*. Boston: Allyn & Bacon.

Buss, D. M., & Kenrick, D. T. (1988). Evolutionary social psychology. In D. T. Gilbert, S. T. Fiske, & G. Lindzey (Eds.), *The handbook of social psychology* (4th ed., pp. 982–1026). New York: McGraw-Hill.

Caporael, L. R. (1997). The evolution of truly social cognition: The core configurations model. *Personality and Social Psychology Review, 1*, 276–298.

Chomsky, N. (1965). *Aspects of the theory of syntax*. Cambridge, MA: MIT Press.

Crook, J. H. (1980). *The evolution of human consciousness*. New York: Oxford University Press.

Csányi, V. (1988). *Evolutionary systems and society: A general theory of life, mind, and culture*. Durham, NC: Duke University.

Csikszentmihalyi, M. (1993). *The evolving self: A psychology for the third millennium*. New York: Harper Collins.

Csikszentmihalyi, M., & Rathunde, K. (1989). The psychology of wisdom: An evolutionary interpretation. In R. J. Sternberg (Ed.), *The psychology of wisdom*. New York: Cambridge University Press.

de Waal, F. B. (1996). *Good natured: The origins of right and wrong in humans and other animals*. Cambridge: Harvard University Press.

Dobzhansky, T. (1962). *Mankind evolving: The evolution of the human species*. New Haven, CT: Yale University Press.

Eccles, J. C. (1989). *Evolution of the brain: Creation of the mind*. New York: Routledge.

Erikson, E. (1982). *The life cycle completed: A review*. New York: W. W. Norton.

Huxley, J. S. (1942). *Evolution: The modern synthesis*. London: Allen & Unwin.

Jung, C. G. (1963). *Memories, dreams, reflections*. New York: Pantheon.

Jung, C. G. (1964). *Man and his symbols*. New York: Doubleday.

Kauffman, S. (1993). *The origins of order: Self-organization and selection in evolution*. Oxford: Oxford University Press.

Köhler, W. (1973). *The mentality of apes* (2nd ed). New York: Liveright.

Laszlo, E., & Masulli, I. with R. Artigiani and V. Csányi. (1993). *The evolution of cognitive maps: New paradigms for the twenty-first century*. Amsterdam: Gordon and Breach.

Lorenz, K. Z. (1969). Innate bases of learning. In K. H. Primbram (Ed.), *On the biology of learning*. New York: Harcourt, Brace, & World.

Maturana, H. R., & Varela, F. J. (1987). *The tree of knowledge: The biological roots of human understanding*. Boston: New Science Library, Shambhala.

Mead, M. (1964). *Continuities in cultural evolution*. New Haven, CT: Yale University Press.

Medawar, P. (1960). *The future of man*. New York: Basic.

Nitecki, M. H. (Ed.). (1988). *Evolutionary progress*. Chicago: University of Chicago Press.

Oubré, A. Y. (1997). *Instinct and revelation*, Vol. 10 (The World Futures General Evolution Studies). Amsterdam: Gordon and Breach.

Petrinovich, L. (1995). *Human evolution, reproduction, and morality*. New York: Plenum.

Rosen, D. (1992). Inborn basis for the healing doctor-patient relationship. *Pharos, 55,* 17–21.

Simpson, J. A., & Kenrick, D. T. (Eds.). (1997). *Evolutionary social psychology*. New York: Erlbaum.

Sternberg, R. J., & Davidson, J. E. (1995). *The nature of insight*. Cambridge, MA: MIT Press.

Stevens, A. (1982). *Archetypes: A natural history of the self*. New York: William Morrow.

Stevens, A. (1993). *The two million-year-old self*. College Station: Texas A&M University Press.

Stevens, A. (1996). *Private myths: Dreams and dreaming*. Cambridge, MA: Harvard University Press.

Stevens, A., & Price, J. (1996). *Evolutionary psychiatry: A new beginning*. London & New York: Routledge.

Symons, D. (1979). *The evolution of human sexuality*. New York: Oxford University Press.

Teilhard de Chardin, P. (1965). *The phenomenon of man*. New York: Harper & Row.

Tinbergen, N. (1951). *The study of instinct*. London: Oxford University Press.

Waddington, C. H. (1970). The theory of evolution today. In A. Koestler & J. R. Smythies (Eds.), *Beyond reductionism*. New York: Macmillan.

Wallace, A. F. C. (1966). *Religion: An anthropological view*. New York: Random House.

Wenegrat, B. (1984). *Sociobiology and mental disorder*. Menlo Park, CA: Addison-Wesley.

Index

About the Editors and Contributors

DAVID H. ROSEN, psychiatrist and Jungian psychoanalyst, is the McMillan Professor of Analytical Psychology, Professor of Humanities in Medicine, and Professor of Psychiatry & Behavioral Science at Texas A&M University in College Station, Texas. He is the author of numerous articles (some having to do with evolutionary psychology, medicine, and psychiatry) and five previous books, including *The Tao of Jung* and *Transforming Depression*, and co-author of *Medicine As a Human Experience*.

MICHAEL C. LUEBBERT is a doctoral student in clinical psychology at Texas A&M University. His clinical and research interests include the application of attachment theory to the study of trauma, marital therapy, and the psychology of religion, specifically forgiveness. He is an Editorial Associate with *Clinician's Research Digest*. He currently has several works in press, including a biographical entry on Schopenhauer for the *APA Encyclopedia of Psychology* and co-authorship of a book chapter on couples therapy.

DAVID M. BUSS is a Professor of Psychology at the University of Texas in Austin. He is an internationally known authority in the emerging field of evolutionary psychology. He has published many articles on evolutionary psychology and his books include *Evolution of Desire* and *Evolutionary Psychology*.

LORNE CAMPBELL is a doctoral student in social psychology at Texas A&M University. His research interests involve intimate relationships, evolutionary psychology, and the statistics of non-independence.

JEFFRY A. SIMPSON is a Professor of Psychology at Texas A&M University. He is the author of many articles on attachment, interpersonal relationships, and evolutionary psychology and he is co-editor of the book *Evolutionary Social Psychology*.

MINDA ORINA is a doctoral student in social psychology at Texas A&M University. Her research interests include attachment & interpersonal relationships and evolutionary psychology. She is co-author of one related article.

WILLIAM G. GRAZIANO is a Professor of Psychology at Texas A&M University and co-author of *Social Psychology* and the author of numerous articles and chapters having to do with evolutionary psychology.

RENÉE T. TOBIN is a doctoral student in social psychology at Texas A&M University. Her research interests include personality variables and evolutionary psychology.

JOHN J. SKOWRONSKI is a Professor of Psychology at Ohio State University (Newark). He is co-author of *Autobiographical Memory* and several articles having to do with the symbolic self in evolution.

CONSTANTINE SEDIKIDES is a Professor of Psychology at the University of North Carolina (Chapel Hill). He is co-editor of *Intergroup Cognition and Intergroup Behavior* and has written several articles on the symbolic self in evolution.

STEVEN M. SMITH is an Associate Professor of Psychology at Texas A&M University. He is co-author of *The Creative Cognition Approach* and *Creativity and the Mind* and co-editor of *Creative Thought*.

THOMAS B. WARD is a Professor of Psychology at Texas A&M University. He is co-author of *The Creative Cognition Approach* and *Creativity and the Mind* and co-editor of *Creative Thought*.

BENTON H. PIERCE is a doctoral student in cognitive psychology at Texas A&M University. His research interests include metacognition, recollective memory in the elderly, and evolutionary psychology.

JYOTSNA VAID is an Associate Professor of Psychology at Texas A&M University. She is editor of *Language Processing in Bilinguals* and co-editor of *Creative Thought*.

HOLLY L. HUSTON is a post-doctoral fellow in Psychology at Baylor College of Medicine, Houston, Texas. She is co-author of an article on evolutionary memory.

BRETT COOKE is an Associate Professor of Modern & Classical Languages at Texas A&M University. He is the author of several articles having to do with evolutionary topics and of *Rushkin and the Creative Process*.

JOHN PRICE is a psychiatrist and co-author of *Evolutionary Psychiatry*.

ANTHONY STEVENS, psychiatrist and Jungian psychoanalyst, is the author of *Archetypes: Natural History of the Self*, *The Two Million-Year-Old Self*, and co-author of *Evolutionary Psychiatry*.

ISBN 0-275-96312-8

90000>

EAN

9 780275 963125

HARDCOVER BAR CODE